THE GRENADA
PAPERS

THE GRENADA PAPERS

Edited by

Paul Seabury and Walter A. McDougall

With a Foreword by Sidney Hook

ICS PRESS

Institute for Contemporary Studies
San Francisco, California

Inquiries, book orders, and catalog requests should be addressed to ICS Press, Suite 750, 785 Market Street, San Francisco, CA 94103—(415) 543-6213.

Library of Congress Cataloging in Publication Data
Main entry under title:

The Grenada papers.

     1. Grenada—Politics and government—1974–   —
Sources. 2. Communism—Grenada—History—Sources.
3. Grenada—History—American invasion, 1983—Causes—
Sources. I. Seabury, Paul. II. McDougall, Walter A.,
1946–   .
F2056.8.G77 1984   972.98'45   84-22356
ISBN   0–917616–68–5
ISBN   0–917616–67–7 (pbk.)

TO THE MEMORY OF ARTHUR KOESTLER
(1905–1984)

It was a mistake in the system; perhaps it lay in the precept which until now he had held to be uncontestable, in whose name he had sacrificed others and was himself being sacrificed: in the precept, that the end justifies the means. It was this sentence which had killed the great fraternity of the Revolution and made them all run amuck. What had he once written in his diary? 'We have thrown overboard all conventions, our sole guiding principle is that of consequent logic; we are sailing without ethical ballast.'

–*DARKNESS AT NOON,* 1941

CONTENTS

ILLUSTRATIONS
following page 229

FOREWORD

The documents in this volume will be mined by scholars of various disciplines for many years to come. But they also have great urgency for intelligent laymen interested in public affairs, for key figures in the media, and, above all, for those directly responsible for American foreign policy, especially members of the American Congress and their staffs. The validity of this judgment is sustainable with only a cursory reading of these fascinating archives of the theory and practice of Communist revolution.

At the very least, familiarity with this volume should destroy the assumptions that dominate the thought and action of the many members of the American Congress, as well as private citizens, who believe that revolutions are brought about primarily by poverty, deprivation, and oppression, and are never engineered by subversive political action. If this were true, most of the world would be in a state of convulsive revolutionary activity. It was none other than Vladimir Lenin, the outstanding leader of the Russian Bolshevik Party, who pointed this out, long before he successfully guided his party to the conquest of political power. The leaders of the New Jewel Movement who seized political power in Grenada, for all their differences, were Bolshevik Leninists. Their very language among themselves reveals this. Not only did the leaders of the New Jewel Movement speak of building a Leninist Party, but one of them, Bernard Coard, in outlining a program of harnessing the trade union movement to the Party-State, warns against the dangers of "economism." This is an expression Lenin used to characterize a trade union movement whose orientation is guided by the economic interests of the workers, and not subordinated to the needs of the revolution as understood by the elite, vanguard Communist Party.

This is only one expression of the Communist view that, regardless how ripe society may be for a socialist revolution, without the systematic, organized activity of the Communist Party there can be no basic change. We need not pursue the question of the interrelation between social and economic movements in all its complexity; but any politically literate person who reads as he runs must admit that oppressive conditions, by themselves, whether in Central America or elsewhere do not generate revolutionary subversion, and that the presence of trained Communist cadres may have major and sometimes decisive significance.

Another illusion that should be dispelled by a perusal of this volume, is that the issues in the Caribbean and Central America are purely local, and that a tiny island like Grenada, or a larger island like Cuba, or for that matter the whole of Central America, can constitute no threat to the security of the U.S. This overlooks the extent to which the Soviet Union and its Cuban proxy are involved in the guerrilla disturbances in Central America. To be sure, the global Communist movement is not a monolith. Peking and Moscow probably fear one another more than they currently fear the U.S. But despite this, in the area which the Kremlin seeks to Finlandize, if not directly absorb, the U.S. remains the main enemy. Every Communist-run territory in Central America would be a strategic outpost of the USSR, integrated into its emergency plans. Were it not for the USSR the U.S. could easily shrug off any Communist putsch in Central or South America. But as these documents show, almost every Communist satellite regime under Soviet influence had representatives and observers, at some stage, in Grenada. Even North Korea, which treads nimbly between Communist China and Communist Russia, was there. Despite their differences, they are marked by a consuming hatred of the strongest bastion of the free world. Grenada was being readied as a pawn, like Cuba before it, in the struggle for world hegemony. Elaborate preparations were made not only to receive multiple forms of aid, especially military aid, from the Soviet Union and its satellites, but to train Grenadian political cadres in the Leninist schools of the Soviet Union.

The arts of propaganda, infiltration, and disinformation are one area in which the Soviet Union has indeed caught up with and surpassed the West. The Kremlin has served as an efficient mentor for its acolytes wherever they have come to power. They have learned to use free institutions to destroy them. Realizing that so long as trade unions remain independent and free, Communist rule will be frustrated in reorganizing the economy, Communists have resorted to ruses, stratagems, and overt terror to wrest authority in the trade unions from those elected by the membership. Recognizing, despite propagandistic assertions to the contrary, that Main Street, and not Wall Street, has more weight in the councils of America, Communists have endeavored to picture themselves as genuine democrats, innocent victims of American imperialistic exploitation. They do not hesitate to seek to influence and exploit even those who, judging by Bolshevik Leninist behavior in the past, are slated for liquidation. Nothing is so revealing as the documents presented here, showing that the stalwarts of Communist rule in Grenada sought to win the Socialist International to their cause. In some Central American countries individuals who in the past had formal association with socialist organizations have thrown their lot in with Communist guerrillas, and exploit their former association to conceal the goals of the Communist-dominated movement, mainly directing their efforts at the politically unsophisticated sectors of the American and world press. The papers uncovered in Grenada indicate the persistence and variety of measures adopted by Bolshevik Leninists, first to neutralize, then to eliminate, actual or potential opposition in any country in which they seek or possess power.

This book will likely be ignored by apologists for the New Jewel movement. They may, in accordance with Communist practice, imply that the original papers have been forged.

However, some public figures, although accepting the authenticity of these documents will maintain that they do not justify the action of the American and Eastern Caribbean forces that liberated the people of Grenada from the yoke imposed on them. Some critics of the Grenada intervention have gone so far as to compare the American action with the Soviet invasion of Afghanistan.

A clear case can be made for the intervention of American and Eastern Caribbean forces following the murder of Prime Minister Maurice Bishop. This is not the place for debate, but regardless of differences of interpretation in international law, we may make short shrift of the fantastic comparison between the Soviet invasion of Afghanistan and the Grenada action. The key differences have already been made public by the Caribbean Central American Studies Center, of Freedom House, New York, and its Afghanistan Information Committee.

The assistance of American forces was requested officially by the Organization of Eastern Caribbean States, along with the Governor General of Grenada, Sir Paul Scoon, who exercised his authority according to British Commonwealth law in the absence of a prime minister and government. The members of the Organization of Eastern Caribbean States unanimously approved of the request as being in accord with treaty specifications. This was officially attested to by Prime Minister Eugenia Charles of Dominica, current chair of the Organization.

On the other hand, the Soviet Union has cited as justification for its invasion, a request from the then-President of Afghanistan, Hafizullan Amin. But the very first action of the Soviet forces was the murder of Amin, in whose name they claimed to be acting, by a special assault team.

The further rationalization offered by the Kremlin was that the Afghan government requested Soviet troops to withstand the assault of American, Chinese, British, and "Zionist imperialist" invaders. But not a single American, Chinese, British, or "Zionist" invading soldier has ever been found.

On the other hand, in Grenada the intervening forces found not only Cuban soldiers and officers but high ranking Soviet, Bulgarian, and East German officers, including a Soviet four star general. Although Grenada is English-speaking, materials and signs in Spanish showed that the Cubans were in charge.

Within a week of their entry into Grenada, American troops began a withdrawal, after laying the foundations for democratic elections. By contrast, four years after the invasion of Afghanistan and the ruthless suppression of the civilian population, there is no evidence that the Soviet forces plan to withdraw. The Kremlin, judging by its propaganda, apparently believes that Grenada, too, is subject to the Brezhnev doctrine, according to which no regime characterized by it as socialist can ever be changed by the population over whom it rules.

Finally, there is incontestable evidence that the population of Grenada welcomed the intervention of American troops as a liberation from the murderous tyranny of the Bolshevik Leninists. The Soviet invasion, combatting a nation in arms, is actively opposed by hundreds of thousands of Afghans.

While there are other significant differences between the two cases, these are sufficient to establish the invalidity of the comparison.

SIDNEY HOOK

EDITORIAL NOTE:

Readers of this collection should be aware of the canons of editorial practice that have been observed in its preparation. As noted in Professors Seabury and McDougall's introduction, typographical and grammatical errors in the original documents have been preserved. In addition, some documents have been transcribed from handwritten originals or typed copies of less-than-total legibility. In such cases, interpretative deciphering has been necessary, but is unmarked. Materials in brackets rather than parentheses, e.g., interpretations of initials or abbreviations, were inserted by the editors. Undecipherable items are indicated as illegible. Ellipses (. . .) indicate editorial cuts.

I
INTRODUCTION
A PORTRAIT OF CARIBBEAN MARXISM
Paul Seabury and Walter A. McDougall

To a degree still not widely appreciated by proponents or critics alike, the American invasion of Grenada in October 1983 was an event of major historical importance. Not only did the U.S. action mark the sole occasion, since the Bolshevik Revolution in 1917, in which an established Communist regime was deposed by democratic forces, but it also yielded a treasure trove of captured documents depicting the inner workings of the New Jewel Regime (otherwise known as the People's Revolutionary Government of Grenada). Thousands of party, state, and police documents fell into the hands of U.S. military forces. Together, they constitute a body of records chronicling the internal affairs of the only Communist regime ever to be established in an English-speaking country.

These papers are now being made publicly available. As this collection goes to press, the bulk of the archives is being released to scholars by the U.S. government. Those upon which our collection is based constitute an initial gleaning of materials made available in early 1984 through the United States Information Agency.

In one respect the papers are historically unique. Until now, the central archives of all Communist regimes—most notably the Soviet Union—have been closely guarded state secrets. Only once before has the Western public been able to gain a significant documented glimpse into the inner workings of a Communist government, when, shortly after the end of World War II, the U.S. Army captured from their Nazi custodians the provincial party archives in the city of Smolensk, which German forces had seized.

Our understanding of the inmost character of Communist systems—in dramatic contrast to our understanding of our own—has labored under a censorship so extreme that scholars and publicists have generally been compelled to rely solely upon con-

jecture, rumor, the accounts of defectors, visitors and foreign diplomats, and upon whatever documents and other information
that compulsively secretive authorities have allowed to be published. Today, for example, historians know virtually everything
one would require to know about the American side of the Korean War of 35 years ago; but we have no definitive idea as to
the intentions and decisions of the Soviet leadership in instigat-
ing it. This asymmetry of hard knowledge has left a legacy of
one-sidedness in the study of the Cold War, constantly obscuring
the intentions of our principal antagonist. In our study of the
role of Communist states in world affairs we have nothing
approaching, for instance, the kinds of scholarship generally
available concerning the origins of the first World War. Such
scholarship depended upon a reasonable degree of openness of
the principal European adversaries' archives. Today, as always,
the Communist world—with respect to its inner functioning—
continues to resemble what T.S. Eliot aptly called "the dark side
of the moon." The only true Kremlinologists today could be said
to be those who work inside the Kremlin—yet probably many of
them are little better informed than the most informed of us.

The New Jewel Movement and the People's Revolutionary
Government of Grenada, which it created in 1979, were exper-
iments cut short by an American invasion. What makes these
papers from Grenada doubly valuable is that they permit us intimately to witness both the dynamics of a Marxist-Leninist regime in the early stages of its consolidation and its emerging
relation to broader configurations of political power in the
Communist world. It is now apparent that until 1983, when the
New Jewel Movement suddenly exploded from "internal contradictions," the regime was bent upon imposing comprehensive totalitarian controls upon the people of Grenada by methods
meticulously copied from its mentors in long-established Communist states—the U.S.S.R., Cuba, Vietnam, and East Germany
in particular. Some of these controls were already in place before
the Americans arrived. But what the documents also reveal in
great detail are the long-term strategies of the regime—plans for
the eventual suppression of all resistance and the complete (to
borrow a Nazi phrase) *Gleichschaltung,* or reorganization of
Grenadian society along Marxist-Leninist lines. This new, small,

Socialist planet was in the early stages of adapting to the orbit of a Soviet-dominated cosmos. The papers on Grenadian foreign relations (both party and state) provide an additional dividend to us—a set of fragmentary, very incomplete, yet intimate glimpses into a global system of synchronized Communist states intent upon the expansion of the Marxist-Leninist world.

Western observers have correctly commented on the Communist phenomenon of "polycentrism" (autonomous non-Soviet Communist leadership, e.g. Italy) and intra-Communist rivalries. But it is also true that in the 1970s and 1980s new forms of fraternal collaboration evolved in the expansionist strategies of the Soviet Union, its satellites, and Soviet-dominated movements in Asia, Africa, and Latin America. A new kind of Socialist division of labor in this overall process has been particularly difficult for outside observers to comprehend. The intricate interweaving of Soviet, Cuban, Vietnamese, and Eastern European Communist activities of far-reaching scope, has been witnessed from the outside but not from the inside. These papers, as they bear on the New Jewel Movement's international connections, vividly display on a small scale the reality of this process.

Grenada was one minor focus of this worldwide and planned activity, which involved a burden shared among the Soviets, Cubans, Bulgarians, Czechs, East Germans, Vietnamese, and many others in consolidating the new regime in the Caribbean. A new kind of *Rote Kapelle** is shown in documents ranging from military assistance to ideological instruction, internal security police training, and economic planning for a "New Socialist Society." (The East Germans, for instance, in Grenada as well as in Nicaragua, South Yemen, Ethiopia, Angola, and Mozambique, now seem to have assumed the role of masters of secret police techniques.)

The Grenada papers also vividly illustrate the contrasts of outward appearance and inner reality, between the face of this moon and its dark side. The Bishop regime during these years

*A term used to describe a pro-Soviet espionage ring in Germany during the Nazi period: the "Red Orchestra."

was at pains to be perceived, in sympathetic Western eyes, as
simply a "progressive" regime intent upon eliminating old ves-
tiges of colonialism and racism, its legitimacy based solely upon
the popular ardor of the Grenadian people. This camouflage—
assiduously cultivated by the New Jewel Movement in the U.S.
media and in sectors of the American political system—con-
trasted sharply with the inner genuine purpose and doctrine revealed in these papers. Eager to attract Western capital, the regime displayed a feigned tolerance toward private business at
the very time it was devising long-term strategies for full
socialization of the Grenadian economy and its coordination
with the "Socialist" economic world. The candor and bluntness
with which these strategies were discussed in secret contrast
dramatically with the benign public "line" followed by the
Bishop government in its dealings with Western business firms
and with financial institutions such as the International Monetary Fund. The image cultivated by Prime Minister Maurice
Bishop himself, as a moderate seeking genial accommodation
with the United States, stands in striking opposition to the
close-up glimpses we have here of a profoundly orthodox
Marxist-Leninist leader.

Also, perhaps surprisingly, at a time when much is made in
the West about the declining appeal of Communism within and
without the Soviet-controlled parts of the world, the Grenada
documents attest to the vigor with which the leaders of the New
Jewel Movement embraced the most orthodox and undiluted
version of Marxism-Leninism. The odd Caribbean-style Leninist
jargon and the often illiterate fashion in which concepts were
discussed and formulated, do not hide the origin of the doctrine.
The bosses of the movement were encapsulated not only in the
rhetoric, but also in the operational style of Marxist-Leninist
orthodoxy. To outsiders, some of the minutes of the New Jewel
Central Committee will sound akin to the pretentious discourse
of undergraduate Marxist seminars in the 1970s. This should
not be allowed to obscure the fact of serious zeal and commitment, turning into the cruel fanaticism that ultimately over-
whelmed the movement in its last days. As the gap between this
fanaticism and the temperament of ordinary Grenadians became
more and more pronounced, so also, within the movement, did

the growing frenzy translate itself into demands for more rigorous discipline and control. Maurice Bishop, it would seem, proved an incompetent tyrant, unable to meet the challenge of growing disillusionment and hostility within the Grenadian populace. Those who overthrew and murdered him, while no more and no less orthodox in their ideological convictions than he, were clearly more willing to adopt the most vicious forms of Stalinist control. At the end, waning charisma and ardor gave way to massive repression and murder of party stalwarts as has been the case in many other Communist regimes since Stalin's time.

There is one final aspect of these documents that should be emphasized: Grenada was, as previously noted, the first English-speaking territory to come under Communist rule. For the reader, regardless of the far more important implications of that development, this now has the special advantage of making the documents included here, all originally in English, easy to read, and the nuances more easily understood. As editors we have reproduced the documents as they have come to us, leaving typographical and grammatical errors unchanged.

Yet the linguistically accessible and occasionally poignant character of some of these papers—particularly those written in the "last days"—convey to an English-speaking reader a sense of authenticity missing in the translation of Communist materials. Americans' linguistic parochialism is a barrier to an understanding of a Communist world that speaks different private tongues. One can thus better understand these records than others translated from Russian, German, Czech, Chinese, or Vietnamese. Moreover, Grenada, with its unique history and proximity to the American mainland, culturally is much closer to us than are the remote scenes of Soviet activity in Europe, Asia, and Africa. The first group of Grenadian Marxist-Leninists was not trained in Moscow (although, as documents show, the second wave was being trained there); they were schooled in America and England. Bernard Coard, whose thugs ultimately murdered Maurice Bishop, is a graduate of Brandeis University; Bishop himself briefly studied law at the University of London. The best language contained in these records reflects the influence of British schools; the worst displays a street argot familiar to every American. Between these extremes is the suffocating prose of badly educated sociology students. One reaction to these documents is that, at whichever level, they convey a sense of intimacy—it was really happening here, on a nearby fringe of our North American continent. Its demystified record speaks our own language, rather than that of some exotic, distant land.

With the exception of the Dessima Williams letter on Grenadian dissident activities and her relations with the office of Rep. Ronald V. Dellums (D-California) (document V-1), and the minutes of the NJM extraordinary general meeting of September 25, 1983 (document VIII-6), the documents presented here were released by the U.S. Information Agency following their seizure by the U.S./ Eastern Caribbean states' forces, in the wake of the New Jewel regime's implosion.

We have organized the documents under eight headings: Treaties and Military Aid (II), Domestic Political Consolidation (III), The Special Case of the Churches (IV), Propaganda and Public Relations Work in the U.S. (V), Soviet and Soviet-Bloc Activities (VI), Grenada and the Socialist International (VII), Crisis in the Party: Minutes of the Central Committee (VIII), and The Revolution Devours Its Children (IX). Each section includes a brief introductory survey, and, with the exception of sections II and IX, each individual document is accompanied by prefatory comments; it was our feeling that in the sections covering treaties and military relations, and the collapse of the regime, the documents require no further elucidation.

We wish to extend our thanks to the author of the chronology and dramatis personae, Daniel Berman, of the Political Science Department, University of California, Berkeley; and to Patrick Glynn and Stephen Schwartz, of the Institute for Contemporary Studies, who were responsible for the editorial format of this book. In addition, Mr. Schwartz wrote the document-by-document commentaries. Other ICS personnel, most notably David Givens and Emanuel Rapoport, contributed significant input to the book. To them and to the ICS staff in general go our appreciation for a job well done.

Introductions to sections II, IV, and VI were written by Paul Seabury; to sections III, VIII, and IX, by Walter McDougall; those for sections V and VII are by Stephen Schwartz.

Supplementary sources consulted in the preparation of this book were: "Grenada: A Preliminary Report," issued by the U.S. Departments of State and Defense, December 16, 1983; *Maurice Bishop Speaks, The Grenada Revolution 1979–83,* New York, Pathfinder Press, 1983; *Caribbean Review* (Miami), Fall 1983; *National Review,* November 11, 1983; *Accuracy in Media Report* (Washington), January 1984; and Jiri and Virginia Valenta, "Leninism in Grenada," in *Problems of Communism* (Washington, D.C.) July-August 1984.

CHRONOLOGY

7 February 1974 Grenada becomes a fully independent nation, in a transition marked by violence, strikes, and political controversy around Sir Eric Gairy, who was named Prime Minister.

13 March 1979 Government of Gairy is overthrown in a bloodless coup by Maurice Bishop, leader of the New Jewel Movement.

16 April 1979 The governments of Grenada and Cuba announce they have established diplomatic relations.

16 October 1979 Bishop's government arrests 20 persons, including opposition leader Winston Whyte, charging them with plotting to assassinate the new government's leadership.

May 1980 Deputy Prime Minister Bernard Coard signs treaty in Moscow permitting Soviet long-range reconnaissance planes to land at new airport at Point Salines.

21 June 1980 An apparent assassination attempt against Bishop is unsuccessful.

1 January 1981 In a speech at a meeting of the Commonwealth Caribbean foreign ministers, Bishop charges that the U.S. is trying to overthrow his government and cites a "three-stage CIA plot".

26 August 1981 Bishop charges that recent U.S. and NATO military exercises in the Caribbean were a "practice run" for an invasion of the island.

6 February 1982 President Reagan, at the start of a four-day conference in Barbados with five eastern Caribbean leaders, charges that Grenada has joined with the Soviet Union, Nicaragua, and Cuba in promoting Marxism in the region.

26–28 July 1982 Bishop visits Moscow for talks and signs substantial economic and political agreements with the Soviets.

October 1982 At a plenary meeting of the Central Committee, Bishop is criticized for weak leadership. Bernard Coard resigns from the Central Committee.

November 1982 Grenada rejects pressure from other Caribbean Community members to hold free elections as a dispute over human rights hampers a community conference.

31 May–9 June 1983 Bishop visits Washington, DC and meets with National Security Advisor William P. Clark and Deputy Secretary of State Kenneth W. Dam.

26 August 1983 The International Monetary Fund (IMF) approves a $14.1 million loan for Bishop's leftist government despite opposition from the Reagan Administration.

14 October 1983 Deputy Prime Minister Bernard Coard, assisted by General Hudson Austin, ousts Bishop, placing him under house arrest.

18 October 1983 Foreign Minister Unison Whiteman says that he and three other ministers in the Government of Prime Minister Maurice Bishop had resigned and that Coard was running the country "single-handedly."

19 October 1983 General Hudson Austin reports that Bishop and three members of his cabinet have been killed in a clash with Austin's soldiers.

21 October 1983 The U.S. Defense Department announces that a ten-ship task force headed for Lebanon has been diverted and sent instead towards Grenada as a precautionary measure in the event that Americans on the island there are endangered.

23 October 1983   The five-member Organization of Eastern
                  Caribbean States formally requests U.S. assis-
                  tance in restoring order and democracy on Gre-
                  nada.

25 October 1983   U.S. troops, together with contingents from An-
                  tigua, Barbados, Dominica, Jamaica, St. Lucia,
                  and St. Vincent, land on Grenada.

DRAMATIS PERSONAE

Hudson Austin

A key figure in the 1979 leftist revolution, Austin was a commander of Grenada's army and militia, which overthrew Bishop, and head of the 16-member council installed after the coup. Austin originally met Bishop while a guard at the prison where Bishop was a political prisoner.

Fitzroy Bain

A union leader, Fitzroy Bain was killed with Bishop following the Coard takeover in October 1983. Bain seems to have been the most active opponent of the Coard faction.

Norris Bain

Minister of Housing, Norris Bain was killed by the Coard forces in October 1983.

Maurice Bishop

Bishop was born in Aruba (Netherlands Antilles) in 1944 to a well-to-do family that had prospered in the hotel industry . At the age of 19, Bishop went to study law in London, where he became a barrister in 1966. He returned to Grenada in 1970 to practice law in association with Bernard Coard. An early leader in the NJM (New Jewel Movement), Bishop was elected to Parliament in 1976. Bishop was killed in the aftermath of the coup engineered by Coard in 1983.

Bernard Coard

Deputy Prime Minister in the Bishop government, and Minister of Finance, Trade, Industry, and Planning, Coard had studied at the University of Sussex in Britain and at Brandeis in the U.S., with a full scholarship in economics at the latter institution. He was founder of the Organization for

Revolutionary Education and Liberation, which merged into the New Jewel Movement, but which was later reportedly started anew as the Organization for Educational Advancement and Research. In document VIII-7, it is suggested that OREL/OEAR functioned consistently as a conspiratorial faction supporting Coard's ambitions, which were finally realized with Bishop's overthrow. It has been asserted that Coard was put under house arrest by Bishop early in 1983, following a statement by Jamaican Prime Minister Edward Seaga that Coard diverted Grenadian funds to a private bank account in Jamaica. At the time this book went to press, Grenadian authorities had completed the inquest into Bishop's death and were preparing to bring Coard and his associates to trial.

Phyllis Coard

Bernard Coard's wife, and head of Radio Free Grenada and the National Women's Organization, Mrs. Coard is reportedly an heiress to a Jamaican liquor fortune.

Leon Cornwall

Grenada's army chief and ambassador to Cuba under Bishop, Cornwall was also a leading Coard backer.

Jacqueline Creft

Minister of Education, Youth, and Social Affairs in Bishop's cabinet, Creft also lived with Bishop, with whom she had a son named Vladimir, age 4. She was killed during the Coard takeover.

Sir Eric M. Gairy

Gairy was born in 1922 near Grenville, Grenada. He first rose to prominence in the 1950s as an anticolonial trade union organizer. In 1950 he founded the Grenada Labor Party, becoming prime minister after independence from Britain in 1974. The colorful Gairy, a former nightclub owner and spiritualist, was in New York to speak at the United Nations about UFOs when he was overthrown in absentia in a coup led by Maurice Bishop.

George Louison

Minister of Agriculture under Bishop, Louison strongly defended Bishop during the Coard coup, but was not killed.

Vincent Noel

A union leader, Noel was killed during the Coard coup.

Kenrick Radix

Minister of Legal Affairs, Agro-Industries and Fisheries, Radix was another survivor of the October 1983 Coard coup.

Lyden Rhamdany

Minister of Tourism and Civil Aviation under Bishop.

Selwyn Strachan

Minister of Communications, Works and Labor under Bishop, he supported Coard's 1983 takeover.

Unison Whiteman

The son of a farmer in St. David's Parish, in the eastern part of the island, Whiteman attended a Roman Catholic secondary school in St. Georges and then studied at Howard University in Washington, DC. A co-founder of Grenada's New Jewel Movement and foreign minister under Bishop, Whiteman was in his late 30s when he was killed by the Coard faction.

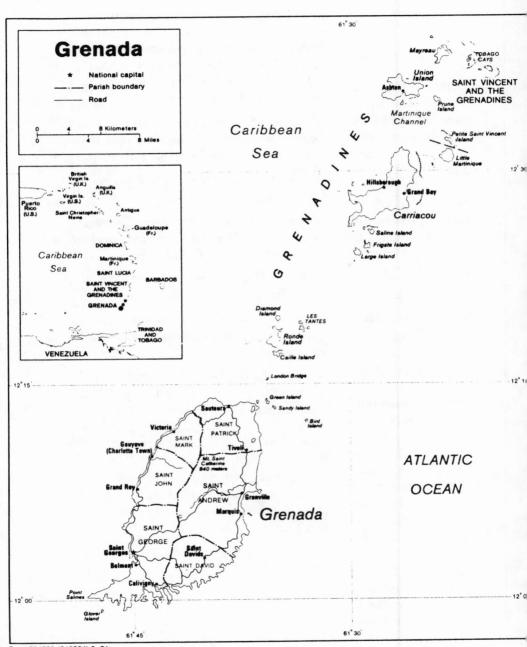

Grenada

★ National capital

—·—·— Parish boundary

——— Road

0   4   8 Kilometers
0   4   8 Miles

Caribbean Sea

Caribbean Sea

British Virgin Is. (U.K.)

Anguilla (U.K.)

Virgin Is. (U.S.)

Puerto Rico (U.S.)

Saint Christopher-Nevis

Antigua

Guadeloupe (Fr.)

DOMINICA

Martinique (Fr.)

SAINT LUCIA

SAINT VINCENT AND THE GRENADINES

BARBADOS

GRENADA

TRINIDAD AND TOBAGO

VENEZUELA

Mayreau

TOBAGO CAYS

Union Island

SAINT VINCENT AND THE GRENADINES

Ashton

Prune Island

Martinique Channel

Petite Saint Vincent Island

Little Martinique

Hillsborough

Grand Bay

Carriacou

Saline Island

Frigate Island

Large Island

G R E N A D I N E S

Diamond Island

LES TANTES

Ronde Island

Caille Island

London Bridge

Green Island

Sandy Island

Bird Island

Sauteurs

Victoria

SAINT PATRICK

SAINT MARK

Gouyave (Charlotte Town)

Tivoli

Mt. Saint Catherine 840 meters

SAINT JOHN

Grand Roy

SAINT ANDREW

Grenville

Marquis

Grenada

SAINT GEORGE

Saint Georges

Saint Davids

Belmont

SAINT DAVID

Calivigny

Point Salines

Glover Island

ATLANTIC OCEAN

61° 30′

12° 30′

12° 15′   12° 15′

12° 00′   12° 0′

61° 45′   61° 30′

II
TREATIES AND MILITARY AID

Before the American invasion of Grenada, few Americans were aware of the intricate web of Soviet-bloc treaties and agreements in which the People's Revolutionary Government of Grenada had become entwined. Perhaps most important among these pacts were those which bestowed arms and other logistical equipment upon the PRG. Even immediately following the American invasion, skeptical Congressmen were reluctant to lend credence to reports that the island had become repository to vast amounts of military equipment far beyond the capacity of Grenadian forces to employ. Senator Daniel P. Moynihan was among these skeptics. "We heard that Grenada was a Soviet and Cuban arsenal," said Senator Moynihan. "Today I pick up the newspaper and read that many of the weapons kept in storage were made 100 years ago and are valuable historical pieces, including 19th-century carbines."

The reality, as the following documents show, was very different from cutlasses and carbines. By the time of the U.S. invasion the Bishop regime had made agreements with the Soviet Union, Vietnam, Czechoslovakia, North Korea, Cuba, and East Germany for supply of modern sophisticated military equipment and technical logistical assistance. Much of this had been already delivered. Much more was to come. The magnitude of these supplies may be judged from the documents excerpted here. At the time of the Americans' arrival, nearly 900 Cuban, Libyan, Soviet, North Korean, East German and Bulgarian personnel were in Grenada to assist in the transformation of the island into a major military camp; artillery, anti-aircraft weapons, ammunition, armored personnel carriers, and rocket launchers were discovered. Cuban forces were the most numerous, yet as these documents also reveal, long-term PRG-USSR programs were being developed for the training of PRG forces chiefly in the Soviet Union, but in other Soviet-bloc countries as well.

Moreover, the People's Revolutionary Army went so far as to request from the Soviet Union aid to expand their army to a total of four regular and fourteen reserve battalions by 1985. This ambitious program would have placed as much as 15 – 25 percent of the entire Grenadian population under arms, and would have given the tiny island country probably the largest army in proportion to population in the world.

These agreements also display the eagerness of the New Jewel Movement for assistance in problems of internal security. Most striking in this regard is the correspondence undertaken by the PRG Minister of Interior, Hudson Austin, in February 1982, to "Commander Andropov," then Chairman of the Committee of State Security (KGB) and later Soviet chief executive. Austin requested that the KGB undertake the training of Grenadian police intelligence officers. Equally of interest is the PRG's concern to learn from Hanoi the techniques of Gulag re-education successfully imposed upon the people of Vietnam (see document VI-1).

II-1
Letter from Austin to Andropov
2/17/82

MINISTRY OF INTERIOR

[BUTLER HOUSE]
ST. GEORGE'S
[GRENADA]
WEST INDIES

TEL: 3383   3020   17th Feb 1982

TO: Commander Andropov
         Chairman of the Committee of State Security
         Member of Politiburo

FROM: General of the Army Hudson Austin

Dear Comrade,

Warmest revolutionary greetings to you, the Communist Party of Soviet Union and all Soviet people, from the Political Bureau of the New Jewel Movement, Government, Armed Forces and all the Grenadian people.

Let me first of all extend our deepest sympathies to your Party and people on the passing away of comrade Suslov, a true Bolshevik and hero of revolutionary people worldwide.

[I write at this time to] request assistance in the strengthening of our Ministry of Interior. This request stems from discussions *[held between]* Cde. Vladmir Klimentov, then attached to the Soviet Embassy in Jamaica, *[illeg.]* Comrade Maurice Bishop, Chairman of the Central Committee of our Party the New Jewel Movement, Prime Minister and

Minister of Defence and Interior of the People's Revolutionary
Government, Comrade Liam James, Member of the Central
Committee of our Party and Head of the Ministry of Interior
[*and myself. Peoples Revo. Govt.* illeg. *formally request the following*] training courses for four (4) [*of our*] comrades: —

a) Basic course in Counter Intelligence for the period of
one (1) year - three (3) comrades

b) Basic course in Intelligence for a period of one (1) year -
one (1) comrade.

We thank you once again for the tremendous assistance
which our Armed Forces have received from your Party and
Government in the past. We recognise the tremendous internationalist obligations of your people, yet we sincerely hope
that these courses will be made available to our comrades in
1982, given the pressing needs in our Ministry and the continuing threat being posted to the Grenada Revolution by
United States Imperialism.

I close by once again extending our greatest warmth and
embrace to you and your Party - Sons and Daughters of the
heroic Lenin. I look forward to hearing from you soon.

Yours Fraternally,

....

General Hudson Austin
Member of the Political Bureau of NJM
Secretary of Defence and Interior.

II-2
Letter from Bishop to Ustinov
2/17/82

MINISTRY OF DEFENCE

FORT RUPERT   ST. GEORGE'S
GRENADA   WEST INDIES

TELEPHONE: 2263 2378   17th February 1982

TO: MARSHAL DIMITROV USTINOV,
     MINISTER OF DEFENCE
     USSR

FROM: MINISTER OF DEFENCE, MAURICE BISHOP.

Dear Comrade,

Revolutionary greetings to you, the Communist Party of the Soviet Union and all Soviet people, from the Political Bureau of the New Jewel Movement, Government, Armed Forces and all the Grenadian people.

I am writing this letter to you in reference to training for personnel of the Grenadian Armed Forces in your country.

Based on Article Three of the Signed Protocol between the Government of Grenada and the Government of the USSR of 27th October, 1980 in Havana, Cuba, I hereby make the following request -

1. Military preparation for twenty (20) Junior Officers in the following areas in courses lasting a period of one year;

a) General Troops   - 6
b) Exploration   - 3
c) Communication   - 2
d) Engineering   - 2
e) Logistics   - 3
f) Anti-Aircraft Artillery - 2
g) Terrestrial   - 2

2. Training for five(5) senior officers of the General Staff of the armed forces on a rotational basis in courses lasting three to six months.

The comrades who will be prepared in these courses are the leaders of our armed forces and as such cannot stay away for long periods at this time.

The areas of preparation for the comrades will be -

a) General Troops - 4
b) Political work in the Armed Forces - 1

We are hope ful that these courses will commence in 1982 and as such we are commencing all the preliminary work for the departure of our comrades.

Comrade Marshal, I want to thank you once more for all the assistance our armed forces have received from your country and say that we are extremely thankful for that.

Finally, I want to say that our Party and Armed Forces look forward with the greatest expectations to our comrades receiving training with the glorious Red Army, in the land of the Immortal Lenin and the Great October Revolution which opened a new world to mankind.

We thank you in advance for your kind co-operation and look forward to hearing from you soon.

Maurice Bishop,
COMMANDER IN CHIEF,
CHAIRMAN OF THE CENTRAL COMMITTEE
OF NJM,
PRIME MINISTER AND MINISTER OF
DEFENCE AND INTERIOR.

II-3
Agreement between U.S.S.R. and Grenada
7/27/80

Top Secret
AGREEMENT
between the Government of Grenada and the Government of the Union of Soviet Socialist Republics on deliveries from the Union of SSR to Grenada of special and other equipment

The Government of Grenada and the Government of the Union of Soviet Socialist Republics,

guided by aspirations for developing and strengthening friendly relations between both countries on the principles of equality, mutual respect of sovereignty and non-interference into internal affairs.

proceeding from the desire to promote strengthening the independence of Grenada

and in connection with the request of the Government of Grenada

have agreed upon the following:

Article 1

The Government of the Union of Soviet Socialist Republics shall ensure in 1982-1985 free of charge the delivery to the Government of Grenada of special and civil equipment in nomenclature and quantity according to Annexes 1 and 2 to the present Agreement to the amount of 10,000,000 Roubles.

Article 2

The delivery of the equipment listed in Annexes 1 and 2 to the present Agreement shall be effected by the Soviet Party by sea, at the port of the Republic of Cuba.

The order of the further delivery of the above equipment from the Republic of Cuba shall be agreed upon between the Grenadian and Cuban Parties.

Article 3

The Government of the Union of SSR at the request of the Government of Grenada shall ensure rendering technical assistance in mastering of the equipment under delivery by receiving in the USSR Grenadian servicemen for training in the operation, use and maintenance of the special equipment as well as by sending Soviet specialists to Grenada for these purposes.

The Grenadian servicemen shall be sent to the USSR for training without their families.

The expenses connected with the Grenadian servicemen's training, upkeep, meals in the Soviet military educational establishments as well as with their travel fare from Grenada to the USSR and back shall be borne by the Soviet Party.

The Government of Grenada shall provide at its own expense the Soviet specialists and interpreters with comfortable furnished living accommodation with all the municipal utilities, medical service and transport facilities for the execution of their duties and shall ensure their having meals at reasonable prices at the places of their residense.

The Soviet specialists and interpreters shall not be imposed by any taxes and duties on entering or leaving Grenada and during their stay there. All other expenses connected with deputation of the Soviet specialists to Grenada shall be borne by the Soviet Party.

Article 4

The Soviet Party in periods to be agreed upon between the Parties shall depute a group of Soviet specialists to Grenada to determine expediency, opportunity and scope of rendering technical assistance in the creation of the stationary shop for repair of the special equipment and transport, commanding staff trainer school, training facilities for Armed Forces as well as the deliveries of missing building materials for construction of the storehouses and road.

The deputation of a group of Soviet specialists shall be effected on the terms and conditions of Article 3 of the present Agreement.

Article 5

The Government of the Union of SSR shall ensure free of charge the transfer to the Government of Grenada of necessary technical descriptions, instructions and manuals in standard composition on operation of the special equipment delivered under the present Agreement.

Article 6

The appropriate Grenadian and Soviet organizations shall conclude contracts in which there shall be stipulated the detailed terms and conditions of deputing Soviet specialists, receiving for training Grenadian servicemen and other services connected with the implementation of the present Agreement.

Article 7

The Government of Grenada shall not without the consent of the Government of the Union of Soviet Socialist Republics sell or transfer, formally or actually, the special equipment, delivered under the present Agreement, the relevant documentation and information or give permission to use the equipment and documentation by a third party or any physical or legal persons but the officials and specialists of the citizenship of Grenada being in the service with the Government of Grenada.

The Government of the Union of SSR and the Government of Grenada shall take all the necessary measures to ensure keeping in secret the terms and conditions of the deliveries, all the correspondence and information connected with the implementation of the present Agreement.

Article 8

The present Agreement comes into force on the date it is signed on.

Annexes 1 and 2 are an integral part of the present Agreement.

Done in Moscow on July "27", 1982 in two originals, each in the English and Russian languages, both texts being equally valid.

FOR AND ON BEHALF

OF THE GOVERNMENT OF
GRENADA

[signature]

FOR AND ON BEHALF

OF THE GOVERNMENT OF
THE UNION OF SOVIET
SOCIALIST REPUBLICS

[signature]

Top secret

ANNEX

to Agreement of July 27, 1982

LIST

of special equipment to be delivered to the Army of Grenada
from the Soviet Union in 1983-1985

Description	Unit of measure	Quantity-total	Years of delivery		
			1983	1984	1985
Armour material					
BTR-152V1 armoured personnel carriers, used, repaired	piece	50	—	30	20
7.62-mm rifle cartridges without clips:					
with steel core bullet	thous. pieces	100.5	—	60.3	40.2
with B-32 armour-piercing-incendiary bullet and steel case	thous. pieces	37.5	—	22.5	15.0
with T-46 tracer bullet	thous. pieces	49.5	—	29.7	19.8

Top secret
ANNEX
to Agreement of July 27, 1982

LIST

of special equipment to be delivered to the Army of Grenada
from the Soviet Union in 1983-1985

Description	Unit of measure	Quantity-total	Years of delivery		
			1983	1984	1985
Artillery armament and ammunition					
76-mm 215-3 guns, used, repaired	piece	30	18	12	
76-mm rounds:					
with fragemntation and high-explosive-fragmentation grenade	thous. pieces	9.3	5.6	3.7	
with armour-piercing-tracer shell	piece	540	330	210	
with sub-calibre armour-piercing shell	piece	450	270	180	
with hollow charge shell	piece	540	330	210	
57-mm 215-2 anti-tank guns, used, repaired	piece	30	10	12	
57-mm rounds:					
with fragmentation grenade	thous. pieces	5.4	3.2	2.2	
with armour-piercing-tracer shell	thous. pieces	4.0	2.4	1.6	
with sub-calibre armour-piercing shell	thous. pieces	1.3	0.0	0.5	

II-4
Protocol between U.S.S.R. and Grenada
10/27/80

Top secret

PROTOCOL

to the Agreement between the Government of
Grenada and the Government of the USSR of
October 27, 1980 on deliveries from the USSR
to Grenada of special and other equipment

The Government of Grenada and the Government of the
Union of Soviet Socialist Republics

have agreed upon the following:

Article 1

The Government of the Union of Soviet Socialist Republics
shall ensure free of charge the delivery in 1981-1983 to the
Government of Grenada of special and other equipment in
nomenclature and quantity according to the Annex to the
present Agreement to the amount of 5,000,000 Roubles.

Article 2

In all other respects the Parties will be guided by the provisions of the Agreement between the Government of Grenada
and the Government of the USSR of October 27, 1980 on deliveries from the USSR to Grenada of special and other equipment.

Article 3

The present Protocol comes into force on the date of its signing.

The Annex is an integral part of the present Protocol.

Done in Havana on February "9th", 1981 in two originals, each in the English and Russian languages, both texts being equally valid.

FOR AND ON BEHALF

OF THE GOVERNMENT OF
GRENADA

[signature]

FOR AND ON BEHALF

OF THE GOVERNMENT OF
THE UNION OF SOVIET
SOCIALIST REPUBLICS

[signature]

II-5
Letter from Bishop to Ortega
7/17/81

[*17.7.81*]

TO: COMMANDANTE DANIEL ORTEGA SAAVEDRA
COMMANDER OF THE NICARAGUAN REVOLUTION.

[*My dear Daniel*]

Warmest fraternal and Revolutionary greetings!

On the occasion of the second Anniversary of the glorious
Nicaraguan Revolution Our Party, Government and People extend our total and complete solidarity with the FSLN, your
Government of National Reconstruction and the fighting children of Sandino.

Cde Hudson Austin, Member of our Political Bureau and
General of the People's Revolutionary Army, will be representing our Party and Government at your second Anniversary.
Cde Austin will be very anxious to discuss the present situation in Nicaragua and to inform you of our present situation. I
am certain, from the reports we have been receiving, that our
two situations are under similar pressures. It is clear that U.S.
Imperialism has decided to make an all-out onslaught on our
two Revolutions. The propaganda war, the economic aggression, the Political and Industrial destabilisation and the threat
of mercenary invasion all lead to the unmistakeable conclusion that imperialism has decided to attempt to overthrow our
popular Revolutions this year. That is their decision; but we
have made our own decision that our Revolutions will continue and undoubtedly we will win out. As our People say in
Grenada—A UNITED, CONSCIOUS, ORGANISED AND VIGIL-
ANT PEOPLE CAN NEVER BE DEFEATED.

In whatever way we can, and at whatever cost, the Grenada Revolution and the People of Grenada will always stand with the Nicaraguan Revolution and the People of Nicaragua.

LONG LIVE THE NICARAGUAN REVOLUTION:

LONG LIVE THE FSLN!

LONG LIVE THE UNBREAKABLE BONDS OF FRIENDSHIP BETWEEN THE PEOPLE OF GRENADA AND NICARAGUA!

FORWARD EVER, BACKWARD NEVER!

A Warm Embrace,

[*Maurice*]

II-6
Agreement between Bulgaria and Grenada
(no date)

A G R E E M E N T

for cooperation between the Bulgarian
Communist Party and the New JEWEL
Movement of Grenada for the period
1982 - 1983

The Bulgarian Communist Party (BCP) and the New JEWEL
Movement (NJM) guided by their mutual desire for
strengthening and enhancing the links of friendship and
cooperation between them, for promoting the friendly relations between the Bulgarian and the Grenada peoples, between the People's Republic of Bulgaria and Grenada, in the
interest of the unity and cohesion of all progressive and anti-
imperialist forces in the world in the struggle against imperialism, for peace, democracy and social progress, have
reached agreement on the following plan for cooperation for
the period 1982 - 1983:

I.

The Bulgarian Communist Party shall receive:

A. In 1982:

1. A two-member delegation of the New JEWEL Movement
for [illeg.] days, to become acquainted with the experience of
the [illeg.] issues of interest to the Party.

Term: second half of the year

B. In 1983:

1. A two-member delegation of the NJM for seven days, to become acquainted with the experience of the BCP on issues of interest to the Party.

Term: second half of the year

The New JEWEL Movement shall receive:

A. In 1982:

1. A two-member delegation of the BCP for seven days, to become acquainted with the experience of the NJM on issues proposed by the BCP.

Term: second half of the year

B. In 1983:

1. A two-member delegation of the BCP for seven days, to become acquainted with the experience of the NJM on issues presented by the BCP.

Term: second half of the year

II.

1. The Bulgarian Communist Party shall grant the New JEWEL Movement yearly, 10 allowances for training cadres in the ten-month specialized courses at the Academy of Social Sciences on Management at the Central Committee of the Bulgarian Communist Party.

2. The Bulgarian Communist Party and the New JEWEL Movement shall exchange delegations which shall participate in the congresses, conferences and other major events organized by them.

3. The Bulgarian Communist Party and the New JEWEL Movement shall assist in the promotion of more intensive cooperation between the public and mass organisations in the People's Republic of Bulgaria and Grenada.

4. The Bulgarian Communist Party and the New JEWEL Movement shall carry out mutual consultations and shall exchange regularly publications, bulletins, films and other materials related to the activities of the two parties.

5. The Bulgarian Communist Party and the New JEWEL Movement may reach agreement on initiatives which have not been included in the present Agreement and which, in their opinion, would help to further strengthen and enhance the relations of friendship between the Bulgarian Communist Party and the New JEWEL Movement, between the People's Republic of Bulgaria and Grenada.

III.

The present Agreement is drawn up in two copies, each in Bulgarian and in English, both texts of equal validity.

FOR THE BULGARIAN COM-   FOR THE NEW JEWEL
MUNIST PARTY: MOVEMENT:

[signature]   [signature]

II-7
Note from Czechoslovakian Embassy
(no date)

EMBAJADA DE GRANADA EN CUBA

Sta. AVENIDA No. 8409 Esq. 84   Telefonos:
MIRAMAR, CIUDAD HABANA   29-5429
CUBA   29-3913

I have received the following note from the Checoslovacian Embassy:

Consequent upon a request from the Deputy Prime Minister Bernard Coard, presented during his visit to Checoslovacia in June of 1980, the Government of Checslovacia has agreed to provide to the Government of Grenada free of cost the following items listed below:

3,000 - 7.62mm automatic rifles type: 52/57

30 boxes of spare parts (SZY 1 KU 100) for automatic rifles type 52/57

1 million cartrages for 7.62 type 43 .

50 bazoocas P 27

5 boxes of spare parts (SZV II) for P 27

5,000 projectiles for bazooca P 27

These pieces of equipment will be sent to Cuba between the latter part of September and the early part of October and transhipped to Grenada. We are making the necessary arrangements through the Embassy with the Ministery of the Armed Forces.

   As I understand it, you have already received information about the agreement of the Government of Bulgaria to provide other military equipment.

Typed by Richard Jacobs seen also by Otto Marero

[several lines of illegible handwriting follow.]

II-8
Agreement between Grenada and E. Germany
6/10/82

Agreement
on cooperation between the New JEWEL Movement of Grenada and the Socialist Unity Party of Germany for the years
1982 to 1985

Guided by the desire

to deepen the friendly relations between the New JEWEL
Movement of Grenada and the Socialist Unity Party of Germany in the spirit of anti-imperialist solidarity and proletarian internationalism;

to mutually exchange information on the development of national and social liberation in Grenada and the construction of
the advanced socialist society in the German Democratic Republic, and

to conduct a constant exchange of views on the international
situation and the foreign policy of both Parties,

both sides agree on the following fields of cooperation for the
period up to 1985:

1. The New JEWEL Movement and the Socialist Unity Party
   of Germany attach great importance to the mutual study
   of their experiences of the revolutionary struggle. Both
   Parties shall exchange material on the political, social,
   economic and cultural development of their countries.

2. The Socialist Unity Party of Germany declares its readiness to assist the New JEWEL Movement in the training
   and political qualification of its cadres. The Socialist
   Unity Party of Germany will aid the drawing up of a

study programme for the acquisition of a knowledge of scientific socialism.

3. The New JEWEL Movement and the Socialist Unity Party of Germany shall exchange information of mutual interest on the development and lessons of the revolutionary process in both countries and also on international questions.

4. Both Parties proclaim their reciprocal solidarity in the struggle against imperialism and reaction and declare their readiness to promote understanding for both revolutions within the world revolutionary movement.

5. Both Parties shall promote the development of cooperation between the mass organizations of their countries.

6. The central organs of the New JEWEL Movement and the Socialist Unity Party of Germany shall enter into a mutual exchange of experiences and shall support each other in their journalistic activity.

7. Both Parties shall promote and support the development of friendly relations between the Governments and peoples of the German Democratic Republic and Grenada.

The New JEWEL Movement and the Socialist Unity Party of Germany shall further concretize these measures by means of annual working plans which shall be drawn up and agreed upon by authorized representatives of both Parties.

For the New JEWEL
Movement of Grenada

[signature]

George Louison
Member of the Political
Bureau of the Central
Committee of the New JEWEL
Movement

Berlin, 10 June 1982

For the Socialist Unity
Party of Germany

[signature]

Hermann Axen
Member of the Political
Bureau and Secretary of the
Central Committee of the
Socialist Unity Party of
Germany

Working Plan
for cooperation between the New JEWEL Movement of Grenada and the Socialist Unity Party of Germany for the years
1982/1983

On the basis of the long-term Agreement on Cooperation
between the New JEWEL Movement and the Socialist Unity
Party of Germany, the following measures are laid down for
the years 1982/1983:

I

The Socialist Unity Party of Germany shall receive:
1. a study delegation of the New JEWEL Movement consisting
   of two comrades who shall acquaint themselves with the
   experiences of the Socialist Unity Party of Germany.

2. in 1982 two comrades and in 1983 five comrades of the
   New JEWEL Movement to study at the Karl Marx party
   college.

3. two representatives of the New JEWEL Movement each
   year for a holiday visit to the German Democratic Republic.

The New JEWEL Movement of Grenada shall receive:

1. a study delegation of the Socialist Unity Party of Germany consisting of two comrades for a period of ten days to study the political work of the New JEWEL Movement in 1983.

2. in line with its wish, a temporary adviser from the Socialist Unity Party of Germany on questions of building up the Party (duration of stay to be agreed).

3. annually two representatives of the Socialist Unity Party of Germany for a holiday visit to Grenada.

Both Parties shall inform each other in good time on the dates, the subject matters and the respective representatives responsible for the fufilment of these tasks and others which may be agreed.

III

The Socialist Unity Party of Germany shall continue to assist in the operation of the New JEWEL Movement's printing press and the training of personnel in this area.

II-9
Letter from Carames to James
(no date)

REPUBLICA DE CUBA
MINISTERIO DEL INTERIOR

Havana City

Lieutenant Colonel Liam James
Director of Security and Internal Order
Granada

Dear Comrade:

I am pleased to inform you that in compliance with the offer-
ings of help to the security of your country, expressed by the
Ambassador of the German Democratic Republic in Cuba,
Harry Splinder conveyed in its occasion to the Prime Minister
Maurice Bishop, the Minister of the Security of the G.D.R.
has decided to give in a free way to the Security Bodies of
Granada, the means and equipments that appear in the enclosed list, which, without any doubt will help to strengthen
the operative capacity of the Security Bodies of your country.

These materials, which we have at hand already, will be sent
to your country as soon as there is an opportunity of transportation available.

Comrade James, we hope that this modest assistance will help
to strengthen the operative capacity of the Granadian Security
in its struggle against the imperialism and the enemies of the
country.

We do not want to say good by without stating before, the interest shown by the Comrade Ambassador of the G.D.R. to realize this assistance.

Wishing you success in your work and in the important tasks assigned to you.

Whit revolucionarity greeting,

Colonel Luis Barreiro Carames
J'Estado Mayor Central

	UNIT
1.-MAGNETOPHONE	20
2.-APPARATUS TO PROJECT FILM (PROYECTION MACHINE)	10
3.-TYPEWRITER	15
4.-IRON HELMUT	10
5.-HAND COMPASS	300
6.-BINOCULARS	10
7.-GAS MASK	25
8.-BICYCLE	32
9.-COTTON UNIFORMS	500
10.-UPPER SHEET	500
11.-LOWER SHEET	500
12.-PILLOWCASE	500
13.-KNAPSACK	500
14.-RAINCOAT	500
16.-PISTOLS (WITH CARTRIDGES)	28
17.-SANITARY BAGS	40
18.-TELEPHONE "MB"	40
19.-SHALE "MB"	10
20.-BATTERY	200

II-10
Request for Military Assistance
7/2/82

TELEPHONE ....   2nd July, 1982

Revolutionary Armed Forces
Grenada

Request for Military assistance to the Peoples Revolutionary
Armed Forces of Grenada from the Armed Forces of the
U.S.S.R.

The present request we are asking is to conclude an agreement between the People's Revolutionary Government of Grenada and the Government of the U.S.S.R. to Arm, Feed, Clothed
Equip and provide the necessary storage and study base for
the consolidation and further development of the Revolutionary Armed Forces of Grenada over a period of three years.

This agreement is to take into consideration all previous
assistance granted, and other existing means and facilities of
the Grenada Armed Forces.

The agreement is to be reviewed on a yearly basis, at which
delivery arrangements will be decided.

The plan for the development of the Armed Forces during
the three (3) year period 1983 to 1985 for which the assistance is required is as follows:-

1983   - (i) Further consolidation of:-
                (a) One Permanent Infantry Batallion.
                (b) Five (5) Reservist Infantry Batallions plus
                    assurance and support units.

      (ii) The creation of:-

          (a) Two (2) more regular Infantry Batallions

          (b) Four (4) more reservist Batallions plus assurance and support units.

1984 - Formation of one additional regular Infantry Batallion, together with two (2) reservist batallions plus assurance and support units.

1985 - Formation of three (3) additional reservist batallions plus assurance and support units.

The appendices (1-3) to this letter deals with the details of our request.

$$\left[\begin{array}{c} 4\ regular\ Bt \\ +\ 14\ reservist\ Bt \end{array}\right]$$

II-11
Agreement between Grenada and C.P.S.U.
7/27/82

AGREEMENT

In cooperation between the New JEWEL Movement
of Grenada and the Communist Party
of the Soviet Union

The Central Committee of the New JEWEL Movement of Grenada and the Central Committee Communist Party of the
Soviet Union,

Guided by the desire to deepen relations between the two parties in a spirit of friendship solidarity,

[illeg.]offing that common commitment to the ideals of peace,
national liberation, democracy and [illeg.]c socialism creates
favourable opportunities for cooperation,

Proceeding from common goals in the struggle against imperialism, neocolonialism, racialism [illeg.] reaction in all
their forms and manifestations,

Reasserting their constant striving to render internationlist
support to all peoples fighting for freedom, independence and
social progress,

and considering that inter-party cooperation is a most important basis for the development of [illeg.]y relations between
the peoples of Grenada and the Soviet Union,

have signed the present Agreement under which both parties
declare their intention:

1. Steadfastly to extend and deepen their cooperation at all
levels.

2. Continuosly to exchange experience in party work and
party guidance of the social, economic and cultural development of their countries, including regular exchange of information and materials on the aforesaid topics.

3. Regularly to exchange delegations of party workers, to
conduct consultations and exchanges of opinion on interna-

tional matters, problems of the world revolutionary process
and present-day social development, and other matters of
mutual interest.

4. To promote cooperation in the training of party and government cadres and in furthering political competence.

5. To develop contacts between the party press and other
mass communication media, to inform the public of their
countries about the activity of the two parties, and of their
home and foreign policy, and resolutely to combat hostile imperialist and reactionary propaganda.

6. To promote all-round development of inter-state relations
and ties between mass organisations of their countries.

7. Periodically to coordinate and implement concrete plans of
inter-party ties, including initiatives that are not covered by
the present Agreement.

FOR THE NEW JEWEL   FOR THE COMMUNIST PARTY
MOVEMENT OF GRENADA   OF THE SOVIET UNION

[signature]   [signature]

Moscow, 27 July 1982

II-12
Agreement between Grenada and N. Korea
(4/14/83)

AGREEMENT

between the People's Revolutionary Government of Grenada and the Government of the Democratic People's Republic of Korea on the free offer of military assistance to the People's Revolutionary Government of Grenada by the Democratic People's Republic of Korea.

For the purposes of further cementing and developing the friendship and solidarity between the peoples and armies of the two countries established in the common struggle to oppose against imperialism, consolidate the national sovereignty and safeguard independence, and strengthening the national defence power of Grenada, the People's Revolutionary Government of the Democratic People's Republic of Korea have agreed as follows;

Article 1

The Government of the Democratic People's Republic of Korea shall give, in 1983-1984, the free military assistance subject to weapons and ammunitions covering US $12,000,000 indicated in Annex to this Agreement.

Article 2

The Grenadian side shall be responsible for the transport of weapons and ammunitions to be rendered to the People's Revolutionary Government of Grenada by the Democratic People's Republic of Korea.

Article 3

Both sides shall strictly keep the secrecy of the military assistance to be executed according to this Agreement and have

an obligation not to hand over any matters of this Agreement
to the third country.

Article 4

This Agreement shall come into force on the day of its signing.

This Agreement has been prepared in duplicate in the Korean and English languages and signed in Pyongyang on April
14, 1983, two original equally authentic.

[signature]   [signature]

By the authority of the   By the authority of the
People's Revolutionary   Government of the
Government of Grenada.   Democratic People's
                                     Republic of Korea.

ANNEX

of Agreement on the free offer of military assistance to the
People's Revolutionary Government of Grenada by the Democratic People's Republic of Korea.

Hand flares	200	pcs
Ammunition for hand flares	4,000	rds
7.62mm automatic rifle	1,000	pcs
7.62mm light machine gun	50	pcs
Ammunition for 7.62mm auto. rifle	360,000	rds
7.62mm blanks	300,000	rds
7.62mm heavy machine gun	30	pcs
Ammunition for heavy machine gun	60,000	rds
RPG-7 launcher	50	pcs
RPG-7	500	rds
Hand grenade	200	rds
Instruction hand grenade	20	rds
Binoculars (8ˣ)	30	pcs
Anti-gas masks	1,000	pcs
Sirens	50	pcs

Tactical drawing instruments	15	sets
Coast guard	2	boats
Uniforms	6,000	suits
Knapsacks	6,000	pcs
Camouflage nets	50	pcs
Ultrashort waves wireless set (= −3)	3	pcs
Ultrashort waves wireless set (= −4)	3	pcs

II-13
Cooperation Agreement between Cuba and Grenada
6/29/83

TOP SECRET

PARTIDO COMUNISTA DE CUBA / COMITE CENTRAL

SECRET

COOPERATION AND EXCHANGE OF PLAN BETWEEN THE
COMMUNIST PARTY OF CUBA AND THE NEW JEWEL MOVE-
MENT OF GRENADA, FOR THE 1983 PERIOD.

INTRODUCTION

The Communist Party of Cuba and the New Jewel Movement,
brotherly united by the same ideals of struggle in their respective countries, as well as of active solidarity in favor of the
peoples that struggle for national liberation, and likewise,
sharing the same convictions against imperialism, colonialism, neocolonialism, Zionism, and racism, become aware
of the need to unite efforts and coordinate actions of cooperation in the different activities within their scope.

.   .   .   .

Both Parties, on agreeing that the many-sided relations of
cooperation be governed by the widest and justest spirit of
cooperation, solidarity, and internationalism, reach agreement on the following:

b) The CPC expresses its willingness to send, according to the
   requests formulated by the NJM in this sense, technical

advisers for the organization of public meetings and propaganda of the Party in Grenada.

c) Regarding the political upgrading and professional assistance, the NJM and the CPC express their willingness to receive, at the "Nico Lopez" School, the NJM cadres that will be decided on mutual agreement.

d) The CPC and the NJM of Grenada will exchange information of mutual interest, both on the field of the development of the two revolutions and their experiences, as well as on the international situation and, fundamentally, that of the Caribbean in its struggle against imperialism, neocolonialism, racism and Zionism. Likewise, they will exchange information on the liberation movements as well as coordinate actions and positions of mutual interest to be adopted at events, conferences, and other Party activities of an international character, with special emphasis on the problems in the Caribbean.

.   .   .   .

The CPC and the NJM will coordinate the positions of the governments of Cuba and Grenada at international events, conferences, and agencies where they participate, in attention to the political, economic and social interests of both Parties.

.   .   .   .

The Communist Party of Cuba and the New Jewel Movement of Grenada, satisfied by the discussed and agreed aspects, which fully correspond with the fraternal relations between both Parties, underwrite this document in the City of Havana, Cuba, June 29th, 1983.

[signature]   [signature]

The Communist Party   The New Jewel
     of Cuba   Movement

II-14
Letter from Bishop to Assad
10/4/79

4th October, 1979.

H.E. Hafez El Assad,
President of the Arab Republic of Syria,
Arab Republic of Syria,
C/O The U.N. Ambassador from Syria,
Syrian Embassy,
New York,
U.S.A.

I am very happy to take this opportunity to write to you concerning the discussions we recently had in Havana during the Non-Aligned Conference.

You will recall that during our discussions, we agreed on the need for our countries to establish diplomatic relations at the earliest opportunity and thereafter for your country to ac-credit your Ambassador to Havana to Grenada.

We also agreed that a Technical Co-operation Team from your country should visit Grenada at an early opportunity with a view to assessing areas of possible technical and economic co-operation and assistance between our countries. Needless to say, I am very anxious for further discussion on these areas of possible co-operation and as such, on behalf of the People's Revolutionary Government of Grenada and the people of Grenada, I am inviting you to send such a team to Grenada as soon as possible.

I want you to know that it was a real pleasure for me to have had the opportunity to discuss so many matters of mutual concern to our countries with you. I sincerely hope that you will be able to come to our country on a state visit at a mutually convenient date in the future. At the same time, until that visit, I am asking you to assist our people in Grenada to learn more about The Republic of Syria and as such we would very much appreciate receiving, if possible, copies of any radio tapes, television video tapes, 16mm or 35mm films or printed matter that your government may have on your country and your struggle for true independence.

We would also welcome a visit to our country by any cultural group from your country that might happen to be coming to this region.

You can rest assured of the continued support of our government and party to the just cause of the Palestinians under the leadership of the P.L.O., our commitment to continue resisting the manoeuvrings of imperialism and the Israeli Zionists and our continued opposition to the treacherous Camp David Agreement.

On behalf of my government, party and people I send warmest fraternal regards to you, your government and people.

Long live the just struggle of the Arab Republic of Syria for social progress, genuine independence and peace with justice in the Middle East!

Yours fraternally

....
MAURICE BISHOP,
PRIME MINISTER.

III
DOMESTIC POLITICAL CONSOLIDATION

Maurice Bishop began his political career as co-founder of the Movement of Assemblies of the People during the last years of British rule in Grenada. In 1973 he merged his movement with the JEWEL (Joint Endeavor for Welfare, Education, and Liberation) organization of Unison Whiteman and Selwyn Strachan, as well as the Organization for Revolutionary Education and Liberation (OREL) of Bernard Coard, to form the New Jewel Movement (NJM). Its task was to win control of the island following Grenadian independence in 1974, but the first elections, held in 1976, ratified the rule of the eccentric and authoritarian Prime Minister, Sir Eric Gairy, and his armed bodyguard, the "Mongoose Gang." Bishop recounts in his 1982 "Line of March" speech that the NJM's reversal at that juncture was due to its failure to take a "deep class approach." In April 1974, therefore, the NJM solemnly dedicated itself to the building of a "Leninist Party," and the pursuit of "mass mobilization" and alliance with the "petit-bourgeois." The Party made its move in March 1979, taking advantage of Gairy's absence overseas. Armed cadres seized the radio station and the barracks of Gairy's defense force, and proclaimed Bishop prime minister of a People's Revolutionary Government. Bishop consummated the coup d'etat, the first in an ex-British colony in the New World, by suspending the Constitution and replacing it with "People's Laws" decreed by the new party-state.

From the moment of assuming power the leaders of the NJM described themselves privately as a "Leninist party" dedicated to the building of socialism under a one-party dictatorship. The presentation of the movement as a National Democratic Party in alliance with farmers and shopkeepers is described in Bishop's speech as a mere tactic necessitated by Grenada's socio-economic under-development and the primitive stage of the Revolution (document III-1). In its years of struggle under Gairy, however, the NJM seems to have been a syncretic amalgam of West Indian

nationalist, populist, and Marxist elements. Its original manifesto
of 1973 characterized the tourist industry, for instance, as
"national-cultural prostitution," and promised "decentralized village assemblies" of free peasants. By 1979 the Marxist strain was
clearly dominant, and Bishop's strict procedures for Party
recruitment and promotion ensured the Leninist sympathies and
discipline of party members.

Once in power, the Bishop regime undertook a broad program of
mass mobilization with the apparent aim of subordinating every
activity, institution, and social group to the party-state. The police
and People's Revolutionary Army were vastly expanded and
politicized, trained and equipped with the aid of Soviet-bloc countries. The Central Committee's Political Security forces anchored
the campaign of domestic surveillance. Routine monitoring of
neighborhoods, schoolrooms, church services, workers' gatherings,
and businesses led to the detention of hundreds of persons (perhaps
over a thousand, or one percent of the population) on suspicion of
political disloyalty. The Party's centralized propaganda apparatus
sought to "[d]eepen the consciousness of the masses as to the history of the vanguard role of the party and the heroes of the revolution. . . . Deepen the internationalist spirit and socialist consciousness of the Grenadian masses." This was pursued through man-
datory indoctrination classes and national "movements" for workers, farmers, youth, and women (documents III-4, 7, 8). Their publications included "Fight" (National Youth Organization), "The
Scotilda" (National Women's Organization), "Fork" (Productive
Farmers' Union), "Workers Voice" (Workers' Committee), "Fedon"
(People's Revolutionary Armed Forces), and "Cutlass" (Agricultural and General Workers' Union). A vast citizens' militia on the
model of Cuba's National Labour and Service Army was planned,
and apparently grew to some 2500 members. In economic policy,
the NJM dispensed with "village assemblies" and planned the
gradual collectivization of agriculture (document III-10). It also
sought to expand tourism (the ostensible justification for the new
airport), encouraged exchange of tourists and students with Cuba
and Eastern Europe, and established a government monopoly of
foreign trade oriented toward Soviet bloc countries (document
III-11). The NJM's own internal documents testify to its rejection
of Social Democracy (see Part VI below). Its 1982 "Line of March"

speech pointed to the assumption of total power by a "Leninist Party." And in an island of 110,000 people, this ambitious program seemed attainable. Yet, by Year 3 of the revolution, the Party's failure to indoctrinate and mobilize the masses was so glaring as to provoke the split and collapse of the Party itself (see Part VIII below). The incompetence of the NJM lends events in Grenada an air of *opera bouffe*. But that should not obscure the reality of the movement's goals: to build a thoroughgoing Marxist-Leninist state in the Caribbean.

III-1
"Line of March" Speech
9/13/82

In this crucial oration, Maurice Bishop bluntly describes the totalitarian regime set up by the NJM, as well as the movement's intention to maintain and extend the undemocratic character of its rule. Bishop admits that the NJM had "hegemonic control on power" and outlines how non-NJM elements, originally part of the PRG, had by 1982 been removed: "Lloyd Noel is in detention; Pam Buxo is out of the country; Lyle Bullen is no longer involved." In a particular display of braggadocio, Bishop proclaims the ethos of NJM justice in Grenada: "You get detained when I sign an order ... once I sign it, like it or don't like it, it's up the hill [to Richmond Hill prison]." On freedom of the press, Bishop states: "When they want to put out a newspaper, and we don't want that, we close it down ... if the truth is told, they have been repressed by the dictatorship. They have lost some of the rights they used to have." He finally describes the specific mechanism of political repression: "We pretend we don't know what is happening and let the trade unionists do it."

Although Bishop here outlines a proposal for an NJM alliance with "elements of the upper petty bourgeoisie and the national bourgeoisie," it is clear that this "alliance" was never perceived as a partnership of political equals. Rather, Bishop proposed to ally with these elements only in the effort to improve the country's economic situation, while continuing to consolidate a Soviet-model government. Bishop clearly intended to dispense with the "national democratic" phase of the revolution and to proceed to a more total dictatorship within a relatively short time.

CONFIDENTIAL

LINE OF MARCH FOR THE PARTY
PRESENTED BY
COMRADE MAURICE BISHOP
CHAIRMAN, CENTRAL COMMITTEE
TO
GENERAL MEETING
OF
PARTY
ON
MONDAY 13th SEPTEMBER 1982

Comrades of the Political Bureau and Central Committee of the Party, Comrades of the Party.

I will like to join with Comrade Strachan to say on behalf of the Central Committee that we are very happy to have all the comrades here this afternoon. As Comrade Selwyn has pointed out, essentially what we want to do today is to deal with the proposed line of march as examined by the C.C. of the Party in the last few weeks.

In our view the line of march needs to take into account four specific features: —

Firstly, the present character and stage of the Revolution. We regard that as fundamentally important. We must decide what exactly is a correct characterisation of the present stage of the Revolution!

Secondly, the line of march must address in a serious way the question of the main tasks facing the Party and Revolution at this time.

Thirdly, we must determine a correct prioritisation of those tasks; we must establish priorities bearing in mind particularly, the comments, criticisms, suggestions, proposals etc. which have been made by Party members and, of course, taking into account the totality of the objective and subjective situation.

The fourth and final factor is the need to emphasise the further development of the subjective factor, the need to place great emphasis and importance on the further development of the subjective factor, that is to say, the Party. In other words, we must look at the Party itself, review the history of the Party very briefly and deal with the question of criteria for membership into the Party and for remaining as members of the Party.

Comrades, in terms of the character of the Revolution, the first aspect to the line of march, we believe it is important for us to look at this question at this time for several reasons.

Firstly and obviously, because we must as a Party know where we are. As Party members, candidate members and applicants we have to face the broad masses out there; we have to answer questions about where we are, what we are trying to do and so on and therefore we must be able to answer those questions in precise terms. We believe further that there is some confusion on this question, that it has not been sufficiently dealt with in the past and therefore we want today to look at it that much more carefully. It is extremely important for us to get a better understanding of where we are, of what we are trying to build and of how we will be able to build it. That is why we feel that this whole question of what exactly is the present stage is so important.

Before looking at that, a few words on the question of where we have come from, in other words, the inheritance of the Revolution. All comrades know of course that we inherited a backward, undeveloped economy, with a very low level — one can say in fact, a primitive level, of technological and economic development in the country. There was a very low level, and there is still a low level of development of the productive forces, that is, of living human labour, objects of labour and instruments of labour. This low level of development of the productive forces in turn resulted in very underdeveloped class formations.

What we have in Grenada primarily of course, is a very large petit bourgeoisie, particularly a large peasantry — the rural petit bourgeoisie — small farmers who own small means of production and who must therefore work as they cannot live off their own plot of land alone. Some of them employ labour; some do not. So a large peasantry or bulk of our rural petit bourgeoisie. Then there is the urban petit bourgeoisie in terms of shopkeepers, garage owners, craftsmen, small restaurant owners and such like. The whole range of the petit bourgeoisie in our country. That of course is by far the largest class formation in the country.

We also have a working class which is very small and made up of agricultural workers based mainly in the rural areas, transport and communication workers on the docks, in telephone, electricity, etc., manufacturing and industrial workers (the smallest section of all) who produce garments, cokes, beer, that sort of thing. Some sections of the working class are employed by Government — garbagemen, the lowest clerical workers, the daily paid workers and so on. And of course we also have the commercial workers. Some of these comrades of the working class are also small owners of the means of production, but do not rely on that to support themselves — at least not as their main means of support.

In terms of the inheritance I also want to emphasise the low cultural level of our population at large as part of that inheritance and in particular the lack of technical skills and technical expertise of the working people. We must emphasise also the 19th century type of capitalist that we have in the country, capitalists engaged primarily in comprador activity, in other words largely in the importation and thereafter distribution of goods. This is a particularly parasitic type of capitalist in the full time service of international capitalism on which they must depend for the manufactured goods which give them their profits. They produce nothing and the vast majority of them engage in no form of manufacturing or industrial activity at all.

As part of the inheritance too, we must also note the very low level of infrastructural development of our country. Further, very backward agricultural development is also part of our inheritance and has relevance to the present stage of the Revolution. This inheritance of ours does have negative implications for the road that we are travelling on, for our objective to build Socialism in our country.

First of all, having a small working class is a very very serious disadvantage because only the working class can build Socialism. We know this is so because the working class is the class that is always growing; in fact, it has been historically, and it still is part of capitalist development that the working class gets larger and larger. Again, it is the working class that is most prepared for organisation and discipline because of having to work every day, having to arrive on time, having to engage in collective organisation and collective bargaining in their trade unions and so on. The working class too owns no means of production, in fact owns nothing except their labour and therefore they are the ones who most of all have to fight to end the oppression that comes about as result of the private ownership of the means of production which of course enslaves them and ensures that their own development is stultified and, finally the working class does have the key role in building socialism because of their role in production.

This inheritance is a problem also because of the large petit bourgeoisie that it has left us. We of course have that number of petit bourgeoisie in our country precisely because of economic under-development, precisely because capitalist production was so undeveloped that they did not need much labour and therefore people were by large forced to try to make a living however they could and wherever they could. But because the petit bourgeoisie is a vacillating class it is more difficult to build Socialism when there is such a large amount of petit bourgeoisie in the country, precisely because

they are in the middle and you have to fight hard to win them.
Many of them of course have bourgeois aspirations, many
more are deluded and [illeg.] by bourgeois ideology and propaganda and therefore the struggle to win the petit bourgeoisie
has historically been a very serious intense struggle in all
countries that have embarked upon a path of Socialist transformation.

The question we must now pose comrades is whether a society
such as ours with their primitiveness, with so little infrastructure, with so little development of productive forces, with
such a small working class can really build socialism. This is
a question that many other countries before us have posed
and many other countries in the future will continue to pose.
Of course, this question arises because socialism requires a
good level of development of the productive forces, it requires
infrastructural development, it requires agricultural development, it requires industrialisation, it requires a high level of
cultural development of the people, it requires an even higher
level of political development and political consciousness, it
requires central planning of the economy and society as a
whole, it requires a serious Marxist Leninist vanguard Party
leading, guiding and directing the whole process. All of these
things are prerequisites for the building of Socialism, and, of
course, the vast majority of these either do not exist at all or
are at a very low level of development, at this time. Nonetheless, the answer is yes, it is possible for a country like ours to
build Socialism. That of course we all know. It is possible, but
the question is how and we think that this can be seen if we
examine some of the possibilities or models for economic development in our country.

We believe that there are four main possibilities for economic
development of Grenada and countries like Grenada. The first
of these is a total private sector free enterprise system of
economic development, your Seaga of Jamaica or your Puerto
Rico model of development, where free enterprise is given full
rein, where the private sector is able to rule uncontrolled. The
second model is a total state sector approach where just about
anything important is owned by the State, where the State

owns virtually everything that matters. The third type is a
mixed economy, but with a private sector dominant, and of
course, that is the model that we have chosen in Grenada, the
mixed economy-state sector dominant type model. But even
after having said that, there are still questions of why we have
chosen that form and the question of precisely how will that
form assist us to build socialism are two such questions that
come to mind. Obviously, if we are speaking of building
Socialism and we are, then it is clear that our objective as
Marxist-Leninist must in the first instance be to construct
socialism as rapidly, but scientifically as possible. That being
so, clearly we cannot choose the path of capitalism. We cannot
choose the path of a total private sector free enterprise model
because that will be inconsistant with what we believe in and
what we have been and are struggling for. We could not
likewise choose that path of the mixed economy, with the private sector dominant because that will have tremendous dangers for the successful construction of Socialism and will have
us without the effective possibility of guiding and regulating
economic development through the imposition of taxes, the
granting of credits and concessions and the use of all arms of
the State apparatus. This must necessarily be so because it is,
as we know, the objective material basis of the economy that
determines and directs the political, social and cultural development of the society as a whole.

Equally, we cannot opt for the total state sector model as the
state does not have the necessary material of financial resources, management and skills resources, access to markets,
international contacts and so on. All of this should be obvious,
but for those who have any doubts, please reflect on the tremendous difficulties that we have in finding the dollars necessary to pay the downpayment to the British Company — Ples-
sey's — that will be installing the radar, communications and
navigational equipment for our new international airport, or
reflect on how difficult it has been to find guaranteed markets
for our primary products and our agro-industrial products, or
how difficult it is to find engineers or architects or science
teachers or managers — and note I did not even say good

managers, I just said managers. No, it would be impossible at this time for the state on its own to build Grenada.

That, of course, means that an alliance is necessary, an alliance in the first place between the working class and the petty bourgeoisie, in particular the rural peasantry, and in the second place an alliance with those elements of the upper petty bourgeoisie and the national bourgeoisie who, for different reasons, are willing to be involved in building the economy and the country at this time.

DEFINITION OF PRESENT STAGE OF GRENADA REVOLUTION

And this leads me at long last to the answer to the question — what is a correct characterisation of the present stage of development of the Grenada Revolution? And the answer, of course, as we all know, is that the Grenada Revolution is a national-democratic, anti-imperialist Revolution, involving the alliance of many classes including sections of the small bourgeoisie but under the leadership and with the dominant role being played by the working people and particularly the working class, through their vanguard Party the NJM.

That comrades is how we define the present stage of the Grenada Revolution today. Obviously National Democratic, anti-imperialist means what it says. I did not say a socialist revolution as some comrades like to keep pretending that we have. Obviously we do not have a socialist revolution and it is not socialist precisely because: —

(1) The low level of development of the productive forces. You cannot have a socialist revolution with this low level development.

(2) Our working class is too small and too politically underdeveloped.

For these primary reasons we cannot proceed straight away to the building of socialism but must first pass through a stage where we lay the basis, where we create the conditions, including the socio-economic and political conditions, for the building of socialism and the creation of the socialist revolution, that is, for the full coming to power of the working class. In other words, comrades, what we are into now (this national democratic stage) really means two things. What we are speaking about now is not socialist construction, not the socialist revolution, we are speaking about the national democratic revolution, we are speaking about socialist orientation. So the important things to contradistinguish here are socialist construction the second stage versus socialist orientation the first stage, which is the stage we are in at this time.

.   .   .   .

We want to point out too, comrades, that the national democratic anti-imperialist stage can be led not just by the working class, not just by the petty bourgeoisie, but even by the bourgeoisie. It can be led by the bourgeoisie, petty bourgeoisie or the working class — any of these class forces can lead the Revolution. If it is led by the bourgeoisie, obviously, it could never go on to build socialism — that will be an impossibility; no bourgeois can build socialism. If it is led by the petty bourgeoisie, the only basis on which it can build socialism is if the petty bourgeoisie leadership in the course of the class struggle is transformed into a revolutionary Marxist-Leninist leadership and therefore develops a Marxist-Leninist Party that then guides and directs the process. Without that transformation, it would also be impossible.

Therefore, obviously it is only the working class that can build socialism. It is only under the leadership of the working class, led by a Marxist-Leninist vanguard Party that the process can be completed and we can go on to socialist construction. That is the only time it is possible.

That again, comrades, needs to be understood by us because of its tremendous relevance to the nature of the alliance we have and what we need to do from here on.

This national democratic stage of the revolution has, broadly speaking, two main components — a political aspect and an economic aspect.

POLITICAL ESSENCE OF THE NATIONAL-DEMOCRATIC PARTY

In terms of the political aspect, the essence of that political aspect is the dictatorship of the working people, dictatorship of rule of the working people — that is the essence. This essence implies a change in the balance of forces that presently exists, a change in the balance of forces that will usually be involved in the anti-imperialist struggle of the national liberation movements. In other words, in your Angolas, Mozambiques, etc., what you would normally find happening is that there is a class alliance involved in the fight to end colonialism. And that class alliance will involve the bourgeoisie, the petty-bourgeoisie and the proletariat (the working class) — all three.

And in countries like ours, after independence, just like in Grenada today, what you usually find happening is that state power is wielded by an alliance of the bourgeoisie, the petty-bourgeoisie and the working class through a particular Party or combination of Parties, and usually comrades, as you know, the situation is that it is the bourgeoisie and the petty-bourgeoisie that is pre-dominant, the combined bourgeoisie and petty bourgeoisie that is pre-dominant, and the working class is the minority influence. That is the usual situation in countries like ours even after independence. That is what is happening right now. Right through the English-speaking Caribbean — in all of them — you can see that the bourgeoisie and petty-bourgeoisie are ruling and that working class representation is very small.

But when countries start to move to develop this essence I was talking about — the dictatorship (or rule) of the working people — is that in the course of class struggle, the bourgeoisie begins to become subordinated and the influence of the petty-bourgeoisie and working class together becomes pre-dominant. In other words a drift begins to take place, at first imperceptible, but gradually observable and at a certain moment when quantity becomes quality, that shift becomes very clear and very noticeable. And at that time, the

bourgeoisie becomes the minority force and the petty
bourgeoisie and proletariat begin to rule. And when that hap-
pens, it becomes the first time at which it is possible to shift
the country away from the path of capitalist development, because a combination of bourgeoisie and petty bourgeoisie
pre-dominant necessarily means that the emphasis will be on
capitalist development. And equally, once the shift takes place
then the potential is there for the first time to begin to move
along the path of socialist orientation and away from the path
of capitalist development. That comrades, is our situation in
Grenada, and that was the situation when we took power on
March 13th, 1979.

When we took power on March 13th 1979, as comrades know,
we did not take power as an alliance — we took power as
NJM. But within the first few hours of taking power, we tried
to build an alliance and we begun to build that alliance for two
main reasons: — Firstly to hold on to power in the first few
seconds, minutes, hours, days and weeks. And the second
reason was to defeat imperialism, in the months and years
thereafter, because defeating imperialism is a complex process, that requires a political orientation and an economic
transformation that involves crushing the rule of the
monopolies and of big business in your country, that involves
taking control of the commanding heights of the economy and
so on. And we cannot do that on our own and that is why the
alliance was and is needed.

.   .   .   .

From the start too, comrades, we had an alliance with sections of the upper petty bourgeoisie and national bourgeoisie
right from the word GO. Within the first few hours of the Revolution, we began to put that alliance in place. I can remember all of us making phone calls to different sections of
the Petty-bourgeoisie and the National bourgeoisie, inviting
them to come down to Radio Free Grenada and in some cases
beginning to feel them out as to whether or not they were
willing to serve on the ruling council of the People's Revolutionary Government.

I can remember very well that the first set of names we announced for the ruling council was fourteen (14), not twenty-three (23). And these fourteen names were made up mainly (outside of the immediate leadership), of the petty-bourgeoisie, the upper petty-bourgeoisie and the national bourgeoisie. You remember that? Simon Charles and Sydney Ambrose — peasantry, Bernard Gittens — professional middle strata, Lloyd Noel — professional middle strata; Palm Buxo and Norris Bain — middle capitalists; Lyden Ramdhanny — big capitalist; that is who the People's Revolutionary Government was. And this was done deliberately so that imperialism won't get too excited and would say "well they have some nice fellas in that thing; everything alright." and as a result wouldn't think about sending in troops.

That was the mistake, for example, the comrades in Gambia made a few months ago. Remember the Gambia Coup E'tat a few months ago? What was the first thing those comrades did? They say "we are Marxist-Leninists and have just had a Marxist-Leninist Revolution and we go wipe out the bourgeoisie." The same day they overthrow them — same day, they didn't even give them three days. So fortunately, NJM had a little more sense than that. And like I said comrades, the first fourteen names were bourgeoisie, big capitalist, petty-bourgeoisie, middle capitalist, peasantry and professional middle strata — that is who made up the People's Revolutionary Government. It is only after about a week and a half (if I recall correctly), when we held the Party General meeting in Radio Free Grenada's studio (and some comrades here would have been present at that meeting) that we finally got around to pulling some more Party comrades. You all remember that meeting down in Radio Free Grenada studio. It was then we chose nine more comrades to make up the twenty-three. But the first set of names were Lyden, Pam Buxo, Norris Bain, Lloyd Noel and so on. That is what I mean by saying that the alliance began from the first few hours and the first few days. And that alliance was and is extremely important.

From our point of view comrades, why do we need the alliance?

We need the alliance firstly, as we pointed out already, to hold power in the first few days and weeks.

We need the alliance, secondly, to consolidate and build the revolution and to ensure the defeat of imperialism. This time we can't do this effectively without the alliance.

We need the alliance, comrades, because we don't have enough managers, because we don't have enough capital, because we don't have enough international contacts, because we don't have enough markets. For all of these reasons, we need the alliance.

.   .   .   .

But there is absolutely no doubt that we have a hegemonic control on power and over all the capital areas of the State. We can see this in several different ways. If you consider the question of Cabinet. The Cabinet of our country has ten (10) ministers and nine of these ten ministers are members of the Party; the only non-member of the Party is Norris Bain. If you look at the ruling council of the People's Revolutionary Government, you will see it no longer has twenty-three people because Lloyd Noel is in detention, Pam Buxo is out of the country, Lyle Bullen is no longer involved. There are three people who are out, there are now twenty (20) people who are in the P.R.G. And if you look at the Party and the Cabinet and you analyse them carefully, you will discover an over 90% direct control by the Party of the ruling council of the P.R.G. and Cabinet.

Secondly, to see further this hegemony or control I am talking about comrades, look at the composition of our army and militia. We don't have any upper Petty-bourgeoisie or bourgeoisie in our army or militia. When you look at the officers in the army it is Working class comrades or petty-bourgeois revolutionary democrats or communists who are the officers in the army — that's the situation in our Army.

Thirdly comrades, consider our Zonal Councils and our Workers Councils and so on. The bourgeoisie is not invited deliberately and consciously, so they don't have the opportunity to come and try to confuse people inside the councils. When we're having a Zonal Council in this building or a Workers Parish Council, we send out the invitations, we decide who we want to invite and we live the bourgeoisie out deliberately and consciously.

Consider the trade unions in our country, five of the eight leading trade unions are under the direct leadership and control of full members, candidate members and applicants of our Party. There is no doubt about it; what we have is hegemony; we have full control.

I want to think of another area. Just consider, comrades, how laws are made in this country. Laws are made in this country when Cabinet agrees and when I sign a document on behalf of Cabinet. And then that is what everybody in the country — like it or don't like it — has to follow. Or consider how people get detained in this country. We don't go and call for no votes. You get detained when I sign an order after discussing it with the National Security Committee of the Party or with a higher Party body. Once I sign it — like it or don't like it — its up the hill for them.

It is also important to note comrades, that while we are in an alliance with sections of the bourgeoisie and upper petty-bourgeoisie, they are not part of our dictatorship. They are not part of our rule and control — they are not part of it. We bring them in for what we want to bring them in for. They are not part of our dictatorship because when they try to hold public meetings and we don't want that, the masses shut down the meeting. When we want to hold Zonal Councils and we don't want them there, we keep them out. When they want to put out newspaper and we don't want that, we close it down. When they want freedom of expression to attack the Government or to link up with the CIA and we don't want that, we crush them and jail them. They are not part of the dictatorship. In fact, if the truth is told, they have been repressed by the dictatorship. They have lost some of the rights they used to have. Now it is the working people who have these rights, not the bourgeoisie. When the working people want to hold a public

meeting, we don't stop them. When the working people want
to go and hold a picket, we don't stop them. When they want to
Picket Bata, that is good, but if Bata want to picket workers we
jail Bata. The workers could Picket Bata, but Bata cannot picket no workers. When Torchlight workers want to take over
the company, we support them, not publicly and through
making noise because that would not be in our interest. We
pretend we don't know what's happening and let the trade unionists do it. But if the Torchlight owners try to crush the
workers, we jail the Torchlight owners.

The point is all rights are not for them, all freedoms are not
for them, but all rights and freedoms are now for the majority
who are no longer oppressed and repressed by a tiny minority. That is very important to understand because that is what
dictatorship or rule means. And that is how every state operates. That is why the state came about in the first case; so that
there would be a dictatorship and a minority, in the case of
the capitalist state, would crush and oppress the majority. In
the case of the Socialist State, the majority will crush, oppress
and repress the recalitrant minority. That is what it is, and
that is what the nature of the dictatorship is, so they are not
part of that. And that is very important for us to understand.

Comrades, as we see it, this political essence — this dictatorship of the working people — is what we have to continue to
develop and to build rapidly if we are to make substantial
progress in building the national democratic anti-imperialist
phase of the Revolution. And I would say, there are six (6)
things to watch and to emphasise in terms of the political essence.

First, it means control by the Party and the working people.
So we have to be guided by that at all times. The Party and the
working people; the Party acting in the name of the working
people and particularly, of course, the working class must
control, guide and direct [line missing]

Secondly, it means an alliance has to continue to be maintained, firstly, with the peasantry and other elements of the

petty-bourgeoisie, and secondly with sections of the upper petty-bourgeoisie and the national bourgeoisie.

. . . .

The third thing, comrades, the question of our people; their education (political and academic); the development of further democratic mechanisms and organisations and means and methods of getting them to be involved and to participate and so on. The need for greater training in democracy for them. In other words, the preparation for them to rule. That, of course, primarily refers to the working class but it applies in general to the working people and also to the broad masses in terms of the development of democracy, in terms of the involvement in mass organisations, in terms of participation in the organs of popular power.

The fourth point, the necessary emphasis we have to give at all times to the working class (we are going to come back to that so I don't want to say too much on it). But for this political section, it has to be emphasised.

And the fifth point, the building of the Party, because again it is the Party that has to be at the head of this process, acting as representatives of the working people and in particular the working class. That is the only way it can be because the working class does not have the ideological development or experience to build socialism on its own. The Party has to be there to ensure that the necessary steps and measures are taken. And it is our primary responsibility to prepare and train the working class for what their historic mission will be later on down the road. That is why the Party has to be built and built rapidly, through bringing in the first sons and daughters of the working class.

And finally comrades, the need always for firmness and inflexibility on political questions that affect the building of socialism. On the economic front, you can have a lot of flexibility; on the political front the fexibility must be very little. We have to be firm because we are walking a real tight rope. On the one hand, you have to give encouragements and incentives and build the confidence of the bourgeoisie. But on the other hand, when they step out of line, we still have to crush them. So it's that kind of tight-rope that has to be walked.

ECONOMIC ESSENCE OF THE NATIONAL DEMOCRATIC PATH

I want to come comrades, to the economic essence in the non-capitalist path, or more precisely the path of socialist orientation. That is what the economic essence of this national democratic business is — the non-capitalist path of economic development, the path of socialist orientation. That involves in particular building the state sector along particular lines which I now want to describe quickly.

Firstly, the state sector must be built to be the dominant sector. As comrades know, that's happening already. Last year over 90% of all investments in this country were by the public sector, by the state and at this time the state controls about a quarter of the total economy. Building the state sector to be the dominant sector means a number of things: —

(a) We must assume total control of all financial institutions over a period of time. I did not say total control tomorrow morning or next year, but equally over a period — that must happen:

(b) We must assume total control of all foreign trade and also of some aspects of internal trade. The MNIB, of course, is helping us in that area already. This year, the MNIB will have a turnover of $20m. Right now MNIB has $35m in stocks (quite a staggering figure). Right now, MNIB is buying over 78 agricultural items from the farmers is Grenada. Right now, one in every ten farmers is selling his produce to MNIB. Right now, the three main depots for the MNIB (Young Street, Hillsborough Carriacou, and Petit Martinique), in January, February, March of this year together, sold something like 300,000 lbs of produce. And I'll give you something that's even more staggering than that which was told to me by the Manager of the MNIB depot in Petit Mar-

tinique — Linus Belmar. Belmar told us that the Petit
Martinique depot has a monthly turnover of $60,000 —
a quite staggering figure. The role of the MNIB, both in
the area of imports and exports, will have to be stepped
up in the coming period.

(c) We must assume total control of all Public Utilities —
electricity, telephone, water, National Transport Service. And here again, as comrades know, we already in
fact control those four. The missing one for us now is
Cable and Wireless and the Satelite Dish from the
Soviet Union will be one aspect of the timing in relation to Cable and Wireless.

(d) We must continue the building of the infrastructure —
air port, sea ports, roads etc. — all aspects of infras-
turcture.

(e) We must ensure the further development of tourism, of
the manufacturing and industrial sectors; of the agricultural sector; of the agro-industrial sector; of
fisheries. In other words, all of the main pillars of the
economy — agriculture, agro industries, fisheries,
tourism, manufacturing and light industry.

(f) We must develop central planning mechanisms for the
economy and the society as a whole. But first of all we
must start with the economy. In terms of the development of the economy comrades, over the next 10—15
years; as we see it, the next 5 years — emphasis will
undoubtedly be tourism. That is not to say that we like
tourism. That is because we have no choice. Tourism is
the sector that has the greatest potential for giving us
the profits to invest in the areas we really want to invest in — agriculture, agro industries, fisheries, and
non-agro industrialisation generally. That's really
where we will like to go, but those cannot produce the
money at this time, while tourism can. We estimate that
we will spend about $350m in just tourism alone over
the next couple of years, including the cost of the New
International Air-port.

.   .   .   .

It is important to observe comrades that all of this lays the
basis for the development of capitalism. And that of course is
a major problem because it means that if we are not careful
capitalism rather than socialism will be the end product, just
like when Lenin had formulted NEP right after the Great October Socialist Revolution, the Bolsheviks too had that same
problem and concern.

Simultaneously we will be nurturing the shoots of capitalism
and the shoots of socialism and the question is which one becomes predominant and how you control and ensure that
socialism is what comes out and not capitalism. We have the
same problem as the young Soviet State faced but a million
times more difficult, because our state sector is much smaller
and does not have the potential in this immediate period for
providing the profits to build the economy and the country.
And of course, we have a much smaller and less ideologically
developed working class. On top of that we have this massive
petty bourgeoisie; you have this low level of development of
class consciousness; you have this total backwardness and
primitiveness in the economy. In other words comrades, we
have a tight rope that we have to monitor very carefully as we
walk it — every single day, understanding clearly that all of
this infrastructural development, and all of this activity we
are describing not only can build socialism but also
capitalism.

What this means is that our primary task must be to sink the
ideas of Marxism/Leninism amongst the working people so
that their own ideological level can advance and they can
begin to better understand what we are trying to do and why
their class consciousness can be raised in this way. Secondly,
of course we can control the development of capitalism
through the use of laws and regulations; because one thing we
do have is political control (and we have that firmly) so we
can decide on how much taxes to charge, we can decide who
get credits, we can decide who gets concessions and pioneer
incentives, we can decide what kinds of Laws to pass and

when, we can decide who to "manners" and when. In other words, we can use the apparatus of the State in order to effect those controls. But it is a tight rope and we just need to be careful and understand what we are involved in.

TASKS OF THE NATIONAL DEMOCRATIC STAGE

Comrades, the tasks of this national democratic stage can perhaps be summarised in ten points; and I want to just quickly list them.

(1) Ensure the leading role of the working class through its Marxist/Leninist Party backed by some form of the dictatorship of the proletariat. But please note that I said some form of the dictatorship of the proletariat, because obviously at this stage we cannot have the dictatorship of the proletariat or the working class, but the form we would have at this first stage is the dictatorship of the working people.

(2) Build the alliance between the working class and mass of the working people.   .   .   .

(3) Ensure over a period, public ownership of the means of production. In other words, build the state sector.

(4) Work towards the gradual transformation of agriculture along socialist lines through development of voluntary co-operative farms and state farms.

(5) Plan development of the economy in order to lay the basis for the building of socialism and to raise living standards.

(6) Begin the implementation of the cultural revolution. And this cultural revolution, as all of us know, is one of the four revolutions we are building at the same time — the political, economic, scientific and technological and the cultural. And in the context of the cultural revolution, I want to emphasise three main points — the spreading of the socialist ideology, the wiping out of illiteracy and the building of a

new patriotic and revolutionary-democratic
intelligentsia.

(7) Build the defence capacity of the country so as to protect it and to protect the revolution from internal and
external enemies.   .   .   .

(8) Develop proletarian internationalism. As representatives of the working class in Grenada, we have to ensure that our working class and the working people
always demonstrate maximum solidarity with all international working class struggles. That is a fundamental responsibility.

(9) Develop equal and friendly relations with all governments in the world, except the fascist military dictatorship and apartheid types.

.   .   .   .

(10) Build rapidly our links with the Socialist World, especially the Soviet Union. And here I should hardly need
to say more; we have just come back from an important visit to the land of Lenin, the Soviets in the last
two days have arrived, nine of them including the
Ambassador and their Embassy is about to be opened
and so on. So these links and relations are building
reasonably satisfactory.

TASKS FOR THE PRESENT PERIOD

Coming out of all of this comrades, what are the tasks as seen
by the Central Committee?

1) The first task is sinking the ideas of Marxism/Leninism
among the working class and the working people. The
main vehicle for this comrades is socialism classes. The
Central Committee feels very strongly that this is the
Number One task. And of course, there can be only one
Number One task, and this the Central Committee regards as Number One — sinking the ideas of Marxism-

Leninism among the working class and the working people. The fact of the matter is that a national democratic revolution can be turned back easily. For example in the case of Nasser's Egypt, not withstanding the years of hard work put in by Nasser and his party into trying to build the national democratic revolution in Egypt. After his death it took only a few years to roll back all that had been accomplished. And there were several reasons. One, the party was not in fact built along Leninist vanguard lines and secondly, because the ideas of Marxism/Leninism had not taken root, there was no deep class consciousness in Egypt. We know that in many of these national democratic revolutions — in Iraq, Somalia, Algeria and so on — the fact is that the ideas of Marxism/Leninism were and are not being spread. And therefore, with the ideological work being weak, at a certain point it becomes easy for forces opposed to revolutionary transformation to overturn what had been accomplished.

2. The second task, comrades, the organisation of the working class and the working people through their trade unions, their organs for popular power, their mass organisations and through sports and culture — the Organisation of the working class and the working people.

3. Thirdly, comrades, strengthening the Leninist character of the party by bringing in the best elements of the working people and in particular the working class, and through building the internal organisation of the Party.

4. Fourthly comrades, building the economy along the path of socialist orientation, thus providing more material benefits for the masses and laying the basis for the construction of socialism.

5. The fifth task, developing the defence capacity of the country through building the militia both quantitatively and qualitatively by strengthening the influence of the Party in the militia.

. . . .

THE SUBJECTIVE FACTOR — THE PARTY

Comrades I want to close, but what I want to close by saying
will take another fifteen minutes or so. I want to close by
going into the question of the subjective factor, in other words
the party, a very brief history of the party's development and
the criteria for party membership at this time.

Over the past nine and a half years, our Party has passed
through many stages of development; all of us know that. We
have analysed recently that there have been six major stages
that the Party has gone through. The first stage began on the
11th March, 1973, with the merger, when came NJM out of
JEWEL and MAP led by intelligentsia and rural petty-
bourgeoisie. The Strategy adopted was one of mass mobilisation with seizure of power coming through mass mobilisation,
general strike, street marches and thereafter insurrection.
Mistakes were made, a deep class approach was not taken, no
attempt was made to build a Leninist Party, there was an
over-reliance on spontaneity and the possibilities of crowd
politics. That period cmrades, March '73 to April '74 is the
period of mass mobilisation in action. Using the issue of
Gairy's incorrect approach to the question of independence as
a base we went around the country agitating the masses for
popular insurrection. During that same period in fact, within
the first two months of the Party being formed, we liberated
51 rifles from Gairy. It is true we did not hold them for as long
as we would have liked; we had them for one year and then
Belmar took them back, but in fact we stole 51 rifles as part of
that preparation.

During this period of mass mobilisation, we held the People's
Convention of Independence and the massively attended
People's Congress where five historic, but nonetheless ultra-
leftist, decisions were taken. You remember the decisions?
Firstly, we tried Gairy, found him guilty of 27 crimes and gave
him two weeks to resign. We suggested that a National Unity
Council should be elected and a National Unity Council was
elected and we said it would have the task of supervising the
orderly transition to power of the new regime. We also decided

that the people would take steps to remove the Gairy dictatorship if he did not resign within 2 weeks. So undoubtedly, this
was ultra-leftism in action. Nonetheless the major weakness
of this period was the subjective factor, the fact that a Leninist
approach to party building and to strategy and tactics were
not adopted; and this is notwithstanding the notable achievements of the period, including the publication of our Manifesto.

.   .   .   .

In the time period, July '77 to August '78, the party did make a
qualitative leap forward in terms of Leninist standards and
principles. That is the period when we stepped up our work
among the working class, the work was not sufficiently deep,
but at least it was starting. We tried to organise the agricultural working class but did not get very far because of Gairy's
use of repression in protecting his base among the agricultural working class. But we did some work during that period
with the urban working class and with sections of the rural
petty bourgeoisie — the farmers and the fishermen. That is
the period too when the Organising Committee of the Party
was formed, thus taking some of the strain off the Political
Bureau and leaving matters of discipline, party organisation
and so on, for the Organising Committee to handle — a critical
step forward.

And then we came to the next period, the fourth period from
August '78 to March '79, when the Party really moved into top
gear. The timing was fortuitous for us because at the exact
moment that a revolutionary situation was developing a
number of key work committees of the Party began to function. Inner party democracy was also being strengthened;
party study was going on, and a mass scientific approach to
organisation was beginning to develop.

And from March '79 to this period, the fifth (5th) we have had
a lot of mass activity. It is the period when we broadened and
deepended our links with the working people and the masses
in general, through the mass organisations — women, youth,
pioneer —; through the organs of popular power — workers,

parish and zonal councils —; through the socialism classes, very critically and also through our greatly expanded work in the trade unions. In this period, we have considerably deepended, broadened and expanded our links with the working people and the broad masses in general. This is the period too when the Party began to develop a number of critical new structures and committees, including the C.C. itself, PCB's and a Committee on the economy for the first time. They have not all done well as we would have liked but the fact is that important new structures have been set up and have begun to function.

During this period too, the Party has also been involved in supervising many aspects of the State Apparatus and in running the state generally. The party is involved in all the key programmes of the Revolution, the Centre for Popular Education Programme, the Land Reform Programme, Youth Employment Programme, and recently in the discussions around the Budget and the Economy. So this is a period that has seen a number of new mechanisms, new structures and new work committees and greatly expanded work in dozens of different areas at the same time.

But we believe very strongly, comrades, that as from now, Sptember '82 the Party is definitely entering a new stage of the revolution and of our Party's development. We feel that because of the growing internal and external complexity of this period, because of the growing quantity of work required of the Party and in order to cope with the new complexities that once again we have to change gears and step up the pace. This year we have a major role to play in the development of the Economy because this is the essential basis for progressing on our path of socialist orientation. Furthermore, the question of the Armed Forces, especially the militia and of the Party assuming leadership of the key positions there is something that we have to be involved in a lot more this year. The question of increasing the quantity and quality of our socialism classes, as our priorities demand is also, something that we must take much more seriously. The CPE Programme, in its second phase, must also get a lot of attention this year.

The Youth Employment Programme and the Land Reform Programme are central to agricultural and overall Economic development.

In other words, we are required to work on a dozen critical fronts at the same time, and that is going to require a lot more application of Leninist standards of discipline, consistency and seriousness. All of this, comrades, means that our ideological and organisational level as a Party will have to rise considerably. It is clear that if we had not insisted higher standards we would not have reached where we have reached. But it is equally clear, comrades, that holding power is much more difficult than taking power. There is no doubt that the Party can be built more rapidly on the basis of lower standards but this will mean that the tasks we have set ourselves, including our historical task of building socialism, would not be accomplished. As Lenin told us a long time ago "better fewer but better". Immortal words that we must never forget.

During the Party's history, there are members who have dropped out; some for opportunist reasons; others because they were not willing to make the sacrifices required in the particular period; in other cases, as the Party's ideological outlook developed, they came to realise that they did not share the desire to develop socialism; some others just could not take the level of disciplines, of organisation, of strain, of hard work, of sacrifice. But no one is a member for life in the serious Leninist Party and, at this point, the Central Committee would like to enumerate the criteria for party membership and to go into some details as to the qualities required for promotion in the Party.

. . . .

POTENTIAL APPLICANTS TO APPLICANTS

From our experience, comrades, these are the people who are most likely to move to Marxism/Leninism. These comrades are then invited to join classes where they are tested to see whether they are hostile to, or accepting of the ideas of Marx-

ism Leninism. If they are not anti-communist, and if they
continue to work well and show an honest approach, they are
admitted as Applicants. And as all comrades know the period
of applicancy is one year. That gives both the Party and the
applicant the time to judge whether the applicant really accepts the science of Marxism/Leninism and is willing to make
the sacrifices necessary to become a Party member.

APPLICANTS TO CANDIDATE MEMBERS

When assessing an applicant for promotion to Candidate
Member the following five points are looked at:

(1) Whether the applicant accepts the principles of Marxism Leninism and shows willingness to continue to
develop.

(2) Whether the applicant has been working consistently
and effectively in his/her [illeg.] of political work and
developing in terms of organisational skills.

(3) Whether the applicant has in practice accepted party
discipline, in practice.

(4) Whether the applicant has good relations with the
masses, including party members and non-party members with whom he works in his Union, Mass Organisation, Army, Workplace etc.

(5) Whether the Applicant continues to be of good character so as to present an example to the masses he/she
comes in contact with; whether certain petty bourgeois
traits such as individualism, hostility to criticism, arrogance, indiscipline and so on are being eroded; and
whether proletarian qualities such as respect for the
working class, co-operativeness and co-operation, discipline, modesty, self criticism are being built. If accepted as a Candidate member, another year would
now elapse before the comrade is eligible for consideration for full membership.

CANDIDATE MEMBERS TO MEMBERS

At this stage, the stage of moving from Candidate Member to Member, the Party looks for the fullest possible development of six factors.

(1) Ideological development as seen in a development of the ability to analyse and cope well with many different situations and to correctly apply strategy and tactics — the essence of correct Marxism/Leninism Leadership.

(2) The development of correct leadership. A professional approach to his/her political work, expressing Leninist organisational standards in all aspects of the work.

(3) The development of an ability to supervise and guide the work of junior party comrades.

(4) The removal of petty bourgeois character faults and the development of a character which provides an outstanding example to other party comrades and the masses alike.

(5) The development of very good relations with the masses and other party comrades.

(6) The development of the technical and professional skills needed by the comrade in his or her job.

Comrades, some comrades feel that it takes too long to become a full member in our Party. Some comrades feel it is rough enough to have applicants, then candidate members and then members so that on top of that to have Potential Applicants is really just pushing the pace too much. And yet the truth is that some comrades in the Party are right now proposing another new category of not just Potential Applicants but of Prospective Potential Applicant, to make it even more difficult to gain entry. The fact is, comrades, that we feel it is correct in our situation for us to have this long process of what, at one level, can be seen as probation before comrades can become full members. We think it is important now because at the level of party leadership we want to keep the number down; in fact at the level of the Central Committee of the Party, our anxiety and concern is to see the Party lifted in terms of quantity and quality in the shortest possible time. But we also know from experience that this whole question of coming to accept full membership in the party and really internationalism and operationalising in a serious way party discipline and party duties is something that does take time to really sink home. Sometimes comrades might last two or three years but then on a certain issue when the class struggle is really heightened they break and then leave the Party.

The truth is that it is not really a case of the Party Leadership laying down harsh conditions; it is real life and the demand of the struggle that make it necessary for us to have these difficult conditions and for us to ensure that comrades who are full members, and also candidate members, are truly the finest representatives of the working class and the most steeled in struggle, in discipline, in dedication, in commitment and in total commitment for the working class and their interests. That is not the C.C. laying laws down, that is real life laying the laws down. And that is why comrades, we feel very strongly that these criteria are critical and necessary.

We believe it must become more and more difficult for comrades to become full members and candidate members and it must become more difficult for new comrades to remain as members and candidate members; and those who are unwilling to live up to the demands of this membership would have to be moved. We believe comrades that this stage of our process requires this. Being a Communist, comrades means becoming a different kind of person. Our society is deeply petty bourgeois and this means the majority of our people are deeply individualistic, ill-disciplined, disorganised, unproletarian, hostile to criticism and so on. Many in the middle strata and intelligentsia often find it difficult to relate as equals with the working people while at the same time many working people lack confidence in dealing with certain types of people. It takes time for a new proletarian person to be built. It takes time for a Communist to be built. So in reality, comrades, promotion is not decided on by the Party but by the development of comrades themselves.

On behalf of the Central Committee of our Party, I want to congratulate all the comrades who have been recently promoted from applicants to candidate members who are here with us today for the first time in that capacity, and who as a result of that new status have assumed new rights, duties and responsibilities. I also want to congratulate in advance those comrades in this room who will shortly be promoted from candidate members to full members. Comrades now know the basis on which they have been promoted. Those comrades who have not been promoted at this time will also, we hope, understand and accept the reasons why they have not been promoted.

We believe comrades, that this line of march will equipt us to go into the field and to move rapidly to ensure that this first stage of the path we are on — the socialist orientation stage — is rapidly built. We believe that we have correctly defined the new tasks required to handle the new situation that has developed. We believe that as Party, individually and collectively, we must now develop ourslves into becoming more professional, more disciplined, more Leninist so that we would be able to meet the demands of this period. We also believe firmly that the path we have chosen is the <u>ONLY</u> correct one. We believe that this path would <u>certainly</u> bring us to our second major historical objective to seeing socialism, of seeing socialist construction achieved in our country, thus ensuring that the working class in Grenada would assume their rightful role and become fully emancipated for the first time.

LONG LIVE THE NEW JEWEL MOVEMENT!

LONG LIVE THE MEMBERS, CANDIDATE MEMBERS AND
APPLICANTS OF OUR PARTY!

LONG LIVE THE THE REVOLUTIONARY HISTORY OF OUR
PARTY!
LONG LIVE THE WORKING CLASS OF GRENADA!
LONG LIVE THE INTERNATIONAL WORKING CLASS!
LONG LIVE PROLETARIAN INTERNATIONALISM!
FORWARD FROM SOCIALIST ORIENTATION TO SOCIALIST
CONSTRUCTION!

      FORWARD EVER! BACKWARD NEVER!

III-2
"Belmont" Surveillance Report

This is one of a considerable number of unsigned and undated reports, prepared by security forces, analyzing areas of potential dissident activity throughout Grenada. It is of interest that in Belmont only the dock workers were considered possible significant opponents of the NJM "dictatorship of the working people."

SECRET

BELMONT

ANALYSIS:

Belmont is one of the largest area in the south. Most families earn a living due to the father or the male in the house being a Dock worker. There is some commercial workers and agricultural workers.

Belmont before the Revolution was a Gariy strong area. Gariy had organise the Dock workers around him resulting in a strong base for his Government. The former government had a strong support base among the elderly people. Due to these facts there was still some conflict among the Dock workers and some of the elderly people that was supporting his Government, because there was constant clashes between the Mongoose Gang and the Belmont Dock workers during the reign of his Government. Although these clashes, some of the Dock Workers still remain loyal to the Gariy Government. During the latter years of Gariy ruling the middle class section of the people in the area was anti Gariy, but there is a few middle classs elements who still loyal to Gariy.

After the Revolution the area have benefit from the programmes being put out by the P.R.G. In the beginning of the
Revolution period many people came out in support of the
overthrow, mainly the youths. The majority of these youths
still give full support to the Revolution. The majority of mass
activities organise by the P.R.G., there is always a large turn
out to these activities.

ECONOMIC OBJECTIVES:

   Butler House
   Ministry of Agro Industries
   Bryden and Minors (Lagoon Rd)
   Grenada Yacth Service (Lagoon Rd)
   Genreal Control (Lagoon Rd)
   Gleans Garage (Lagoon Rd)
   Grenada Tyre Service (Lagoon Rd)
   Mc Intyre Bros. (Lagoon Rd)
   Patio Bar (Lagoon Rd)
   Ross Combine Workshop (Lagoon Rd)
   Univeral Supplies (Lagoon Rd)
   The Ware House (Jean Anglias)
   Maitland Garage
   Papaty Garage
   8 private shops
   St. Ann Guest House
   Skyline Guest House
   Cresent Inn

SOCIAL OBJECTIVES:

   International Mediation Society
   Robertson Convalescent Home
   Mrs. Black Pre-Primary School
   Picker Patch Pasture (Lagoon Rd)
   Reservoir (Jean Anglais)
   Pandy Community Center
   Belmont Soceity Hall

MILITARY OBJECTIVES:

Ministry of Interior Unit

POPULATION:

1,863 people

CHURCHES:

Grenada Baptiste Church — Paster James —
Catholic Church now under construction

ENEMY FORCES:

Vernon Edwards — Worker — Very Dangerous
Mr. Maitland (Lagoon Rd) — Petty Boug — Dangerous
Linclon Ross — (" ") — Petty Boug — Less Dangerous
[*Phinsley St. Louis – Petty Boug – Dangerous*]

OUR FORCES:

Pioneer Group — 1
N.Y.O. Group — 1
N.W.O. Group — 1
Parish Council members — over 50 members
[*P.S.G.*]

CONTACTS:

Ian Wilson
Isiah Trail
Kelvin Howell
Sharon Coutain
Brian Birzan
Nicholas St. John
Mrs. Beryl Coutain
James Eddie

III-3
Plan of G.I. (General Intelligence) Operations

This brief, undated report, issued by the Grenadian Ministry of Interior, describes plans for wholesale monitoring of political trends within the country – including checking "the mood and movements of the [medical] school hierarchy and professors."
"Counters" is short for "counter-revolutionaries."

MINISTRY OF INTERIOR
BUTLER HOUSE,
ST. GEORGE'S.

PLAN OF G.I. [General Intelligence] OPERATIONS

Setting up of command post comprising Major Keith Roberts. Cpt. H. Romain, Lt. B. Pivotta.

Responsible for analyzing all information that are coming in, in order to pass on to members of the Central Committee.

— Also, one Comrade who we can send to verify situations and incidents that have been reported.
— Recorder of all the information coming into the Centre.

MONITORING REGIONALLY — ST. GEORGE'S

City — three (3) Officers
Dock, Carenage — one (1) Officer
St. Paul's — two (2) Officers

ST. JOHN'S

One (1) Officer plus Party Cadres — Valdon

ST. PATRICK'S

(R)eports from Jan

T. ANDREW'S

Two (2) Officers plus Party Cadres — Re Gill
Regular hourly report from all officers and Party Cadres being
[illeg.]ed for this purpose.

(i) Monitoring of all Embassies and Diplomats in this
period.
(ii) To control the movements of all diplomats, with the
purpose of revealing the links with possible counter
elements.
(iii) Stop any possibility of them actively using this period to
create distrubances and confusion and a major
counter-actions.
(iv) Monitoring of all visitors who have been in Grenada
over four weeks and more.
(v) Study the incoming visitors of the various counters to
see the composition of visitors.
(vi) Checking and controlling the key middle class elements
who have links with diplomats and influence in some
section of the society.
(vii) Check the hotels to see if visitors are leaving before
their scheduled time or the booking question.

MEDICAL SHCOOL

Monitor all students during this period.
Check the mood and movements of the school hirachy and
professors during this period.

CHURCH

Monitor all sermons by the various parish priests and
preachers in the society.
The controlling of all hirachy meeting of the church in par-
ticular the Catholic and Anglicans.
Controlling all elements of the society that pay visits to the
Hirachy.
Tapping of the Hirachy of all the leading counter churches
phones.

ESSENTIAL SERVICES

[illeg.] protection of the key installations against sabotage. [illeg.] on confidence people to ensure that any signs of [illeg.] may be identified.

Getting a general operative picture of the area in which the key installations are located.

Checking of mails of dangerous elements.

Tapping and disconnection of dangerous elements phones.

Check all Heads of Ministries to see if they have any important documents which needs to be secured.

Special control over technicians who are not very firm and cannot be replaced.

COAST GUARD

Establish communication with watch towers.
Boat patrols on a nightly basis.

Documentation of all telephone calls and security reports from various regions.

III-4
Propaganda Work Plan

This extensive, undated report, developed by the New Jewel Propaganda Department, specifies the intention of the Bishop regime to concentrate press activities on the distribution of Soviet propanda.

WORK-PLAN OF THE PARTY'S PROPAGANDA DEPARTMENT

I. <u>OBJECTIVE</u>: Organise propaganda campaigns around important events and activities of the party.

<u>WAYS AND MEANS</u>:

   (i). Identify key events and activities of the party for 1983.

   (ii). Develop work plans and schedules for specific events and activities.

<u>OBJECTIVE 2</u>: Lift the political, academic and ideological levels of the masses.

<u>WAYS AND MEANS</u>:

   (i). ENCOURAGE participations in the CPE programme, Worker education classes and the work-study programme.

   (ii). Recommence publication of all the leading Party Organs.

   (iii). Publish theoretical articles in all Party publications.

<u>OBJECTIVE 3</u>: Coordinate the publication and distribution of all Party organs.

WAYS AND MEANS:

(i). Prepare articles in conjunction with the editors of the respective organs.

(ii). Hold regular meetings with the editorial committees of the respective organs to review strength and weaknesses.

(iii). Set up a central distribution system.

OBJECTIVE 4: Document all speeches and publications of the party and leadership.

WAYS AND MEANS:

(i.) Tape edit and reproduce major speeches of Party members.

(ii.) File all publications and other documents of the Party.

OBJECTIVE 5: ENSURE press coverage of all public party activities.

WAYS AND MEANS:

(i). Obtain list of party activities every month.

(ii). Co-ordinate with SPC — attend the weekly meetings.

OBJECTIVE 6: Deepen the consciousness of the masses as to the history and vanguard role of the party and the heroes of the revolution.

WAYS AND MEANS:

(i). Research, document and publish information on the heroes of the revolution.

(ii). Prepare booklet on the history of the party — 10 years.

(iii). Prepare materials on specific historic events of the party — peoples congress. etc.

(iv). Provide general information on the party and its leadership (profiles ect).

OBJECTIVE 7: Deepen the internationalist spirit and socialist consciousness of the Grenadian masses.

WAYS AND MEANS:

(i). Distribute progressive materials received from the Soviet Union other Socialist countries and progressive parties.

(ii). Highlight the struggles of National Liberation Movements.

(iii). Highlight the struggles of other countries against imperialism.

(iv). Highlight the immense benefits to workers under socialism.

(v). Expose the evil and warmongering policies of imperialism.

(vi). Highlight the struggles of the working class under capitalism.

(vii). Promote the life of people under socialism.

OBJECTIVE 8: Deepen the Patriotic [word missing] of the masses and cultivate even stronger desires to participate in National defence.

WAYS AND MEANS:

(i). Highlight activities of the people Revolutionary Armed Forces (PRAF).

(ii). constantly expose the [word missing] of imperialism towards the Grenada Revolution.

(iii). Consistently highlight the critical importance of National Defense.

(iv). Highlight the message to be delivered by solider of the PRAF.

(v). Propagandise the new programme of technical and academic training in the PRAF.

OBJECTIVE 9: Encourage the masses to actively participate in economic construction and stress the need to constantly lift the levels of production and productivity.

WAYS AND MEANS:

(i). Develop specific programs around the National budget and plan.

(ii). Extensive promotion of the emulation programme in the different party publications.

(iii). Constantly remind the masses of the economic problems inherited by the revolution and the pressures of imperialism.

(iv). Highlight the numerous economic projects of the revolution.

(v). Promote the views of workers on ways to lift production and productivity.

OBJECTIVE 10: Defend the party and revolution against counter revolutionary, backward and reactionary attacks from inside and outside of Grenada.

(i). Respond to all attacks against the party and revolution.

(ii). Consistently promote the achievements of the revolution in all areas.

OBJECTIVE 11: Ensure that fraternal parties — regionally and internationally — receives news, speeches and other documents of the party.

WAYS AND MEANS:

(i). Obtain names and addresses of all progressive and revolutionary parties in the region.

(ii) Regularly send out news, speeches and other documents of the party.

OBJECTIVE 12: Deepen the awareness and strengthen the resolve of Grenadians to struggle for World Peace, detente and
disarmament.

WAYS AND MEANS:

(i). Highlight the activities of the peace movements around
the world.

(ii). Promote the effects of the party and revolution on the
question of world peace and for the Caribbean to be declared a zone of peace.

(iii). Publicise the activities of the socialist and democratic
world for peace, disarmament and detente.

OBJECTIVE 13: guide and co-ordinate the propaganda of the
mass organisations and other party bodies.

(i). Regular meetings with propaganda representatives and
leadership of Party Committees.

(ii). Assist in drawing up propaganda plans the different
bodies.

RADIO AND TV PROPAGANDA

(1) Interviews
(2) News
(3) Special Programmes
(4) Promos
(5) Music
(6) Announcements
(7) Poetry
(8) Extracts from Speeches

ASPECTS OF PROPAGANDA

(1) Newspapers
(2) Pamphlets
(3) Bill-boards
(4) Badges

(5) Leadership speeches
(6) Radio and Television
(7) Posters
(8) Statements
(9) Jerseys and Pens
(10) Photography/Cartoons
(11) Letters to the Editor
(12) Photographic Exhibitions
(13) Newspaper displays reflecting the role of the party
(14) Use of Public Address Systems
(15) Use of Almanacs
(16) Booklets
(17) Photo stories
(18) Use of films and videos

PARTY PUBLICATIONS

(1) New Jewel   - N.J.M.
(2) Fight   - N.Y.O.
(3) The Scotilda   - N.W.O.
(4) Cutlass   - A.G.W.U.
(5) Fork   - P.F.U.
(6) Pioneers Voice   - N.F.M.
(7) Workers Voice   - W.C.
(8) Fedon   - P.R.A.F.

III-5
Ideological Crash Course

This report, dated September 17, 1983, outlines efforts to develop introductory studies in Marxist-Leninism for chosen industrial and administrative personnel. We should note the presence at this session of a Soviet observer, Boris Pirchgun. That NJM instructors were having difficulty putting over their ideological lessons is suggested by the fact that the only two student concerns addressed by "Brother Pirchgun" were whether the Soviet Union had, in fact, a classless society, and the Korean airline incident.

REPORT ON IDEOLOGICAL CRASH COURSE 17/9/83

ATTENDANCE:

The session started at 2.03 with the following W/C [Working Class] Comrades present.

COMRADES PRESENT:

Chester Humphrey (Tutor)
Vincent Noel
Trevor Noel
John Jones
Timothy Toursaint
Carl Johnson
Derek James
Derek Allard
Anslem De Bourg
Michael Prime

ABSENT WERE:

John Ventour
Jennifer Donald
Perron Lowe

.   .   .   .   .

Course Content: The concept of "Class Struggle" was taught for
the second time.

SOME QUESTIONS AND ANSWERS:

TUTOR: In order to fully grasp the essence of Class Struggle in
our present society it is important to fully understand the
class struggle between the slaves and the slaves masters.

TUTOR: How many classes existed in the slave society?
MASS PARTICIPATION: Two main classes — Slaves/Slave
Owners
George Best: Slaves lived under very bad conditions.
TUTOR: What are these bad conditions?
Victor Julien: No freedom of speech.
Anthony Lewis: Forced Labour for no wages.
Dollis Mc Kenzie: Slaves were compelled to work without
    choice.
Jacqueline Charles: Poor housing facilities.
Leroy John: Slaves were made to work 24 hours without food
    or very little food.
Cleaver Williams: Harsh penalities for resisting work/poor
    medical care.
Antoinette Martin: Slaves owned nothing not even them-
    selves.
TUTOR: Why do you think that the class of slave masters put
    the slaves under these kind of conditions?
Keith Jeremiah: They did this in order to maintain their slave
    system.
Terence Mc Phail: The whole system is geared to benefit one
    class. All the benefit goes to the slave master.
Nola Nelson: Because he can make much more for himself.
TUTOR: Did slavery remain forever?
    Mass participation: No! slaves rebelled, slavery lasted for
    over 400 yrs.
TUTOR: We agree that in Modern Capitalist society there are

two main classes — Capitalist/Working class.

Is there class struggle under Capitalism?

Mass participation: Yes — the struggle between the capitalist and the workers.

TUTOR: Why is there class struggle under capitalist capitalism?

Mass Participation: It is the interest of the capitalist to take the lion share of what is produced and give the workers less.

TUTOR: More for the capitalist means less for the workers and less for the capitalist means more for the workers.

TUTOR: Do you think it is fair for the capitalist to get the lion share?

Wharwood: Workers use their strength to create the wealth — they should get the biggest share.

Soniania Frederick: We should get a good share but not the lion share.

Anthony Lewis/Ambrose Smith: Capitalist owns the means — workers own the labour.

Sharon De Bourg: [missing word] power so profits should be equally divided.

Dollis Mc Kenzie: If the capitalist did not buy the machinery, the workers could not work, so worker should not get the biggest share but a reasonable share.

TUTOR: The most important thing here is to show that class struggle arose as result of exploitations of one class by another class.

TUTOR: What is the main objective of the exploiter class?

TUTOR: How does the capitalist make more profits.

Anthony Lewis: Cheaper Labour.

Leroy John: Longer working hours.

George Best: Increase in prices.

Errol Antoine: Cutting staff (more work for workers — less wages paid out)

Anthony Lewis: non recognition of Trade Unions.

TUTOR: If workers don't struggle — what will happen to their share of the cake.

Mass participation: It will get sam a smaller.

TUTOR: 1. It is important to understand, that to struggle is a necessity — struggle leads to progress.

2. In a class society, there is always class struggle.

3. Class struggle is the engine of progress.

Anthony Lewis: Is there class on a universal scale?

Is there class struggle in the U.S.S.R.?

TUTOR: In response to the above questions, tutors started that these questions will be looked at in the next session.

At this state a short address was delivered by A.U.C.C.T.U. Representative Bro. Boris Pirchgun who focussed on these two areas. 1. Class in the U.S.S.R. 2. Korean Airline.

ANALYSIS: Overall the participation was very good. From a scale of 0.5 participation can be rated as 3.5. Generally the mood of the workers was good.

III-6
Complaint of Russell Budhlall
9/30/80

This memorandum on charges of torture, put forward against the Grenadian prison administration by detainee Russell Budhlall, was transmitted by special investigator Victor Husband to security chief Kenrick Radix, dated October 1, 1980.

MT. ROYAL
ST. GEORGE'S
30th September, 1980

COMPLAINT OF RUSSELL BUDHLALL

On the 16th September 1980 I complained to my Lawyer Tillman Thomas that I was beaten on my abdomen and I received punch, kick and they beat me with Gun butt. They had an instrument burning me with. They burn me all different parts of my body and then push it up through my bottom. They handcuff me from behind. My hand was behind my back and they handcuff it there and they pull the handcuffs tight then they held the handcuff and pull it and I get two cuts on both wrists from the handcuffs. I receive a kick on my face and I bleed through my nostrils. Some of the spots of blood can still be seen on the wall. That is all I told my Lawyer on the 16th September 1980. It was the first time I told him about it. These incidents took place on the 2nd July 1980 when you were arrested.

I complained to a Security Officer by the name of Chicken sometime around the 24th July 1980 and as a result, Doctor Purcell came and examined me a few day after. The Doctor gave me some treatment.

I also complained to a Security Officer named Francis around the same time I complained to Chicken. I also told

Francis what they did me when I was arrested and asked him to get some magnesia for me. I did not get the magnesia.

The reason why I did not tell my Lawyer about these incidents before is because I did not get a good chance to do so. On the 16th September 1980, I was allowed an interview with my Lawyer, a private interview and it was then that I told him about it.

I think that the reason why the matter was brought up in court this morning, 30th September 1980, by my Lawyer for the first time is due to the fact that I told my Lawyer that I was having some problem with my abdomen which I feel was caused by the incidents of the 2nd July 1980 when I was arrested and asked my Lawyer to request the Magistrate to order that I be examined by a Doctor. That is the reason why I think the matter was raised in Court this morning.

When I was arrested on the 2nd July 1980 I was taken to a place that I don't know. I don't know the place because I was blindfolded. In that place I was questioned by some persons but I do not know who they were. They questioned me about the bombing in Queens Park. I told them that I don't know about it. I started receiving punch, well say blows and burns. Then the blindfold came off from my eyes, it fell off and I manage to see about six to eight men around me. Two of them had something in their hand that they was burning me with. Justin was one of the men but I don't know the name of the next one. While they was burning me the others was punching me and some was hitting me with gun butt. Then I receive kick and the feller that kick me name Bread, I don't know he right name. I receive a kick on my nostril when I bleed. The same Bread is who kick me because he show me the boots a few days afterwards that he kick me with. After the blindfold fell off I was sitting on a chair and while they were burning me I fell on the floor lying on my back. They take off my underpants and what they had burning me with was pushed up through my bottom. Since that I am seeing some trouble to pass my stool.

Signed: [signature]

III-7
Leninist Komsomol — National Youth Organization

These notes, prepared by NJM-NYO Chairman David Tan Bartholomew, undated, reveal an overall plan for youth in Grenada borrowed from the Soviet model of youth indoctrination. "Leninist Komsomol" is an official Soviet term for the Leninist Communist League of Youth, the youth organization of the Soviet Communist Party.

ISSUES FOR DISCUSSION BETWEEN LENINIST KOMSOMOL AND THE NEW JEWEL MOVEMENT-NATIONAL YOUTH OR-GANISATION NJM-NYO.

The former Leader of the New jewel Movement — National Youth Organisation (NJM-NYO), comrade Leon Cornwall, held discussions with Leninist Komsomol during his visit to the Soviet Union to attend the Komsomol Congress in May 1982. The discussions centered on, among other things, the question of desperately needed material assistance to NYO. This Delegation has the responsibility of following up on discussions held between Comrade Cornwall and the Leninist Komsomol.

THE FOLLOWING WERE DISCUSSED BETWEEN KOMSOMOL AND NYO.

1. Leninist Komsomol agreed to receive a four (4) man Delegation from NYO in November, to further study Y.C.L. activities. This presant NYO Delegation is the fulfilment of this agreement. We attach tremendous significance and importance to this visit, because we think we can learn from the tremendous experience accumulated by the Komsomol, which we may be able to creatively apply to our local situation.

2. Leninist Komsomol offered a Scholarship to one (1) Gre-

nadian Youth to study an academic subject in the USSR for
three (3) years. NYO now proposed that the area of study
be Journalism given the importance of this area to us and
the unavailability of this skill. Our propaganda work is
seriously affected by the absence of comrades with skill in
Journalism.

3. Leninist Komsomol had invited two (2) Pioneers and a
Guide to attend a Pioneer Camp, in USSR in July 1982, this
took place. The experience and knowledge gained during
the Camp has helped our young comrades in their work at
Home.

4. Leninist Komsomol had proposed for consideration a
friendship festival with NYO with all expenses to be paid
by Komsomol. The proposal was that two (2) festivals one
(1) 1983 in Grenada and two (2) 1985 in Soviet Union.
NYO now proposes a rescheduling of the festival to 1984 in
Grenada and 1985 in USSR.

5. Komsomol agreed to assist NYO with Sporting equipment,
Camera, Loud Speakers and Marxist-Leninist literature. We
have already received Literature earlier this year from
Komsomol. This is being used as part of the NYO Library
where comrades can borrow books to be used for ideological study. The thirst for Marxist-Leninist ideas is very intense among our Youth, we are unfortunately far from
being able to satisfy this positive demand. However, the
most important thing for the NYO at this point in time is
Sporting equipment. Our Youth are sport fanatic. Sport
remain and will remain for a long time the main vehicle
around which we can mobilise and organise our youth. Unemployment is one of the main social and economic problems facing Grenada. The rate of unemployed people are between 10% of the work force. But 65% of all unemployed
people are between the ages of 16-25 years. This large reserve Army of unemployed youths are turning to drugs to
ease frustration. We are concerned that opportunist,
bourgeois elements in alliance with imperialism will use
the frustrated youth against the Revolution.

In 1980 left-opportunist were able to organise a section of
the unemployed youth against the Revolution. This was
firmly crushed, but the unemployed youth has remain a potential reserve for Reactionary activities. Sport is the vehicle through which we can mobilise and organise these
youths and divert them from the negitave tendancies. The
organisation of sport is our number one strategic priority.
We will provide a list of the specific equipment we need
desperately.

6. Komsomol had promised also to look into the possibility of
giving assistance with clothing for the Youth Agricultural
Training Schools. These schools are organised by the
Ministry of Agriculture and NYO where unemployed youth
live in Schools set up to teach new methods of Agriculture.

7. Komsomol had also promised to investigate the possibility
of assisting NYO with two (2) Jeeps. Our second most crucial problem is Transportation. Our youths are organised
in hundreds of base groups throughout the Country. These
Groups cannot be serviced effectively without Transport.
We will appreciate greatly assistance in this area.

8. Komsomol also promised to contact us on the possibility of
giving ideological training to youths in USSR or to send a
lecturer down to Grenada for a week or two.

NEW PROPOSALS

1. Assistance with (a) films and Projectors (b) Typewriters.

Film/Projectors

Ideological education is presantly one of the main priorities
of our Party. Experience have proved beyond doubt that the
most effective methods of ideological education for our Mass
Organisations is through Film Shows. Assistance in this field
will greatly enhance our ideological work among youth and
students.

Typewriters

Our administration department suffers from the shortage of type writers. With the expansion of our work the administrative department will also have to be expanded. Assistance with typewriters will help us tremendously.

The assistance requested will help our organisation to solve serious objective problems that has been holding back the development of our work. We are convinced that assistance requested could qualitatively improve our work among the Grenadian youth and student thereby preparing them to play a major role in building the new Society.

Comradely,

[signature]

DAVE TAN BARTHOLOMEW
CHAIRMAN — NJM — NATIONAL
YOUTH ORGANISATION

III-8
Draft Protocol on Youth

This agreement between the youth organizations of the Grenadian and Czechoslovakian governments, prepared in June 1982, lays the basis for further integration of Grenada into Soviet-bloc political mobilization activities.

The World Federation of Democratic Youth and the International Union of Students, both headquartered in Czechoslovakia, consist of mass-participation institutions in the Soviet-bloc countries, along with youth and student wings of the pro-Soviet Communist parties outside the bloc. It should be noted that although the NJM youth organization was linked to these Soviet-controlled groupings, the NJM also was affiliated with the Socialist International, which officially defends Western democracy.

DRAFT PROTOCOL ON YOUTH

Between the Socialist Union of Youth of Czechoslovakia and the NJM National Youth Organisation of Grenada.

The Socialist Union of Youth Czechoslovakia (SSM) and the NJM National Youth Organisation of Grenada (NJM-NYO) on this day of June in the year 1982 formally established relations and agreed on the following principles as the basis of their fraternal relations.

A. Recongnition and support of the Union of Soviet Socialist Republics (USSR) as the bulwark for peace in the world and preparedness to combat antisovietism as a reactionary policy of imperialism and being dangerous to the progressive forces.

B. Consistent struggle for world peace, disarmament, detente and the policy of peaceful coexistence between nations of different social system; specifically struggling for peace and security in Europe, against nuclear deployment in

Europe, against the manufacturing of the nuclear bomb, for an end of imperialist military base and manoeuvres in the Caribbean area.

C. Support for Czechoslovakia in its struggle to build an advanced socialist society and support for Grenada in its national democratic stuggle to lay the basis for socialism.

D. Supprot to the World Federation of Democrative Youth (WFDY) and the International Union of Students (I.U.S.) and active work to make these two (2) Youth and Students bodies stronger in drawing the broadest sections of democratic youth and students into the struggle for World peace.

D. Support for the broadest antimonopoly and democratic forces in the developed capitalist society in their struggle for broadening democracy.

E. Support for the National Liberation Movement having in mind, that the work and tasks of the youth are growing in these Movements.

The SSM and NJM-NYO agree that in the period 1983 to 1985 the following programme would be embarked on;

A. Assistance from the SSM to the NJM-NYO in its youth employment programme (YEP)

B. Provision of musical instruments to NJM-NYO by SSM.

C. Hosting Friendship and Peace festivals with the people and youth of each country NJM-NYO to host first festival in 1984 and SSM to host the other in 1985.

D. Reconise and celebrate the liberation dates of each country and revolution.

E. Exchange of delegations to study the experience and work of the youth organisations of each country.

F. Assistance from SSM to NJM-NYO's political education and prograganda work by giving assistance in film and slide projectors, films, small printing press and Marxist literature with a van that can serve as a mobile libarary unit.

G. Assistance from SSM to NJM-NYO in building seven children's playgrounds.

   It is hereby agreed and confirmed by;

_____   _____

Chairman SSM   Chairman NJM-NYO
Dated; June 1982.

III-9
National Service and Labor Army

*This undated "progress report" by a Grenadian governmental
subcommission discusses the possible adoption in Grenada of the
Cuban concept of an obligatory national service and labor army. It
was prepared by A. John for limited circulation among Grenadian
officials.*

*The term "petit-bourgeois," originally referring to small mer-
chants and professionals in urban, industrial societies, has been
transformed by Communist ideology from a sociological category to
a highly-damaging political insult. It is usually considered, in the
Marxist context, to denote habits of individualism or self-interest on
the part of those who, it is felt, might normally embrace an outlook
more in conformity with the duties of the average person living
under a Marxist state.*

TOP SECRET
COPY NO. __ OF __

PROGRESS REPORT OF COMMISSION NO. 5

The Commission had met on the 7th and 8th and the following matters were dealt with: —

(1) Study of review of the implementation of National Service
and Labour Army in Cuba.

(2) Study of the present political trend in Grenada, the particular of our society and the possibilities of implementation of the National Service and the Labour Army.

(3) Political and economic consequencies.

On the Cuban experience, we discovered that the real difference between the Labour Army and the National Service is

that the Labour Army is for production and the National Service is for defense. The National Service were implemented in 1963 while the Labour Army was implemented ten (10) years after.

In those days when the Cubans had implemented the National Service there was a form of restriction on people leaving the country. People had to get authorization to leave the country.

A number of people had tried to avoid the National Service and the Labour Army. Even some churches tried to argue that their young men are not to hold gun and wear military uniform. Some people tried to escape from the country (though in a small minority) and others pretended sick and mad.

The Cuban leadership had foreseen all the above reaction and had passed a law called "Law of Obligatory National Service." Anyone who refused to do their national service were jailed for a minimum of five (5) years. They had also passed a law on Labour Army.

The methods at which persons are called into the National Service and the Labour Army are basically the same. Persons are called into the National Service at the end of pre-university. They would spend three (3) years in the National Service and depending on their discipline and work in general, they can then continue their studies at university level.

If one should not do well at the National Service and has displayed illdiscipline, then at the end of his service he is transferred to the Labour Army. Also one can be transferred to the National Service from the Labour Army if he is doing well.

Initially, the Cubans have excluded women from the National Service and it was not until the late seventies that they decided to include women into the Service. They had foreseen that a too early inclusion of women into the Service would pose a big logistical problem that would be a heavy burden for the economy in that time.

Also, they did not take in persons leaving primary school because in the early days they had to lay much emphasis on developing the intelligencia.

Both the National Service and the Labour Army has its discipline regulations, but the regulations at the National Service are more rigorous. A military tribunel is formed to unlease punishment on those that broke the regulations at the National Service. For those breaking the regulations at the Labour Army, a civilian tribunal is formed among the masses that can unlease punishment of five years imprisonment as a minimum.

Together with other basic necessities, the person at the National Service receive six (6) pesos (dollars) monthly, while those in the Labour Army seventy six (76) pesos monthly and still receive basic necessities. Recreational facilities such as games hall and playing field are provided for both National Service and Labour Army. Also nightly passes are given to the Labour Army and weekly passes are given to those in the National Service.

Present Political Trend, Political Background, Present Situation:

The Commission has concluded that our society is largely petit Bourgeois in mentality as well as socially. Such a mentality, we concluded, is by law rebellious to any form of strict discipline and organisation. A number of persons are interested with the mentality of wanting to have their petit means of creating wealth they would automatically rebel against the idea of National Service and Labour Army.

Because of our geographical location the idea if National Service and Labour Army is going to be under much attacks and falsification by the reactionary neighbouring islands. It is in our view that there would even be open attacks by internal counter-revolutionary if we are not careful in how we handle the matter.

Imperalism well understand the significance of National

Service and Labour Army for our process and would not cease from their effort of destabilisation and may even lend open support to stop our process.

In terms of the political trend, we conclude that with all the revolutionary programmes like C.N.B., Housing schemes, International Airport, Preo milk, better roads, MNIB etc. etc. coupled with an expanding socialism classes, the political consciousness of the masses should rise, and if the Party do away with its subjective weaknesses, the masses can be prepared to accept National Service and Labour Army in the not too distant future.

Particularity of our Country:

In the first place, we conclude that our country does not have a military tradition and as a result it is not all that easy for people to accept National Service and Labour Army.

Our people, as a tradition, believe in going overseas to work for more money and there is at present an unsatisfactory level of patriotism among the masses. In other words, we have grown up with a visa mentality.

The question we now pose is, can we apply restriction to people wanting to leave the country?

Our country is a very open country. Anyone can turn on to say Radio Station and listen to all of the imperialist propaganda. They can turn on to look at imperialist television. They can read any magazine, books, etc. and have access to all the ways and means in which imperialist can influence the mind.

A good many of the poor families would not readily understand their children after leaving school should give a military service to their country and not bringing any financial gains to the family.

We are now faced with the question: What salary should be given to the person in the National Service and the Labour Army? How much persons should we take in the National

Service and the Labour Army yearly? Given the economic condition of our country, can we embark be National Service and Labour Army simultaneously? How soon can the economy afford national Service and Labour Army.

The amount of persons we take in yearly for the National Service would definitely have to be according to what the structure is calling for. We have already concluded that whatever the amount would be, (be on the Cuban experience) we would have to take in one-third of that amount every year if we are going to make the period of National Service a duration of three (3) years.

Given all the particularities of our country, we conclude that the first and the best time to introduce the idea of National Service and Labour Army should be at the fifth (5th) Anniversary in which the Commander-in-Chief would spell out the gains of the Revolution and explain the necessity for defending these gains against the permanent enemy, imperialism.

This March 13th introduction must be followed by a series of useful propaganda to prepare the masses for the implementation of the National Service and/or the Labour Army.

Finally, in looking at the particularity of our country we have seen that our people had known no war. The majority of our people is complacent and only respond in times of crisis. They does not understand the reason for National Service.

.   .   .   .

III-10
Central Committee Resolution
on Agriculture

This undated document outlines the strategy of the NJM leadership in dealing with agriculture, the mainstay of the Grenadian economy. Simultaneously, the Bishop regime sought to impose a large state-bureaucratic apparatus on Grenadian farmers while accepting the need for tax and other concessions to them.

CONFIDENTIAL

CENTRAL COMMITTEE RESOLUTION ON AGRICULTURE

From early October the Central Committee and the Political Bureau have been engaged in a long and exhaustive analysis on the Party's Line of March in Agriculture.

During these three months, intensive discussions have been held on working out a correct approach to: —

(1) The overall land question with particular focus on the approximate 600 acres to be declared idle in the coming weeks.

(2) The development and strengthening of the State Sector and the specific role of GPC.

(3) How to build the firm alliance between the working class and the peasantry, begin the process of collectivisation and transformation of the countrysides.

(4) What strategy and tactics must be applied toward the large owners. How to lay the basis for their nationalisation, prevent any land fragmentation while at the same time utilising their managerial skills in production.

(5) What is the best way to utilise the YEP graduates.

As a result of all these discussions the CC resolves Priority
One in Agriculture in the coming period must be:

1. PRIORITY ONE:

    TO MAKE GPC THE LEADING VEHICLE FOR BEGINNING
    TO LAY THE BASIS FOR THE SOCIALIST TRANSFORMA-
    TION OF AGRICULTURE: . . .

2. PRIORITY TWO:

    TO WIN THE PEASANTRY GRADUALLY TO SOCIALISM BY
    BUILDING THE ALLIANCE OF THE WORKING CLASS AND
    THE PEASANTRY THROUGH A PROGRAMME OF CONCES-
    SIONS AND BY BUILDING AND STRENGTHENING PFU . . .

PRIORITY 3:

The CC and PB concluded that joint venture companies should
be established with large estate owners who are willing to
produce, remain in production but may be faced with
economic crisis or bankruptcy. Such joint ventures should be
immediately established with selected land owners. . . .

PRIORITY 4:

The CC concluded that the development and modernisation of
Agriculture hold the key to winning the peasantry to
Socialism and the transformation of the countryside along
socialist lines.

All Party committee are requested to study this resolution
carefully; be guided by its analysis and implement its conclusions in their entirety.

III-11
State Trading Corporation/Socialist Countries

This document presents a proposal for establishment of a government import-export entity designed to expand Grenadian trade with countries in the Soviet bloc.

The New Jewel government clearly aimed at an increasing statification of the island's economy, to the detriment not only of private business but also of such non-private units as the cocoa, nutmeg, banana, and spice marketing cooperatives. Statification was conceived of as much in the context of Grenada's external politics (the references to "imperialism") as of increasing economic benefits. Such proposals indicate a much stronger tilt toward Soviet-based governing models than has been seen in such other regional left-wing states as Jamaica (under Michael Manley) and Guyana.

ON THE POSSIBLE ESTABLISHMENT OF A STATE TRADING CORPORATION FOR EFFECTING GRENADA'S TRADE WITH THE SOCIALIST COUNTRIES

GENERAL CONSIDERATIONS

With the growing disparity between our import bill and our export earnings — and consequently, with the growing un-favourable balance in our terms of trade — as a result of our entanglement in the world imperialist system the question of state direction and control of the country's foreign trade assumes increasing importance. This is so because it is becoming increasingly necessary to restructure and re-align our foreign trade activity so as to bring them in line with our possibilities and our needs. In particular, this need embraces four (4) steps:

(i) Changing the structure of our exports by diversifying the range of items available for exports. This will make us

less dependent on and less prone to the difficulties associated with dependence on one or two agricultural
commodities.

(ii) Diversifying the destination of our exports by actively
seeking and finfing markets in the Socialist Countries
and other developing states and developing trade on a
state to state basis. Taking into account the principles
which guide the foreign trade activity of the Socialist
Countries, this will guarantee new relations of mutual
advantage and stem the worsening balance of trade with
which we are now faded.

(iii) Changing the structure of our imports so as to give
greater emphasis to items required for productive activity and reduce (at least in relative terms) the import of
food and non-essential consumer items.

(iv) Changing the sources of our imports so as to take advantage of better and more favourable terms and conditions
of purchase of essential items and at the same time make
ourselves less vulnerable to the economic aggression of
imperialism. This implies concretely, purchasing, to
greatest extent necessary and possible, more items from
the Socialist Countries and other developing countries on
a state to state basis.

Since March 13th a number of concrete steps have been
taken to realise all of the four objectives. In these notes we
propose to focus on the second (ii) and fourth (iv). In particular, we shall [illeg.] from the standpoint of strategy, the possibilities and prospects for developing and deepening our
trade relations with the Socialist Countries and the steps
which may be taken at the particular point in time. These
possibilities and prospects will be examined especially in the
light of institutional arrangements and will be viewed both
from the standpoint of exports and imports.

(A) EXPORTS

The area of export diversification and export control re-

quires critical and urgent attention at this time for the following reasons: —

(i) Merchandise exports has had and still has great potential for raising the country's foreign exchange earning
capacity — this is particularly so for agricultural exports.

(ii) With only a few commodities constituting the bulk of
agricultural and indeed, merchandise exports, the
managerial and technical skills and experience required to control and direct this activity are relatively
few and less varied.

(iii) At present these activities are in the hands of only
four (4) "Non State" organisations. As such only a
limited amount of people will be severly and directly
affected by state control and direction of these activities, i.e. the political reaction to such a measure is
not likely to be popular in scope. This proposition
must be qualified and is further examined below.

In short, as compared to imports, the possibilities for export control and direction seem greater and apparently can be
achieved in a relatively shorter space of time.

The vast majority of our merchandise exports are ac-
counted for by cocoa, nutmegs, bananas and spices. At present,
the exports of these commodities are controlled by four (4)
separate marketing co-operatives. Taking into account the
present mode of operation of these organisations and the
broad objectives of the Party and Government (particularly as
outlined in (ii) above) it will be necessary for the state to intervene in the activities of these organisations.

STATE INTERVENTION IN (CONTROL OF) EXPORTS

Any form of intervention by the State in the activities now
handled by these organisation will have to take into consideration the following considerations: —

(1) Who presently own/control these organisations?

(2) What are the existing arrangements for purchasing and marketing these commodities?

(3) Which are the existing markets and who are the Agents/Brokers?

(4) What form should the intervention by the state take?

(5) What is likely to be the reaction and implications of those who now control these organisations?

(6) What is likely to be the reaction of the workers in these organisations, to state intervention and what steps can be taken to win or reinforce their support and participation?

(7) What is likely to be the reaction of the farmers to state intervention?

(8) What is likely to be the reaction of those who control the shipping lines handling these commodities?

(9) What advantages can be brought to the farmers through state intervention and what steps must be taken to convince the farmers of these advantages?

(10) What are the overall advantages for the Revolution in taking such a step?

(11) What are the overall disadvantages of taking such a step and what steps can be taken to cushion these.

The first three questions are to be examined in some detail after collecting information form the existing institutions. Every other question should be considered in all possible options of intervention.

WHAT FORM THE INTERVENTION MUST TAKE

These alternatives appear to be opened to the Party and Government: —

OPTION 1: The State establishes a total monopoly on the marketing of these products and set up a new

State Trading Corporation to deal with these products.

OPTION 2: The State establishes a monopoly on the marketing of these commodities and incorporates the existing institutions into MNIB.

OPTION 3: The State establishes a monopoly on exports with the Socialist Countries, takes responsibility for this programme and decide what the exports levels to these countries would be.

OPTION 4: The State localises the operation of these institutions and by legislation adopts majority control over their operations.

OPTION 5: The State simply set the export levels to the Socialist Countries each year.

. . . .

IV
THE NEW JEWEL MOVEMENT
AND THE CHURCHES

In the predominantly Christian countries of Central America and the Caribbean that are now affected by the spread of Communist power, indigenous churches have tended to present a formidable obstacle to the consolidation of control by totalitarian forces. However, this trend must be considered alongside the opposite current within the U.S. and Western Europe, where radicalized factions within mainstream Protestant and Catholic churches now aid and identify with the political goals of Marxism-Leninism in Latin and Caribbean America. The same sympathies for Marxist-Leninist movements have been apparent among activist religious orders such as the Maryknolls who, in the name of "liberation theology," have aided these movements and regimes, attracted by their radical programs and their promises to overthrow "oppressive social structures" and establish a new order of socialism. In this, the Christ of liberation theology is depicted as a guerrilla fighter working alongside objective historical-materialist forces to create a mundane, non-transcendental, and perfect social order. It should be remembered that for Marxist-Leninists, to attempt too vigorously or overtly to repress Christianity in the early stages of revolutionary consolidation is to run the risk of creating a backlash of opposition such as the Polish Communist regime has faced for a long time.

In Grenada, however, it does not seem that "liberation theology" had made any significant impact before or after the Communist seizure of power. The new authorities therefore perceived the existing churches as wholly reactionary obstacles to their ultimate objectives, rather than as potential vehicles to be easily infiltrated, seized, and transformed.

The following documents attest to the intense interest that the new regime displayed in the inner nature of the various churches on the island, Protestant and Catholic alike. In investigating them, the authorities relied on their political police and, interestingly enough, upon Cuban intelligence operatives to penetrate the churches. The original strategy for infiltrating and weakening the churches appears to have been set forth in a paper authored by Cuba's hemispheric affairs (America) department. Bishop himself, as his marginal notations on several documents show, paid close personal attention to police reports on the activities of individual parish ministers and priests, and Christian workers. Evidently, he also was intrigued by the idea of establishing a "progressive" church as a weapon against the opposition. (It is interesting to see that a similar tactic had been used already to crush free trade unions, by establishing state-controlled ones.) In addition, the New Jewel Movement sought to emulate the Sandinista authorities by seeking their advice on how to incorporate "liberation theology" in this process.

Interestingly also, reports of internal security police demonstrate that they regarded the Jehovah's Witnesses and the Baptists as the "most reactionary" of the non-mainstream churches—a view closely akin to that of the KGB in the Soviet Union.

IV-1
Catholic Church Publications Report
2/11/80

This unsigned report, describing ostensibly dissident Catholic Church publications distributed in Grenada, is annotated in Maurice Bishop's handwriting [notes in margin]. The report shows the hostility of the Bishop government to any non-Marxist publishing activities on the island.

TOP SECRET

REPORT   18.30 hrs.   FEBRUARY 11, 1980

A series of publications are being put out by the Catholic Church. Most of those published so far are aimed at showing that Communism is atheistic and should be feared and that our party is Communist. The articles aim at creating fear in the minds of the religious.

So far five have been published in the series - the first three being the small leaflets of track size. No. 4 was Civic Freedoms, No. 5 some notes on Marx-Leninism. The sixth publication is in the making but no definite date has been given as to when it will be out.

[*Who typed?*] The typing of the 5th publication was done by an Irish teacher at St. John's Christian Secondary School.

[*Which priests + any others?*] Father Bernard Kadlec of Czechoslovakia is one of the writers. Father Austin is another. (I don't know which).

Publication is done by Mc Kie's Printery, and Torchlight Printery. A track size publication Brown writing is now being printed [*Where printed?*] in St. Lucia.

Further information could not be had: the Priest was in a haste to leave for St. George's.

However, the Priest said that whenever he publishes any of these things he always send one to the Prime Minister.

[*X*] He seems to have a hunch that the PRG will clamp down on these publications. I told him to ensure me a copy of each of his publications when he replied yet with a statement to this effect.

Father Bernard was the writer of Civic Freedoms, but I have not found out who is the author of the 5th publication.

[*Source*] The Priest is also afraid of these leaving the hands of the PRA soldiers for fear they may lose their jobs.

And so fear to give it to soldiers.

IV-2
Cuban Report on Churches
10/14/82

*This extensive report, prepared by the hemispheric affairs
(America) department of the Cuban Communist Party (PCC), represents perhaps the most dramatic single bit of evidence of Cuban
interference in Grenadian internal affairs.*

*As the report clearly shows, the Cuban government took on,
virtually independently of the Grenadian authorities, responsibility
for developing Grenadian state policy on what could easily have
become a serious internal problem, that of anti-communist sentiment within the ranks of the Catholic church.*

*The report begins by noting that the Grenadian New Jewel per-
sonnel were responsible for a "total lack of informative or unofficial
documentation," increasing the need for the Cubans to work on their
own in their investigation of the situation. It goes on to ascribe to
Catholic Church representatives "aggressive positions. . . against
the revolutionary leadership," a claim that cannot be substantiated
independently, for it is clear that the church remained politically
inactive in Grenada throughout the period of New Jewel rule; this is
supported by the lack of any reportage of actual incidents indicating
friction between the church and the bishop state, much less resistance by the religious community. Clearly, as noted in the introduction to this section and as stated openly in the next document (IV-3),
Cuban and Grenadian "concern" over Catholic activities was based
almost solely on anxiety over the possibility of some kind of "Polish"
situation emerging in the future. Such anxieties may be considered
a logical product of Grenada's pro-Soviet "remodelling."*

*The report notes indeed that the only area of disagreement be-
tween the Catholic hierarchy and the New Jewel government involved the timetable for elections. While the Catholic church had
sought to act as a mediator for political prisoners held in Grenadian
jails, this is a role the church has traditionally played throughout
the world, as part of its original mission. Although the Caribbean
Catholic bishops seem to have supported the demand for "freedom of
the press in Grenada," no serious agitation along these lines was*

undertaken. In effect, as the report admits, it could not be said that the hierarchy had "decided on an open confrontation," and the "contradiction" that was anticipated could only be described as "potential."

Many uncomfortable questions, for the Cubans and the Grenadians, may be derived from this report. As pointed out above, it shows the Cubans involving themselves in the most sensitive problems of the Grenadian state, relative to internal security, with a proposal for direct training of NJM personnel on religious matters. Further, the report reveals a basic Marxist hostility to the independent activity of the Church that strongly conflicts with the claims the Cubans and other Latin American left-wing forces have advanced regarding their commitment to harmony between communist states and religious communities. It shows the Cubans recommending measures for the control of religious activities that can only be described as totalitarian, such as a legal "Register of Associations" in which religious groups would be obliged to list themselves.

Perhaps most importantly, the report also reveals the Cuban presumption of a special role, in the policing of the Grenadian Catholic Church, for "clergymen and members of the laity from Nicaragua and other Latin American circles linked to the theology of liberation." While Marxists and liberation theologists alike have been at pains to deny any direct or active link between the religious and political left, we see here that such a coordination represents an important element in official Cuban government policy in Caribbean and Central American affairs.

REPORT OF THE DELEGATION SENT TO GRENADA BY THE
AMERICA DEPARTMENT WITH THE AIM OF STARTING THE
GATHERING OF SOURCES FOR THE CHARACTERIZATION OF
THE RELIGIOUS SITUATION IN THE COUNTRY, AND THE
CONTACTS FOR FURTHER COOPERATION BETWEEN THE PCC
AND THE NJM REGARDING THE QUESTION.

DELEGATION: Cde. Aurelio Alonso Tejada
DATE: August 13—24, 1982
This report was handed in on October 14, 1982,
"YEAR 24 OF THE REVOLUTION"

INTRODUCTORY NOTE

This report is the result of an initial ten days stay which, as it
coincided with holidays, could not be used to the greatest advantage.

Two more difficulties must be taken into account: firstly, the
total lack of informative or unofficial documentation by the
NJM* comrades, which resulted in the need to find sources
through our visit to the public library, the national museum,
and religious bookstores; secondly, the absence of Judy Williams, the most important person among the Christian lay
people that actively cooperate with the NJM who, in addition
to her personal testimonies, should have arranged our contacts with other positive elements within the laity. This situation caused our interviews to be limited to representatives of
the ecclesiastical institutions.

In spite of these difficulties, it can be considered that the work
showed useful results so that the thought-out objectives were
satisfactorily reached.

We received a decisive support by the revolutionary leadership
through Cde. Selwyn Strachan, member of the Political Bureau
of the NJM and Minister of National Mobilization, whom we
met on three occasions. During the first interview, Cde.

Strachan summarized the recent aggressive positions adopted
by the Church against the revolutionary leadership and we, on
our part, explained the concrete aims we had set for the visit.

---

* New Jewel Movement

.   .   .   .

CONCLUSIONS

The religious situation in Grenada shows a series of characteristics which can be summarized as follows:

1) Since the revolutionary triumph in 1979, the diocese
showed signs of reservation and started to insist on the holding of elections. During the three years of revolutionary government, the Catholic hierarchy has added to its electoral
claim a position of mediation in favor of the 1979 pro-Gairy
prisoners and of advocate of the "freedom of the press" in the
face of governmental measures to stop counterrevolutionary
propaganda. The emphasis of the Church is in harmony with
the campaigns carried out by the reactionary governments in
the Caribbean against Grenada's PRG and now has an institutional argument formalized in the pastoral of the Caribbean
Catholic bishops in February this year. This pastoral marks a
new reference, which goes backward in comparison with that
of 1975, and starting from it, political sectors in the area have
promoted the summons to the Church for a confrontation of
forces with the PRG of Grenada.

2) For the Grenadian Church (particularly the Catholic one)
the moment can be described as one of definitions. It cannot
be said yet (in our opinion) that the hierarchy has decided on
an open confrontation. Although the pressure from the reactionary forces in the region within and outside the Church is
aimed at confrontation, the position of the diocese seems to
lean towards a combination of the pastoral attacks with repeated reference to the disposition to dialogue and the insis-
tence upon the fact that their position towards the PRG is not
uncompromising.

3) There are reasons to think that there is a potential contradiction between the foreign clergy (mainly the British and
the Irish) and the West Indian minority. That majority, whom
the vicar of the cathedral himself think is alien and unadapt-
able to the local realities, is at first sight the most active counterpart of the oppositionist dynamics brought about by the
February pastoral and by the provocations of reactionary
forces in the region.

4) There are no signs of systematic progressive projections
within the Grenadian clergy. It seems that within the institution there is not a trend in the theological and social line
sympathetic to the revolutionary project, and there are no in-
dications of a community organization of this kind at the
grass roots. However, some believers belonging to Catholic organizations, who gather around the Pope Paul Camp (with
whom we could not get in touch during this visit) and who
actively collaborate with the NJM, can constitute a ferment in
this direction.

5) The strong point of the Grenadian churches (both the
Catholic and traditional Protestant ones) regarding their social influence is the educational sector. The religious schools
are, at a very high percent, in charge of elementary and secondary education because throughout the colonial period the
State traditionally neglected this sector. The PRG does not
have a public educational system. In our opinion, the teaching
centers are the stronghold of the ecclesiastical institutions
and the possibility of a reform that should bring about their
exclusion is their main concern.

6) The incorporation of the Catholic churches of the Caribbean to the Conference of Caribbean Churches (CCC), which
also includes over 20 Protestant churches since its creation in
1973, besides being an exceptional characteristic of
ecumenism, establishes an associational link among the
Christian institutions that admits a game of influences in
their projection: the Grenada Catholic diocese is a member of
the Conference of Churches of Grenada (CCG) and with its
positions it can influence on the the Protestant churches, and
the other way around; at the same time, the fact that the

Catholic Church belongs to the CCC means a similar game of influences at the regional level. In this interaction, the most positive positions of the CCC act as a restraining factor to the behaviour of the Catholic Church at the local (and regional) level. However, the CCC is not a homogeneous body and the possibility of a reversal of its positions should no be underestimated, which would be in harmony with the tone of the criticisms to the PRG by the Grenadian churches.

7) The estimated believing population is over 80 percent, made up mainly by Catholics (59 percent), Protestant from the historical churches (Anglicans, Presbyterians and Methodists), and a number of sects among which the Rastafarians seem to be widely disseminated. The level of participation observed in the Sunday service is high. There does not seem to exist a significant difference in the degree of religiosity among Protestants and Catholics. The Charismatic Catholic movement has expanded and it is thought to reach no less than a quarter of Catholics. The African roots and their possible syncretic expressions should be studied.

8) The Catholic Church is organized in a diocese with 20 parish churches. It has one Bishop and 22 priests, with a rate of one priest for every 2,950 Catholics (baptized). Sixteen of the priests are religious and 6 are diocesan; 16 are English, Irish, and American; 4 are from other West Indian countries and 2 from Grenada; 15 are white and 7 are mestizo or black. Thus, because of their origin and race this is a clergy with characteristics that alienate them from the problems of the island.

9) The diocese is suffragan to the archdiocese of Castries (St. Lucia) and belongs to the Episcopal Conference of the West Indies, whose main seats are Jamaica and Trinidad-Tobago. Thus the ecclesiastical organization takes on a supranational character and the projection of the Grenadian Church is linked to the strategy carried out by the West Indian body.

.   .   .   .

RECOMMENDATIONS

1. We underline the importance of the fact that a comrade responsible for the attention to the religious problems be appointed by the New Jewel Movement: This activity would basically include the information work at the beginning and regular contacts with collaborators from Christian organizations. If it is thought to be relevant, this can also include contacts with the clergy. We repeat the recommendation that the person to be appointed should spend 15—20 days in Cuba so as to be able to know our experiences, be trained in the tasks of systematic information on the subject, and exchange ideas on the most controversial aspects of the work. Comrade Strachan expressed his agreement on this proposal.

2. It would be advisable to study the possibility of formally creating a Register of Associations (or a similar mechanism) attached to the corresponding governmental body. Such a body could be legally established on the basis of the public need to make an inventory of the existing associations in the country and their activities (this would not only include the religious institutions, but the Chamber of Commerce, associations of professionals, clubs such as the Rotarians, the Lions, etc.). This would enable the counting of members, posts, premises, etc., the knowledge on special and regular activities, the means of financing of activities, etc. Both the terms of the resolution or law and the concrete contents of the register and modus operandi would be defined according to the specific conditions. This proposal is based on the need to regularize the access by the PRG to systematic factual information on the religious institutions and their activities. Our recommendation does not dismiss the fact that the responsibility regarding the register could be closely linked to the above-mentioned proposal.

3. To promote contacts among clergymen and members of the laity from Nicaragua and other Latin American circles linked to the theology of liberation and, in general, to the idea of a church committed to the revolutionary positions, and the Christian sectors in Grenada through the Pope Paul Camp and

maybe through talks with religious clergymen from a same
order, particularly the Dominicans. These contacts should
positively influence the Christian sectors of Grenada.

.   .   .   .

ANNEX 2
SUMMARIES OF INTERVIEWS HELD AND OF
OBSERVATION CARRIED OUT IN
THE CHURCHES OF ST. GEORGE'S

F. CYRIL LAMONTAGNE.

• Was born in St. Lucia; 55 years old - diocesan with around
  16 years in Grenada - General Vicar of the diocese.

• He explains that in St. Vincent, Barbados, and Antigua most
  of the believers belong to the Anglican and Methodist
  Churches, while in the French West Indies, as in the Spanish
  ones, the majority are Catholic. Grenada keeps the Catholic
  predominance of the colonial period under France, which
  has also culturally left other marks.

• He establishes a difference between the massive level of participation, which includes attendance to Sunday mass, and
  the intense participation, which is by a minority. His view is
  that in Grenada the levels of attendance to the Historical
  Protestant churches are close to those of Catholicism: more
  intense during the festivities - Christmas, Holy Week, Lent.

• As to the liturgy, he says that there are several priests trying
  to assimilate the reforms of the Vatican II.

• On being asked about his opinion regarding the theology of
  liberation, and in general regarding this renewed line of
  thought, he answered that Grenada is not a country with a
  large concentration of wealth; that there are neither the
  very rich nor the extremely poor; that there is a predominance of a poverty characterized by a low standard of living,
  but not by misery (only in unusual cases); he adds that at-

tendance to church is representative of this composition, and that he thinks this specific fact makes a theology of liberation that would adjust to other realities to be less adequate in the country. These observations follow his doubts about the strictly theological character of these theories.

- Composition of the clergy by countries: at present there are only 2 Grenadian priests and another four from the West Indies; there are 16 Irish, British, Canadians and Americans, which complete the present 22 priests.

- In the '70s three priests were brought from Nigeria with the aim of increasing the proportion of blacks, but he says this experience was a failure because they did not have a good adaptation and that 2 of them left, and the third one will soon go back to Nigeria. They chose Nigeria because of the experience and contacts of the Kiltegan friars there.

- On assessing negative reactions on the part of the clergy to social change in Grenada, he puts them down to the difficulties of the transition from a church that rules to a church that serves. He centers the problems on the European clergy whom he thinks should proportionally decrease in years ahead in favour of an indigenous clergy from the region.

- The Catholic Episcopal Conference (West Indies) has two major seminaries: one in Trinidad and another in Jamaica. Both seminaries are - diocesan and the former now has around 20 seminarists, while the latter has around 10. They are affiliated to the University of the West Indies (UWI) so that their level would fit to that what is tought - there and the degree confered would be correspondent.

- He explains the dependence of the West Indian dioceses on the Congregation for the Evangelization of the Peoples and the Propagation of the Faith instead of on the Congregation of Bishops, like in the rest of America, due to financial reasons. The Caribbean Church is not able to finance itself and subordination to the above Congregation assures its financing as the region is considered a territory of Mission.

- He points out that the relations Church-State under Gairy were not easy, but that the Church managed to keep its status because the government knew its social influence. He adds that the Church has to show its capacity to carry out its mission beyond the ideologies being predominant in society.

- He said that at present the Church does not object the changes by the PRG, but that it has critical apprisals. He understands that there have been mistakes both by the PRG leadership and the Church. In the Church the foreign clergy is not as able as to understand the internal questions and reacts hastily, adopting wrong positions. The PRG has interpreted these positions as being those of the Church, but it has been made clear that those manifestations do not express the position of the Church.

- In spite of maintaining these criteria, he admitted that the statement by the journalist Alister Hughes in the Congress of the DFP of Dominica, summoning the Church to exert pressure on the public opinion around this question, was not an appropriate channel; and he says that this is not the Church's position. He recognizes that out of the 400 initial prisoners, over 75% have been set free, and that in this shows that the PRG has not acted intransigently in this sense.

- He is interested in knowing whether Marxism necessarily assumes atheism and whether we understand the building of Socialism as conditioned by atheistic positions. He has the opinion that in the Island (I think he means the political leadership without expressly affirming it) there is the view that religious faith and Socialism are not compatible and that they are willing to accept Socialism as long as one does not start from this criterion of incompatibility. He stresses that he is, above all and first of all, a man of the Church and that he will always react as such, but that he is willing to accept, within this framework, a Socialist transformation. That the Church would also have to facilitate the assimilation of these changes for the believers.

• He asks questions on Cuba, the Church, the training of the clergy (whether there is a major seminary, whether it is integrated to the higher education system, etc.). He says he is interested in visiting Cuba, but that he does not know in what way this visit could take place.

OPINION:

Lamontagne is, as he said, a man of the Church, representative of the positions of the institution. In my opinion, he cannot be evaluated as a progressive clergyman, but as one who could assimilate a Church within the framework of radical social transformations. I think that his willingness to visit Cuba and his interest in doing so should not be underestimated because his visit could contribute, on the one hand, to counteract the effects of propaganda schemes; on the other, it would help in differentiating his situation within the clergy of the diocese. . . .

IV-3
Analysis of the Church
7/12/83

This report was prepared by the Ministry of the Interior's Major Keith Roberts, dated July 12, 1983, and annotated in Maurice Bishop's handwriting (italics at end).

Like the preceding Cuban document, this "analysis" suggests several unpleasant aspects of Grenadian internal policies. Although the churches had done nothing seriously to counter the ideological activities of the regime, religious neutrality was an insufficient guarantee of security for the NJM leadership. Here Roberts explicitly warns of a future "Poland situation."

Should the religious communities fail to produce a current of clerical opinion favorable to governmental and general "left" politics, the Bishop government was prepared to act as if this represented active subversion rather than mere lack of enthusiasm. Among other measures proposed for the handling of the religious problem were introduction of political education in all primary and secondary schools, political education for all teachers, restriction of religious programming on Grenadian radio, and promotion of "contacts among clergymen and members of laity from Nicaragua and other Latin American countries, linked to the theology of liberation and in general to the idea of a church committed to revolutionary positions."

TOP SECRET

MINISTRY OF INTERIOR,
BUTLER HOUSE,
ST. GEORGE'S.

12TH JULY, 1983.

ANALYSIS OF THE CHURCH IN GRENADA

(1) A BRIEF HISTORICAL OVERVIEW:

The real history of the Church in Grenada can be said to have begun with the coming of Columbus to the island and the subsequent attempts by the different religious sects to "christianize" the inhabitants.

With the changing of the balance of power by the constant squabbles between the Colonial powers and the subsequent changing of ownership of the island of the religious institutions of those powers were extended to Grenada; first the English Anglican Church, then the Roman Catholic Church, Methodist and Presbyterian Churches.

All these Churches served the interests of the ruling classes and helped to strengthen the position of the Colonial Governments. While helping the ruling class, these Churches also played a key role in uniting different sections of our society. For example, the Anglican Church traditionally comprised the elite of Grenadian Society while the Roman Catholic Church drew it's members from the poor and oppressed classes. This serves, today, to explain why the Roman Catholic Church is the most powerful in Grenada with approximately 70,000 baptised members.

Poor living conditions, poverty and dispair during the era of Colonialism served to strengthen the position of the Church among the broad masses of our country because the Church is strongest where there exists poverty, illiteracy and an educational system designed to suit the interests of the Church, where religious knowledge was compulsory at schools controlled by the Church, served to entrench further a deep idealism among our people which today, is one of the main reasons for our people's deep and strong religious feelings.

To compound matters more a flood of new-fangled religious sects and denominations came to Grenada just after the Second World War. These are the Non-Traditional American types. This flood continues even to this day. Thus, the bases of the traditional religious have been somewhat eroded and the social composition of Grenadian society further subdivided into a multitude of various sects of different shades and creeds.

In conclusion, we can say that the Church, although at periods in it's history, sometimes played a progressive role if even in it's own interest is nothing but a fetter to our development.

(2) THE CHURCH AS A THREAT TO THE REVOLUTION

March 13, 1979 forced all Churches in Grenada to take a new look at themselves and to analyse their role in a Revolutionary society. At first they played a wait and see game, but, when it became clear where the Revolution was going and what it stood for, they took up a clear position. It is safe, here, to say that there is no clear "left" religion in Grenada, but, since our Revolution enjoys popular support, then the broad mass of church goers are to varing extents supporters of the Grenada Revolution. This cannot be said about the Leaders of the Churches in Grenada and I contend that we have no support among them, all are to different degrees hostile to the Revolution. This is true even though some are less vocal than others. The following analysis of events taken at different periods up to the present time will suffice to here identify the Church as the main potential source of major internal counterrevolution.

1980—1981 - The main line pushed for this period by the Traditional Churches was the question of the Detainees at Richmond Hill and the holding of elections. The Roman Catholic Church in particular used every forum to push this line. This Church organised retreats, seminars and conferences and at every one of these activities, hostile statements were hurled against the Grenada Revolution on so-called violation of Human rights. Every Sunday at one Church or another priests were heard to ask people to "pray for the detainees" whose rights have been denied.

While the Traditional religious were on the human rights/ election line, the non-traditional religions were on a different line. They were preaching the so-called "last days doctrine" and saying that "man has turned away from god" a subtle attack on our ideological positions. This line was particularly strong among the Baptists and the Open Bible Churches.

1980-1981 period saw the Catholic Church making efforts to obtain priest versed in the knowledge of submitting our ideological position, and also saw the Roman Catholic Priests begin to print pamphlets on "civic and Human Rights" and "notes on Marxism". In reality anti-Marxism/Leninism.

1982 - The first half of the year was relatively quiet as the Churches started to plan new strategy and tactics. In November 1982 the Roman Catholic Church emerged as the No. 1 antagonist of the Revolution.

The Bishop, Sydney Charles, began to push the line that the Church will face its biggest "challenge" in 1983. A new strategy was developed that of re-organization of all Catholic Youth under the direct control of the Bishop. Two new organizations were formed for this purpose (a) the Diocesean Youth Commission and (b) the Diocesean Youth Council. The Latter organization whose chairman is appointed by the Bishop, replaces the Catholic Youth Congress (CYC) whom the Bishop saw as "too political".

On 10th December, 1982, 4,365 copies of the Jerusulem Bible arrived in Grenada for the Catholic Church. A very sim-

ple bible it is written in novel form so as to make it easier for
the church masses to read. This indicates the Church's understanding of the ideological struggle. The call by A. Huges for
the church to voice its opinion on matters of human rights,
and the statement that it is the main hope at this time. The
Bishop speaks of the "challenge" to the Church in 1983 in his
Christmas Message.

The situation took on a new turn when Methodist Minister
Ledson refused to officiate at the burial of Cde. Demo Grant
and had to be kicked out of Grenada. All the traditional
Churches saw this as "persecution" and hardened their position against the PRG and Revolution.

In December of the same year, in his Christmas sermon,
Arch Deacon Huggins of the Anglican Church, spoke of the
need to safeguard the right to worship, and acted in a way
that would make anyone feel that this right was about to be
taken away.

1983 - Upsurge in open air crusades, house to house and
tract giving by the non-traditional religions. More house to
house work done by Jehovah's Witnesses. There seem to be
a frenzied drive by these churches to win new members.
This process is continuing now. There has also been a
number of visits to Grenada by pastors and preachers from
abroad to "beef up" the work in "evengelization".

The Roman Catholic Clergy, for the first time, has insti-
tuted a prescheduled list of meetings led by the Bishop for the
year. Nine (9) in all. Three (3) have been held so far, all at
different venues. The fourth meeting will take place on 12th
July, 1983 at the Grand Roy Presbytry. This activity indicates
that the Clergy is becoming more and more organized under
the leadership of the Bishop.

The organization of the youths continue at an accelerated
rate, with all ages included in this drive. The Bishop, at a
meeting of all Catholic youths leaders in May, said that the
enemy was organized and that it was necessary that the
church organize also to combat the enemy. At an early meet-

ing in April, the Bishop again spoke of a subtle form of de-stabilization against the church. The Anglican Church has started to re-organize its Youth Groups after a lapse of three (3) years. This year was the first time the Anglican and Catholic Churches had a joint Corpus Christi Procession.

Based on these developments and the knowledge of the large percentage of Grenadians who have very deep trust in the church and also taking into account the weakness in all our mass organizations and, therefore, our influence over the masses, we see this development as a very dangerous one. We think that in the medium term, if serious measures are not taken, we can find ourselves faced with a Poland situation. In this light, we see the church in the immediate period as being the most dangerous sector for the development of internal counter revolution.

FUTURE TRENDS

1) We forsee the continuation of the organization of all Youths by the Catholic and Anglican Churches.
2) We forsee stronger unity among all G.C.C. churches.
3) We think that the unity among Catholic Clergy will grow steadily.
4) Infiltration of anti Marxist/Leninist from outside.
5) The Bishop becoming bolder in his attacks against the Revolution.
6) The Catholic Church overall hardening its position against the Revolution.
7) More and more foreign Pastors and Preachers of non-traditional religious will want to come to Grenada to work and hold crusades.

RECOMMENDATIONS

a) Ensuring that Michael Roberts continue a permanent and full time way to be in charge of church work.
b) Obtaining a second person to work in this area in order to control all churches, their leadership, membership and their activities.

The establishment of a register of association including
churches and all other organizations e.g. Jaycee, Unions, Association of Professional etc. which will make it necessary
when registering to give some basic fact about the Associations or churches e.g. the knowledge on special and regular
activities, counting of members, different posts within the organizations, means of financing activities, etc.
Continuing to develop the co-operation in this area with the
Cuban Comrades at the level of Party to Party.

• Ensuring that C.P.E. get a majority of working people involved in its classes.

• Build the Mass Organizations - Pioneers, N.Y.O., N.W.O., P.F.U.,
  Militia, to incorporate a majority of working people.

• Organize the community work in the different areas more
  efficiently, start on time, and actively mobilize to bring out
  the masses to participate.

• Removing from Primary Schools, all deeply religious head
  teachers by whatever means most suitable, replacing them
  with more progressive elements. This should be done no
  later that the end of this month.

• Introduce Polical Education as that or Social studies in every
  classroom in the Primary and Secondary Schools from this
  September, use the most progressive teachers within the
  schoosl system (chosen by teachers committee) to teach
  these classes. Use Merle Hodge and Didicus to write up the
  materials for the courses.

• Political Education for all teachers by this September.

• Strengthen Science Education - theory and practical - in
  every school and in the community through C.P.E. and Film
  shows.

• Cut back on all religious programmes on R.F.G. Substitute on
  Sunday morning voice cast of the masses on the progress of
  the projects.

- To promote contacts among Clergymen and members of Laity from Nicaragua and other Latin American countries linked to the theology of liberation and, in general, to the idea of a church committed to Revolutionary positions.

- To implement the visits of Pastors from the Grenada Protestant Churches belonging to the Caribbean Conference of Churches (CCC) of which the Evangilical Churches of Cuban in a number, to short annual course, in light that the comrades can solve the language question.

- More dialogue with West Indian Priests, Nuns and Brothers in the Church and schools by the Leadership.

- Opening up M-L [Marxist-Leninist] Bookshop in different parishes of the country.

- Getting M-L literature into all schools by September.

- Explore possibility of getting Father Martin and La Montague to visit Cuba.

- Step up the systematic monitering of all Religious manifestation in the state, and position being taken as regard the work permit of way-side Preachers entering the country to preach, and immigration position on these way-side preachers.

[signature]
MAJOR KEITH ROBERTS

[open cinemas.
start progressive church (talk with Nicar.. + Cubans)]

V
PROPAGANDA AND PUBLIC RELATIONS
WORK IN THE UNITED STATES

The Bishop regime carried out a surprisingly extensive campaign to gather support within the United States. One important element of the New Jewel strategy was an attempt to draw the Reagan administration into open controversy over Grenada, as a means of polarizing American opinion and generating support for the New Jewel Regime among U.S. liberals.

The regime in fact targeted a variety of groups. It made a serious effort to mobilize the sympathies of Grenadian nationals residing in the U.S., particularly in the New York City area. Beyond that, Bishop and his colleagues sought to build support among American blacks, stressing the image of Grenada as an English-speaking, black, socialist commonwealth. In connection with the latter aim, the Grenadians enlisted the cooperation of black political figures known for left-wing sympathies, notably United States Representative Ronald V. Dellums (D.-CA) and Gus Newport, the mayor of Berkeley, California, which is located in Dellums's district (documents V-1 and V-3).

However, the range of contacts developed in the U.S. extended beyond black, government, and media circles. The Communist Party U.S.A. became part of the effort; party activists Angela and Fania Davis and party official James E. Jackson are mentioned in documents V-2 and V-3. An important role was also played by the Socialist Workers Party, a Trotskyist organization, which sent several of its members to Grenada before the collapse of the New Jewel regime. However, the Grenada papers show evidence of irritation on the part of pro-Soviet NJM figures, and their U.S. supporters, at what they regarded as the interference of the Trotskyists (document V-3).

The final pair of documents in this section consists of briefing notes and minutes from a meeting between Maurice Bishop and a group of U.S. officials including then-national security adviser William P. Clark and deputy secretary of state Kenneth W. Dam. As is manifest from the minutes of the meeting, the U.S. represen-

tatives gave the strong impression of seeking a fresh start in
U.S.-Grenadian relations, although Clark and Dam warned of
their concern over Soviet influence on the island. It has been
suggested that Soviet or Cuban displeasure at proposals voiced in
this meeting played a role in Bishop's overthrow by the Bernard
Coard faction, and document VI-5 in this collection, "Grenada-
Soviet Relations: A Summary" indicates Soviet irritation that the
meeting with Clark and Dam took place without previous consultation between Grenada and Moscow.

V-1
Letter on Grenadian Dissidents
5/16/80

This document, authored by Dessima Williams, Grenadian ambassador to the Organization of American States, describes the receipt of Grenadian dissident material (excerpt annexed) by the office of U.S. Rep. Ronald V. Dellums (D-California). According to Ambassador Williams, Barbara Lee, who was a staff employee of Congressman Dellums, warned the Grenadian authorities of the distribution of such materials.

Telex: 64528   Telephone: (202) 265-2561

PERMANENT MISSION OF GRENADA TO THE ORGANIZATION OF
AMERICAN STATES
Suite 203 - 1424 Sixteenth St., N.W. Washington, D.C. 20036 Tel. 347-3198

TO: Cde. Minister of National Security — Bishop
FROM: Cde. Ambassador Williams
DATE: May 16, 1980
RE: The attached mailing from Prime Minister's Office

Comrade:

On May 14, 1980, Barbara Lee called to say she had received a piece of anti-PRG propaganda stamped from the Prime Minister's Office, post-marked in Grenada. We collected it May 15, and it is herewith attached [excerpt annexed below].

Some obvious questions are: — What concerns us is: How is it possible for such vicious anti-government propaganda to be mailed and stamped from the Prime Minister's Office to a friendly Congressional Office?

Who?
How?

Barbara says that all those U.S. persons who went to Grenada
for The First Anniversary have been receiving G.I.S. News Releases regularly. Should this be so? To her knowledge, no one
else except she has received this particular piece of anti-PRG
material.

.   .   .   .

Please advise us at an early time if this was a known or un-
known error; if a conspiracy and/or sabotage, and how to
handle it.

Neither, 'Shampoo' Norbert Douglas our Security Officer at the
Mission here, nor I have a clue on this. Only speculations:

[signature]

DESSIMA WILLIAMS

ANNEX: "BISHOP AND HIS COMMUNIST NEW JEWEL GANG"

.   .   .   .

BRIEF SUMMARY OF OPPRESSIVE ACTS ALREADY TAKEN BY BISHOP'S COMMUNIST ILLEGAL REGIME IN GRENADA

In the exercise of unauthorised absolute power there are no
limits and Bishop and his Communist New Jewel are already
guilty of the following acts: Terrorism (illegally and violently
seizing power, and causing extreme fear among the people),
Treason (disloyalty to the sovereign in order to compel
change of policy) Murder (giving guns to untrained youths to
kill themselves and paying others to kill) Setting up missile
bases all over Grenada with the help of Cuba, and putting guns
everywhere in Grenada, imprisonment of hundreds of people
in Grenada without trial, including Ministers, Leaders of Opposition parties, Doctors, Lawyers, students, and cancellation
of visiting rights of families and friends, seizing of people's
property (house, car etc) after arrest and imprisonment, seizure of the privately owned Cocoa Cola Factory, Evening

Palace Club, other private homes, etc: closing down the only non-governmental newspaper 'The Torchlight', closing the courts, revoking all recognized laws and substituting their own laws with twice yearly trial by tribunal comprising of people with no legal background, serious violations of all human rights and freedoms, prevention of people from leaving Grenada (scholarship holders and any one suspected of being a threat to the revolution), tapping of all telephones in Grenada and censoring of all mails, etc entering and leaving Grenada, importation of Cuban doctors and other personnel to take over jobs held by Grenadians, sending people without passports for training in Cuba and bringing in another personnel from Cuba under the guise of exchange program, detaining, searching and questioning and then imprisoning any one arriving in Grenada who is known or even suspected to be a family or friend of any member of Gairy's party or any one in custody.

. . . .

V-2
Interim Report on
North American Resistance Movement
3/29/83

This unsigned document outlines some activities of the Grena-
dian regime and its supporters in attempting to mobilize pro-New
Jewel opinion in the U.S.

Perhaps the most interesting aspect of the Grenadian public-
relations offensive in the U.S., as revealed here, is the coordination
with the Nicaraguan Sandinista regime in the United Nations
Security Council.

On "C.P. Comrade Jackson," see the introduction to this section.

TO: POLITICAL BUREAU
DATE: NEW YORK, WEDNESDAY MARCH 29th, 1983
SUBJECT: INTERIM REPORT ON NORTH AMERICAN RESIS-
TANCE PROGRAMME

Generally speaking, Grenada's fight-back campaign in
North America has got off the ground. In terms of the four
zones, New York is moving well; Washington has made a
start; and in concrete preparations to step up their programme by Thursday. The West Coast got off the ground yesterday.

Consistent with the 26 point plan, our objectives are as follows:

1. To mobilize public opinion (including in Congress) in
order to restrain the U.S. Government from attacking Grenada
militarily;

2. To win long-term contacts and sympathy for Grenada,
hence turning attacks to our advantage;

3. To solicit concrete assistance: paper, tape recorders, typewriters, etc.

As you know, Reagan attacked Grenada on national T.V. and radio just as I was about to arrive, showing spy photographs of our airport. We responded the very night and the response was carried on radio, but not widely in the media.

Grenada's address to the Security Council the next day evoked some interest. Many journalists (NBC, TIME, etc.) interviewed Caldwell after his speech, in which he spent five minutes on Grenada, but we have not seen or heard anything come out, except on radio. In fact, minutes after requesting interviews, many T.V. stations changed their minds saying, they "can't find crew". Clearly the word was to, "blank Grenada".

I understand that a few blacks and liberal whites used their influence and got ABC television to arrange the interview with Maurice. The airing of this interview has become the turning point. It is being released in bits. It's a road march. Previously, it was Reagan's speech that was the road march. According to Tom Wicker, N.Y. Times journalist on the David Brinkley (ABC) Show "This Week" Reagan has "lost credibility" for his phoney satellite pictures of Grenada since the airport is open to T.V. cameras. Brinkley agreed and they laughed. (Note that tens of millions view this show). Assistant Secretary of Defence, Ikle, embarrassed himself on National (ABC) T.V. "Night Line" with Ted Copple who shook him up brilliantly - tens of millions of viewers - trying to project Grenada as a threat and had to resort to "Russian style obstacle course", human rights, etc. He stated that unlike Haiti, our type of process is "irreversible".

[Illegible]

Reagan's speech was effective, but not very much so since the "Soviet military build-up" idea is so stale. We were in some "star wars" technology. Therefore, the statements on Grenada were hidden in proposals with far-reaching strategic implications. Of course, the photographs of Cuba, [Illeg.] ads being

visual aids would have helped his case a little, but only a little.
In the end, the administration looked a bit silly, with respect
to Grenada.

Over the past few hours, I note that they are trying to recoup the situation. The same ABC News has come up with a
slanted version of the Grenada item, basically reversing themselves, stating that the airport will be used largely for Soviet
aircraft, including Bear aircraft, especially since we have few
hotel rooms. We have to respond to it. They're fighting back
fiercely, using the same ABC but out of Washington this time.
Very latest reports confirm that ABC has changed their line.
They are now projecting Grenada as a threat, using the sea
lanes and "Cuban troops to Angola" arguments. Our size is
irrelevant, they say. They've bowed to State Department pressure.

(Later changed again - second "ABC" Interview)

. . . .

HERE ARE SOME OF THE ACTIVITIES - AREA BY AREA

(Areas are Washington/Atlanta/South: Dessima; North-East:
Caldwell (plus Burke); West Coast: Ian; Canada: Benjie)

AREA 1 NEW YORK/DETROIT (BASE OF OPERATIONS)

1. Planning meeting with Grenada Ambassador and Ian,
   leaders of work in four zones.

2. Participation in Security Council debate on Nicaragua.

3. Meeting with U.N. Secretary-General. He listened atten-
   tively and appeared somewhat concerned.

4. Radio interviews: WLIB, WBAI (including Maurice's)

5. Meeting with hundred key Grenadians, leaders of
   organisations.

6. Press conference at U.N. Headquarters with large turnout
   of international press.

7. Meeting with C.P. Comrade Jackson. Party will give general support.

8. Meeting with leading white liberals, and progressive blacks, academics, media people, ANC and influential types. Best of its kind for years, over three hundred (double the number expected) attended, coming from all over the region.

9. Substantial Radio, T.V. and newspaper coverage of U.N. Press Conference by national media, ranging from skeptical to favourable, but mostly "balanced", quoting both sides together.

10. Biggest event is rally planned for next Sunday April 3, in New York.

DETROIT (Burke)

Meeting with Caribbean organisations, Grenadians, Students, Press. As of yesterday, Tuesday, the situation with regional/national press/publicity was as follows:

- New York Times article (pg. 7) - Saturday.
- Daily Challenge (only Black national circulation of just over 100,000.)
- Short New York Times piece (Front page) - skeptical.
- WINS, most listened to radio station in New York area gave good reports.
- New York Daily News (Positive story of U.N. Press Conference on prominent position, large circulation close to that of New York Times).
- Daily Challenge again.
- Short story in Wall St. Journal: Front page (from press conference).
- As mentioned earlier, ABC interview with Maurice showing airport in favourable light until the recent twist.
- Large number of radio interviews.
- Small number of short T.V. clips of press conference.

MOOD OF GRENADIANS (GENERAL)

Our nationals are in high spirits. Reagan's attack on their airport has firmed them up. This is true in the U.S., Canada and Britain. We invited seventy-five (75) carefully chosen Grenadians to brief them on their tasks for Sunday's rally and a little over a hundred turned up, inspite of hours of heavy rain (and most didn't have transport). In little time, funds were raised for radio advertisements for the rally. Hundreds are phoning up all our missions expressing support. It is difficult to keep up with the noting of calls.

WASHINGTON (Dessima)

- A brief rap (five minutes) with a hundred leading progressives and Blacks (Angela Davis, PLO Rep., etc.) at a function.
- Half hour rap on Howard University Radio.
- Fascinating meeting with OAS Secretary-General Orfila. His response to Maurice's letter was sympathetic and supportive. "The Americans have closed the door on dialogue" he said. He went on to add that this makes him frustrated. He will meet right away with William Clarke, Reagan's National Security Advisor.
- An ABC T.V. interview on meeting with Orfila (fact of presenting letter, content etc.) has not been aired.
- Caribbean Ambassadors' Caucus. Guyana - supportive; Jamaica - sympathetic; Barbados - skeptical; Antigua - concerned, but in an idealistic way.
- Arrangements are being finalized for meeting with Congressional Black Caucus, Senators/Congressmen, rally, press conference, OAS protocolary session.

CALIFORNIA (Ian)

Tuesday 29th - (1) Interview with Radio, T.V., two newspapers. (2) Meeting with Friendship Society. (3) Address to Oakland City Council with possibility of solidarity resolution being passed later in week.

Wednesday 30th - Major press conference due (Note difference in time) The U.N. Press Conference was front page in San Francisco Chronicle, largest circulation paper in region. Balanced report.

The publicity is also preparing ground, whipping up interest in build-up for Sunday's rally with Dessima, Claudette Pitt etc.

U.K. (Dennis)
- Meeting in Sheffield. Fifty persons - Firm.
- Letters delivered.
- Met with Minister Cranley Enslow who said that this is a figment of our imagination and that he will respond in writing. He also said we've stopped relaying BBC news.
- Demonstration planned in front of U.S. Embassy on Tuesday, first working day after long weekend.
- Black media briefed.
- Large media resisting access to us.

. . . .

OVERVIEW

All in all, the programme is taking shape and we are getting reasonable responses and results. So far tens of millions would have got our version (ABC has a high rating and David Brinkley's "This Week" report and "Night Line" are listened to by tens of millions.) In addition to the news, there have been more than a dozen radio interviews. Many of the radio stations and newspapers reach over a million persons. Also, the attacks (and fightback) have widened and deepened our support and sympathy and the awareness of our situation among progressives, academics and Blacks. We are making progress on building a wider network of friends and allies vital for our future work.

. . . .

V-3
Report on U.S.
4/83

In this lengthy study NJM member Ian Jacobs, a special assistant to Bishop, presents a highly revealing survey of pro-Grenadian activities inside the U.S., in preparation for the Grenadian leader's U.S. tour, in Spring, 1983.

Probably the most important aspect of this document is its discussion of the role played by Barbara Lee, an employee of Rep. Dellums, in organizing support for the Bishop regime. As also noted in document V-1, Ms. Lee kept frequent contact with Grenadian representatives.

On the C.P.U.S.A. and S.W.P., see the introduction to this section.

INTERIM REPORT ON NORTH AMERICA FROM
MARCH 23,–April 21, 1983

BY IAN JACOBS

I. INTRODUCTION:

It will be recalled that the explicit purpose of this visit was to assist in a campaign to counter attack President Reagan's verbal attack on Grenada high-lighted by his speeches of March [illeg.] and 23rd 1983. During my stay I visited eight cities in the U.S.A. and without hesitation I would say that the visit as a whole was a success, I make this assertion for the following reasons:

   a) There was excellent media coverage — see section two of this report and appendix for sample news clippings.

   b) Our North American networks once again proved their worth with excellent short notice organizational efforts.

c) Because of the above we were able to reach thousands of Americans with our message.

d) I anticipate that with the contracts that were made we should be able to raise between three to five thousand U.S. dollars — a figure that should allow us to purchase a word processor within three to six months.

II. [illeg.] OF VISIT:

A. March 23–28: Briefings in New York and Washington with Cdes. Whiteman, Taylor, Williams and Angela Davis.

B. March 29–April 2: Visit to California with stops in San Francisco, Oakland, Berkeley and Sacramento. During this stay there were [illeg.] activities as follows:

1. March 29 — Oakland and Berkeley:

a) Live radio interview with K.P.F.A. — public radio station in Berkeley with a liberal [illeg.].

b) Interviews with People's World — newspaper of C.P.U.S.A.

2. March 30 — Oakland, Berkeley and San Francisco:

a) Phone interview with K.A.L.X. — Berkeley campus radio station.

b) Phone interview with K.S.O.L. — most listened to black station in Oakland.

c) Phone interview with K.B.L.X. — second most listened to black station in Oakland.

d) Press conference at the San Francisco Press Club. Appearing with me was Angela Davis. Press present were the California voice, the Sun Reporter, Bay City wire service — the major regional wire service for the West Coast, Associated Press, Associated Press Radio, K.D.I.A. Radio — a black station, K.P.F.A. — public radio, K.A.L.X., Pacific Sun, K.R.O.N. — N.B.C. afiliate in San Francisco, the San Francisco N.A.A.C.P.

The conference went well with no major problems. The
Press's main concern was my statement's reference to violations of our air and sea space.

e) Interview with the Oakland Tribune — Oakland's
biggest paper which is also Black owned.

f) In the evening I gave a five minute address to the
Oakland city council. I was politely received and one
of the Black members (Wilson Ryles) moved a vote
of thanks. However the original hope was that the
council would pass a resolution in support of Grenada and calling for talks with the Reagan administration. This did not happen however because
of poor advance groundwork by our comrades and
the fact that the council is quite conservative. Added
to this elections were due in three weeks.

3. March 31 — Sacramento:

a) Press conference at City Hall. Appearing with me
were representatives of the Sacramento chapter of
the U.S./Grenada Friendship Society. In attendance
at the conference were representatives from the City's main media. Thus there were reporters from the
Sacramento Bee — the city's main newspaper, the
Sacramento Union — the city's second main newspaper, K.I.X.J. a city television station, K.C.R.A. —
the city's main television station.

This conference went well but there were hostile questions
from the reporter for K.C.R.A. This was not surprising as this
city is viewed as quite conservative.

b) Lunch hosted by the U.S./Grenada Friendship Society Chapter. The lunch was well attended with positive discussions highlighted by a commitment to get
petitions sent to Washington and to raise funds for
a world processing machine. There were some 40
people present representing various progressive
groups such as N.B.I.P.P., S.C.L.C., N.A.A.C.P., Solidarity groups for El Salvador and Nicaragua. Also present were some Black businessmen.

c) Interview with the editorial Board of the Sacramento Bee. This is supposed to be the liberal paper of Sacramento.

d) Interview with the editor of the editorial page of the Sacramento Union. This is the more conservative paper in Sacramento but as the Appendix shows they gave more coverage to the visit.

4. April 1 — Berkeley and Oakland:

a) Meeting with the members of the Latin American division of the Political Science department of the Berkeley Campus of the University of California. This was essentially a briefing session for sympathetic students and faculty.

b) Lunch organised by the Oakland Chapter of the U.S./Grenada Friendship Society.

c) The Black Caucus agreed to pass a resolution in support of Grenada and send it to Washington. In discussions with Barbara Lee on April 20, 1983 she informed me that this had been done and a copy would be sent to us in Grenada.

d) The Black Caucus agreed to circulate a resolution in support of Grenada within the wider assembly and to send this resolution with as many signatures as possible to Washington. On April 20, 1983 Barbara Lee informed me that this resolution is presently circulating.

e) The Black Caucus agreed to visit Grenada in August 1983, with the group being organised by Barbara Lee.

7. April 7 and 8: Los Angeles:

With Extensive Assistance from the National Conference of Black Lawyers and the L.A. chapter of the U.S./Grenada Friendship Society we had a good visit to L.A. with the following activities:

On the evening of the 7th a dinner was held to welcome me.
Sponsored by the N.C.B.I., N.B.I.P.P. and the L.A. chapter of the
U.S./Grenada Friendship Society, the dinner was well attended.
There were representatives from the Southern Christian
Leadership Conference (S.C.L.C.), N.B.I.P.P., C.P.U.S.A., A.N.C.,
Anti-Apartheid Committee, N.C.B.L. and the National Lawyers
Guild. [illeg.] The main outcome of this event was a commit-
ment by this group to help with getting copies of the pro Gre-
nada resolution to Washington (see Appendix), and a com-
mitment to raise funds for the Word Processor project.

The following events took place on the 8:

a) Interview with the Executive editor of the L.A. Sen-
tinel — the leading Black newspaper in L.A.

b) Press conference at the L.A. Press Club. Appearing
with me were representative from N.B.I.P.P. and the
National Lawyers Guild. The conference was not
badly covered with representatives from the L.A.
Times, Channel 18 T.V. — local station, People's
World, Voice of the People and Cable Network News
— C.N.N. — national station. There was no conflict
but the main questions dealt with the location and
size of the counter revolutionary force.

c) Radio interview with K.J.L.H. — the leading Black
radio station in L.A.

d) Radio interview with K.P.F.K. — the public radio
station in L.A.

e) Reception hosted by the N.C.B.I. and the National
Lawyers Guild. The representation of people at this
function was very wide with Liberal, Progressive,
Black Nationalist and Peace Interests all represented. The total number of people was about 75
and there was a commitment to assist with the resolution as well as to raise funds for the Word Processor project.

8. April 13–19: Miami and Washington:

This last period was largely spend in Miami with a visit to Washington for funds and consultations with Cde. Dessima Williams. The visit to Miami was very successful as the following was achieved:

a) live radio interview with [illeg.] an all news station in Miami with a wide listenership. There was a phone-in section and the calls were about 50% in favour of our position. The show lasted one hour.

b) Phone-in interview with the National Black Network news service. This service serves the Black community nationwide. The interview lasted ten minutes.

c) Newspaper interview with the Miami News, Miami's main evening paper owned by Miami Herald. The interview was quite warm but the article that resulted from the interview (see Appendix) contained some inaccuracies.

d) Newspaper interview with the Miami Herald, Miami's main newspaper. The interviewer was [illeg.] who has been to Grenada a few times and Juan Tamayo. Basically the interview was friendly but they said from the outset that they would print nothing unless I had information on the size of the counter revolutionary force and its exact location.

e) a press conference was held with fairly good coverage. [illeg.] present was A.B.C. (their Miami affiliate), N.B.C. (their Miami affiliate), W.I.N.Z. — an all news station with a wide listenership.

f) A phone-in interview with W.G.B.S. an all news and talk station with a wide cross section of listeners. This lasted for five minutes.

g) A taped radio interview with the Haitian Refugee Centre. They have a one hour program every week on a Miami station and this interview would be used

for that program. The interview went well as they
were supportive.

h) A live radio interview on W.N.N.S. an all news station which claims to have a listenership to this particular program (a regular talk and phone-in show)
of between two and three hundred thousand people.
The program lasted three hours and the phone-in
segment was about 50% in our favor. Appearing to
counter my presentation was [illeg.], a Grenadian
counter living in Miami. He was friendly but very
blatant in his lies about our revolution. He is obviously well financed in Miami as he runs a well produced (although full of lies) newspaper which he
distributes free. He also drives a luxury American
car (1983 model) and lives in an exclusive area of
Miami. A copy of the paper has been supplied to Cde.
Bishop with his copy of this report.

i) There was a public meeting held at the Chalet
Centre in the middle of Liberty City, that well known
Black area (the riots of 1981−82) of Miami. The
meeting was covered by the Miami Herald and [il-
leg.] (regional station). There were about 150
people present (three Grenadians — Troy Garvey,
Carol Peterson and Sally [illeg.] Smith) and generally it was a good meeting with positive support.
Apart from outlining the present situation I also
used the opportunity to circulate the resolution on
Grenada (see Appendix). One point to note was that
although the meeting was held in Liberty City, only
about 10−20 blacks were at the meeting.

j) I had a meeting with Mr. Aaron Schecter, a wealthy
Jew who is very supportive of the Peace Movement.
The idea was to get a commitment for a contribution
to the Word Processor project. He agreed to contribute (somewhere between U.S. $1,000−2,000) if I
would get a tax credit organised for him. To do this
his contribution would have to go to a tax exempt

organisation. In this context I spoke to a contact at the American Friends Service Committee in Philadelphia and I intend to follow up with them so that he can send the money to them and then they will send it here.

While the visit to Miami was overall quite successful it must be pointed out that this was inspite of the S.W.P. [Socialist Workers Party] Miami branch which tried desperately to seize the visit for their own purposes. Had this happened we would not have reached so wide a cross section of people but fortunately they were outmaneuovred by both myself and the local organisation that really put together the visit — [illeg.] — a broad front organisation that concentrates on support for anti-imperialist forces in Latin and Central America.

.   .   .   .

The visit's success was due to the ground work of some key people and some key organisations. Among them are:

A. The West Coast:

　1.　Angela and Fonja Davis.
　2.　Gus Newport [Mayor of Berkeley, CA].
　3.　Barbara Lee.
　4.　The National Conference of Black Lawyers.
　5.　The National Lawyers Guild.
　6.　The National Black Independence Political Party.
　7.　The U.S./Grenada Friendship Society branches in Berkeley, Oakland, San Francisco and Sacramento.

B. Philadelphia:

　1.　The American Friends Service Committee.
　2.　Freddy Hill — Professor at Haverford College in Haverford Pennsylvania.

C. Miami:

　1.　The La Casa Group.

IV. IDEAS FOR FOLLOW UP:

  A. Funds for the Word Processor project. These should
      come from L.A. and Miami mainly.

  B. The California Legislator's Resolutions on Grenada
      should arrive soon from Barbara Lee. Also the visit of
      the Black Caucus from the California legislator should
      be followed up with Barbara Lee. This visit is planned
      for August.

  C. The resolution campaign should be monitored so as to
      make sure it takes place. The key person here is Fonja
      Davis.

V. CONCLUSIONS

This particular visit was undoubtedly a success. The efforts
of our organisation on the ground in the various cities is a key
reason for that success. At the same time however, it is clear
that there is much sympathy for Grenada (particularly in the
black community and among liberal and progressive Whites),
a sympathy advanced by Reagan's hostility. Thus I think it is
correct to [illeg.] that we must continue to tap that pro Grenada sentiment [illeg.] of North Americans with a properly
organised [illeg.]. A broad and continuous propaganda campaign that always keeps our revolution in the minds of North
America. From my experience this means that our missions
must organise a year round propaganda campaign that includes:

  a) The proper and regular distribution of news on the Re-
      volution throughout North America.

  b) Planned visits by Embassy officials to various parts of
      North America. Of particular value here would be Em-
      bassy involvement on the Campus circuit — i.e. regular
      appearance at University Campuses for payment of a
      fee.

  c) Close links with important progressive movements like
      the peace movement in particular.

  d) Regular visits from top P.R.G. officials to North
      America.

Certainly not all of these things are happening now, but I would suggest that unless they do (and undoubtedly other activities too) we will lose the momentum we have and more importantly we will lose a constituency that is vital in our battles against U.S. imperialism.

IAN JACOBS
APRIL 27, 1983

V-4
Advice on U.S. Tour

*In this undated and originally handwritten letter, Gail Reed,
U.S.-born wife of Cuban ambassador to Grenada Julian Torres
Rizo, advises Maurice Bishop on tactics for his 1983 visit to the U.S.
Most importantly, Gail Reed recommends that Grenadian leaders
work out their agenda for meetings in the U.S. with Parodi, attached to the Cuban Interests Section, which is the official Cuban
diplomatic representation in the U.S.*

Dear Maurice —

I've given some thought to what you raised over the phone,
and come up with a couple of ideas, although without [illeg.]
the general picture of what the trip looks like and perspectives you have on it — a big limitation. But for what it's worth:

1) I think being pressured into coming up with a major
announcement, declaration, etc. or even a gimmick along
these lines is a bit of a trap. [illeg.] With all due respect to the
power of the U.S. media, once you've got their attention, the
agenda must be yours, not theirs. Although I haven't been in
the States recently, certain things don't change: the U.S. media
go after violence, and when there's no war, controversy will
due just as well — especially in an election year. I would say
say they're most interested in the visit as it fits in to their idea
of a "faceoff" with Reagan and his administration, in the midst
of the election campaign. But, of course, Grenada's interests
are far different. And it seems to me the best idea is to stick
with those interests and objectives, and use the media as far
as possible to advance them, [illeg.] without getting "cor-
nered."

2) Why the visit? (Of course, you've given the answer to this one more thought than I.) But for the media, how does this sound: "Grenada and the United States have a long history of relations — many thousands of Grenadians live in the United States, their work contributing to the development of that country; many thousands of U.S. citizens travel to Grenada to enjoy its hospitality and natural beauty; cultural similarities united Grenada with cultural currents in the U.S.; other economic links, etc., etc. The purpose of the visit is to reaffirm and develop these ties at as many levels as possible, and by so doing to help lessen the tensions that have cropped up at one of these levels: the current White House administration [illeg.]." Thus, the importance of accepting the Black Caucus (<u>another governmental</u> level) and Transafrica invitations — as <u>important in themselves</u> — leaving open the possibility of meeting with the Reagan administration if it were to come off.

I think any suggestion that accepting these invitations is really a "cover" for another (larger) purpose (such as a meeting with Reagan) needs to be denied flatly, and strongly. After all, what is contained in the suggestion, besides the implication that the PRG is opportunist, is the <u>racist</u> and <u>anti-popular</u> implication — "why would he come here just because a bunch of Black folks invited him?"

The strong answer is that <u>of course</u> it is legitimate in its own right — to speak directly to <u>the people,</u> to other levels of their government, etc. That is <u>what the PRG is all about.</u>

3) I still think it might be a good idea to launch the organizing of the "US-Grenada Friendship Flight" (or some such <u>better</u> name), the inaugural flight direct to Grenada's new international airport for March 13th. Beyond a tourism boost, I think it would go a long way to promote the "open-ness of Grenada and its airport to U.S. citizens," as well as the idea that the airport is a normal one, a good thing for U.S. travellers too. Over time, the flight itself could be a focus for publicity — of the important figures that will be on board, the Grenadians going home. (Wouldn't the medical school like to do-

nate cash for a few seats so "prize trips" could be awarded, let's say, to a [illeg.] Grenadian [illeg.] couple from New York, a trade unionist from Detroit? — Anyway, that's just a thought for the future.)

4) On the specific meetings, I think I'm too out of touch to be helpful. [Illeg.] Parodi from the Cuban Interests Section will be the single most clear person on this whole question. (Only comment: I think the contact with Gil Noble is important.)

Reading this over, it's pretty rambling, but I hope of some use.

By the way — the ABC interview was beautiful!

Take care of yourself.
Warm regards,
Gail

V-5
Background Notes for Meeting with
National Security Advisor Clark

This unsigned and undated set of notes, presumably prepared for Maurice Bishop, suggest tactics to be adopted in meeting with U.S. National Security Advisor William P. Clark. On this and the following document, see the introduction to this section.

BRIEFING NOTES ON MEETING WITH JUDGE WILLIAM CLARKE, CHAIRMAN OF THE N.S.C.

Section-1: Background on the N.S.C.:

Originally the N.S.C. had been an advisory board on Foreign Policy. However under Nixon (with Kissinger as Chairman of the N.S.C.) and Carter (with Brezinski as Chairman of the N.S.C.) and now Reagan the council has become a key body in the formulation of U.S. foreign policy.

Indeed it is now widely felt (certainly in the Washington Post and Time Magazine) that the N.S.C. under Clarke has become the chief formulator of U.S. foreign policy. Certainly this is evident in recent U.S. foreign policy decisions in Central America where it is widely felt that the removal of Enders (under Secretary of State for Latin American Affairs) and Hinton (Ambassador to El Salvador) is linked directly to Clarke's recommendations. Significantly it is also widely felt that Clarke (together with Jane Kirkpatrick at the U.N.) is the real formulator of policy in Latin America and the Caribbean.

While this is an apparent reality it should be noted that Clarke has absolutely no background in foreign affairs at all. His only credential is his close friendship to Reagan. Moreover that friendship is based on a shared hard line right wing approach on everything including his limited knowledge on foreign affairs.

This dichotomy of control and limited knowledge has led to
much conflict between the N.S.C. and the State Department
where more real knowledge on foreign affairs exists. Nevertheless it is clear that for now the National Security Council
under Clarke is calling most if not all of the shots on foreign
policy, particularly in regards to central America and Caribbean.

Section II: Talking Notes

1. Comrade Bishop must clearly in practice and also been
seen to take the initiative, even perhaps the offensive in the
meeting. Two main reasons:

1. We asked for the meeting, so we must demonstrate that we
   have issues, topics, an agenda.

2. The psycological struggle will be fierce, but, of course, very
   sophisticated. We must definitely win that struggle.

Section III: Suggested proposals:

Concretely propose the following:

1. Our two countries must exchange Ambassadors this year,
   1983.

2. The United States Government must end its economic aggression and propaganda destabilization against Grenada
   without delay.

Later These two points will be added:

1. Miami-based agents of destabilization

2. Cease your support for countries - those opposed to PRG
   and extradite Gairy.

Section IV: Background on Grenada's Position:

For over three (3) years, Grenada's PRG has been saying we
want to normalize diplomatic relations with the United States:

- Bernard Coard to Pete Vaky, Carter's Assistant Secretary of
  States to Inter-American Affairs

- In almost every multilateral forum e.g. OAS, CARICOM, UN.
- Cde. Whiteman has also made the point on all of his visits here

At the same time the U.S. has refused to respond to many of our overtures.

V-6
Handwritten Notes of Meeting with
National Security Advisor Clark

These handwritten minutes of Maurice Bishop's meeting with U.S. National Security Advisor Clark are unsigned and undated (see previous document.) It has been averred that these notes were written by Grenadian OAS ambassador Dessima Williams.

NOTES OF BISHOP MEETING
WITH JUDGE CLARKE

We must <u>protest</u> the meeting not occurring as we were led to believe —

— Long delay

— Mittendorf the chief host

<u>Clark, Dam, Mittendorf, Bosch, Browne</u>

M. Glad for meeting, been requesting it for some time.

Need to start off on the long history of good people to people relations.

Bottom line: dialogue and normal relations

— Commission: a Discuss differences

b Discuss cooperation

<u>Clarke</u> — No problems with dialogue, more interested in conduct

Concerned with Soviet influence among our neighbors

Soviet influence in region is not acceptable

Can communicate to your our response to your proposals

Agreed to off the record meeting a secret meeting

Not only to refer to this meeting

Expect change in criticisms in future.

Have common strands (history) — legal practice. Hope this can lead to great progress.

M. — Encouraged by his response — that they are willing to accept talks on the normalization of relations.

— Our language (careful) should [be] noted

— toning down of attacks must be mutual

Clarke Their preference is to sit around the table re discussions rather [than] public attacks.

Referred to moving location of the school — not for this conference

Hope that we return to basic form of govt. rather than model of E. Eur.

Judge's departure

M. Time perspective re reply to our pro[posals?]

Dam — Key thing is Sov./Cuban influence

Need to see some change in conduct before the agreement

M.—Will have to look at econ. destabl.

C.D.B., IMF.

—Tourism re res [?]

—We can explore any range of subjects and give fullest assurance that we constitute no threat to the US

Dam — Interested in assurances

"Thank you for coming to meet with Judge Clarke."

— Re shift in venue

— Length of time judge stayed

— Points he made

— Tone/atmosphere

— State Dept. component (Dam)

— Meaning of the press/press state[ment?]

VI
SOVIET AND SOVIET-BLOC ACTIVITIES

The New Jewel Movement took pride in its authentic revolutionary origins. But as the following documents show, its quest for legitimacy and status within the Soviet camp progressively enmeshed it in a system of dependency upon many Communist states, which was not only military but political.

As previously shown in Section II, the Soviet Union and other Eastern Bloc countries had agreed to supply this new people's democracy with vast amounts of military equipment and training facilities to make Grenada a major military installation in the Caribbean. But as these additional documents show, in diplomatic dealings with the Soviet Union and other Moscow-aligned Third World countries, the Bishop regime was to be a supplicant constantly reaching out for symbolic and material support that was not invariably forthcoming. Streams of letters from Grenadian officials went out in all directions seeking assistance of all sorts from Soviet and Soviet-aligned states—North Korea, Vietnam, East Germany, Syria, and so forth. These pleas were for aid in the construction of internal police systems, party ideological training, advice on how to "re-educate" the Grenadian population (sought from Vietnam, incidentally, which had successfully established Gulag-style camps for this purpose after its conquest of South Vietnam in 1975). To oil-rich Libya and to Iraq went requests for financial support in building a huge airport which, as Maurice Bishop wrote, would have "great strategic value in the event of any external invasion. . . . The very survival of our country and our revolution," he wrote to President Hussein, "depends on it."

In its political dealings with the Soviet Union, the new regime was particularly concerned to train the second cadre of revolutionary leaders in the C.P.S.U.'s International Leninist School which, since the 1920s, has served as the principal training center for foreign political operatives. An account included here gives the curriculum of the school, and reveals the reactions of the Grenadian students to and their relations with, other non-Soviet cadres from Mozambique, Ethiopia, South Africa, Syria, Jamaica, Colombia, and Denmark.

Thrust suddenly into the big league, Grenada's small mission to Moscow seems to have rankled under the patronizing slights received from Party and State authorities there. A small frog in a big Caribbean lake, the PRG received a back-of-the-hand treatment from Soviet political authorities. Its relationship with Soviet officialdom was confined to low-level functionaries. The tiny diplomatic staff (Ambassador Richard Jacobs personally typed his diplomatic reports) was rent by feuds no doubt exacerbated by the bleak, uncongenial atmosphere in which they worked. Grenadian diplomats accordingly found relief in the colony of other accredited pro-Soviet Third World emissaries. Jacobs' report from Moscow provides a glimpse of how these minor actors on the world stage tried to gain favor and prestige from their Slavic patrons. Jacobs' analysis of Grenada's role in the Soviet bloc is uniquely sophisticated and candid.

Space limitations permit the inclusion in this volume of only a sample of such party-to-party, state-to-state diplomatic documents. Yet the editors must acknowledge that those in our possession cast but little light upon a crucial question—the differing natures of Soviet and Cuban influences upon their new Caribbean client and the possible friction between them. The Moscow link paralleled the New Jewel Movement's Havana connection. It would seem that almost until the end Castro remained the principal mentor of Maurice Bishop. It would also seem that important military matters between Moscow and Grenada were handled through Havana.

But what the documents now in our possession do not well illumine are the political nuances of Soviet and Cuban relations to their client. The Soviet chief of mission in Grenada, Gennady Sazhenev, is mentioned nowhere in the documents; yet evidently he was a substantial figure in Soviet activities in the Western Hemisphere. A one-time deputy defense minister of the U.S.S.R., Sazhenev had served in Cuba before and during the missile crisis; his subsequent tour of duty involved assignments as Minister-Counselor in Argentina and Colombia in the 1970s, coinciding with outbreaks of guerrilla activities and waves of assassinations in both countries. We can only speculate as to the possible role, if any, which Soviet authorities on the spot played in the overthrow of Maurice Bishop. But, during his last hours, Bishop sadly likened his own impending doom to that of Mohammed Taraki and Hafizullah Amin, the Afghan pro-Soviet Prime Ministers murdered before Russian troops began their invasion in 1979 (see Section IX).

The question of frictions and tensions between Cuban and Soviet authorities in Grenada remains unresolved, yet is a matter of crucial importance to an understanding of bloc relations. Castro appears to have been outraged at Bishop's downfall; after his murder, Castro in a public speech in Havana referred to Bernard Coard, Bishop's successor, as the "Pol Pot of the Caribbean." It is to be hoped that further information on this question will be found in subsequent releases from these archives.

VI-1
Letter from Jacobs to Vietnamese Embassy
5/23/81

This letter by Grenada's roving diplomat, W. Richard Jacobs,
was addressed to the Vietnamese Ambassador in Cuba, dated
May 23, 1981.
"Lumpen" refers to "lumpen proletarians," or "clod proleta-
rians," a Marxist term describing hard-core unemployed and
similar marginalized social elements.

EMBAJADA DE GRANADA EN CUBA

23rd May, 1981

CONFIDENTIAL

Excellency,
   The Embassy of Grenada in Cuba presents its compliments
to the Embassy of Vietnam in Cuba, and has the honour to
inform you that during his visit to Vietnam between June
2nd. and June 16th. 1981, General of the People's Revolutionary Army, Member of the Political Bureau and Minister of Defence and National Security, Comrade Hudson Austin accompanied by Major Bazil Cahagan and Captain Christopher Lowe
wish to include the following items in their programme:

1. Techniques of defence against an occupying force.

2. Tour of appropriate trenches and exposure to the tech-
   nique of trench warfare.

3. Tour of anti-airraid and artillery centres for defence.

4. Counter-intelligence techniques.

5. A study of captured U.S.A. military equipment.

6. An assessment of tactics used by U.S.A. imperialism in
   Vietnam.

7. Techniques of moving warfare.

8. How to counter the naplam weapon.

9. Techniques of dealing with counter-revolutionaries especially in the area of re-education.

10. Methods of dealing with lumpen elements.

As you are aware, Excellency, the delegation returns to Moscow from Mongolia on 1st June. We trust at that time that they will be able to collect their airline tickets from the Vietnamese Embassy in Moscow.

General Austin has asked me to convey to you his great pleasure in meeting and having discussions with you and he looks forward to a successful and rewarding mission to Vietnam.

The Embassy of Grenada in Cuba takes this opportunity to extend to the Embassy of Vietnam in Cuba the assurances of its highest consideration and esteem.

W. Richard Jacobs
Ambassador

VI-2
Draft Workplan of the
International Relations Committee N.J.M. for 1983

In this unsigned and undated document, NJM leaders put for-
ward their goals in the field of relations between their party and
other leftist movements, particularly the "international Communist
and Workers movement," i.e. pro-Soviet parties around the world,
both in and out of power. The Grenada Peace Council, mentioned
here, was set up along the lines of the Soviet-controlled World Peace
Council.

OVERALL OBJECTIVE:

   To develop the International relations Work of the Party
through programmes that raise the Internationalist consciousness of our working people, strengthen the Leninist
character of the International Relations Committee, expand
political tourism and deepen the call for World Peace, friendship and co-operation.

SPECIFIC OBJECTIVES:

(1)   To act as a major force in raising the consciousness of
        the masses on question of peace, the National Liberation
        struggle and other major International questions.

        (a) Prepare a year plan of solidarity activities.

        (b) Plan and organise a series of symposia, panels, de-
             bates, etc. — Influence trade Unions, mass organisa-
             tions and schools to participate in these on the basis
             of competition and emulation.

        (c) Assist in the development of International Relations
             sections in mass organisations, trade unions etc.

(d) Ensure the collection and distribution of progressive literature on international affairs among the working people, particularly the working class.

(e) Effectively utilise the mass media as a means to sharpen Internationalist consciousness of the working people, in particular, the working class.

(f) To strengthen the Grenada Peace Council.

(2) Consolidate our relationship with the Caribbean masses particularly Trinidad and Tobago, St. Vincent, Barbados and Venezuela.

(a) Strengthen our ties with progressive and democratic forces in these countries and influential individuals.

(b) Organise through T & T Committee a plan of exhibitions, cultural and sports tours, and excursions and exchange visits.

(c) Step up the flow of information and propaganda work about the Grenada Revolution.

(d) Develop an efficient network for distributing publications from Grenada Free West Indian, Party papers, organs of Mass Organisations, taped and typewritten speeches of Leadership, posters, etc.

OBJECTIVE 3:   To establish relations with International Communist and Workers Movement.

WAYS & MEANS: (a) Draft a master list of all major activities.

(b) Draft a master list of the member parties of this movement.

(c) Develop relations with our contacts in the movement through exchange of materials.

(d) Seek to have the party represented at selected meetings of the movement.

(e) Giving internationalist support to all peoples fighting for their freedom, independence and social progress.

OBJECTIVE 4:   To ensure the proper supervision and co-ordination of Party Branches overseas.

WAYS & MEANS: (a) Ensure that party study materials and relevant decisions/reports are sent to these groups regularly.

(b) Ensure regular monthly reports from these Party Branches.

(c) Sending of party paper, Fight, Fedon, Cutlass, Worker's Voice, Scotilda, speeches by the leadership of the revolution, F.W.I. and other relevant documents on the revolution, on a weekly basis.

(d) Distribution of posters, pamphlets, video's, pictures on historic celebrations of the revolution.

OBJECTIVE 5:   To maintain links with regional left parties.

WAYS & MEANS: (a) Organise quarterly seminars on organisation.

(b) Organise training sessions in various areas of mass work for cadres of these parties.

(c) Organise exchange visits.

(d) Regular exchange of experiences in party work and party guidance to the political process in the various countries, including regular exchange of information and materials in these areas.

VI-3
Meeting of Soviet and Grenadian
Military Chiefs of Staff
3/10/83

This report, issued by Bernard Bourne, Minister-Counselor of the Grenadian Embassy in Moscow, describes a meeting between top Soviet and Grenadian military personnel, during which Soviet Marshal Nikolai V. Ogarkov declared: "Over two decades ago, there was only Cuba in Latin America, today there are Nicaragua, Grenada, and a serious battle is going on El Salvador."

EMBASSY OF GRENADA IN THE USSR

Dobryninskaya Ulitsa 7   *Telephone*
Apartment 221   *237-25-41*
Moscow   *237-99-05*
USSR

MEETING BETWEEN CHIEFS OF GENERAL STAFF OF SOVIET ARMED FORCES AND PEOPLE'S REVOLUTIONARY ARMED FORCES OF GRENADA

DATE: THURSDAY 10 MARCH 1983 (4.00pm)

Representing the Soviet side were:

1.	Marshal of the Soviet Union Ogarkov N.V.	- Chief of Staff
2.	Colonel General N.A. Zutov	- 10th Department
3.	LT.-General G.A. Borisov	- Foreign relations Department
4.	Colonel Soloviev	- 10th Department
5.	Captain M. Globenko	- Foreign Relations Department

Present on the Grenada side were:

1. Major Einstein Louison   - Chief of Staff
2. Bernard Bourne   - Minister-Counsellor

The meeting commenced promptly by Marshal Ogarkov who
extended a warm welcome to Major Louison. In doing so,
Marshal Ogarkov enquired whether Major Louison was having any problems with his studies and living conditions.

Major Louison expressed thanks for the words of welcome
and explained that he had no difficulty with studies and
thought that he was making progress because there was no
report to the contrary from the professors at the school.

Speaking about the Grenada Revolution Major Louison
pointed out that the economy had grown by 5.5% (percent) in
1982 and living standards by 3 percent. He explained that the
United States continues with its plans to destabilize the revolution, undermine tourism, linking our international airport
with military potential and training of mercenaries in Venezuela, in addition to the United States itself. Major Louison
then emphasized that the Grenada Revolution got around
these problems and still continued to make advances. He also
informed Marshal Ogarkov that at the the Seventh Non-
Aligned Summit Grenada was again elected to the coordinating Bureau of the Movement.

At that moment Marshal Ogarkov said that he was glad for
the information on Grenada. About the situation in the world
Marshal Ogarkov pointed out that the United States would try
now and in the future to make things difficult for progressive
changes in all regions and continents. The Marshal said that
over two decades ago, there was only Cuba in LAtin America,
today there are Nicaragua, Grenada and a serious battle is
going on in El Salvador. The Marshal of the Soviet Union then
stressed that United States imperialism would try to prevent
progress but that there were no prospects for imperialism to
turn back history.

Moreover, Marshal Ogarkov emphasized that in an aggressive
climate the military people have tasks to do. He explained that

since Grenada was located close to US imperialism and was not developed militarily the Grenada Revolution would have to be specifically vigilant at all times. Furthermore, the Marshal declared that once the masses have a burning desire for progress the leadership should move ahead decisively and firmly. On that point Marshal Ogarkov assured Major Louison that the plans outlined by Prime Minister Maurice Bishop during his visit to the Soviet Union in 1982 were good and had the support of the Grenadian people.

Further still, the Marshal of the Soviet Union reminded Major Louison that the Soviet Union would contribute to raising the combat readiness and preparedness of the Armed Forces of Grenada.

He informed the Grenada Chief of Staff that according to the agreement signed in July 1982, one-third of the means for 1983 were already supplied and the rest would be delivered during this year.

In response Major Louison expressed his gratitude for the supplies sent to Grenada and mentioned that he was confident that more deliveries would be sent to Grenada in the future.

However, Major Louison explained that he wished to introduce another matter for discussion which was not included in the protocol. The Chief of Staff of Grenada explained that he was referring to the text of a letter from Prime Minister Bishop addressed to Prime Minister Tikhonov dated 28th July 1982. Major Louison said that in the letter, Grenada was requesting additional assistance in: food, fuel, spare parts, transportation, engineering kits, uniforms and others. He disclosed that the greatest part of the budget was used for food and fuel and that spare parts were also of serious concern because many vehicles were grounded since the basic spare parts were unavailable.

Marshal Ogarkov replied rather jokingly that students should be concerned with studies, but that Major Louison who would graduate on 10th May was also concerned about the problems of his soldiers. Nevertheless, the Marshal indicated that he

was aware of such requests, but hastened to assure Major
Louison that all items contained in the protocol would be
delivered. Marshal Ogarkov further assured Major Louison
that the requests contained in the letter to P.M. Tikhonov
were presently under consideration and that even though
they were handled by GKS and Ministry of Foreign Trade, the
Ministry of Defence would exercise some control on the solution. He said, with confidence, that his Ministry would participate in the settlement of these requests.

Further still, the Marshal disclosed that there was a possibility that some of the main questions would be solved and as
soon as a decision was taken, the Ministry of Defence through
Col-General Zutov would inform the Embassy.

Additionally, referring to the question of deputation of Soviet
specialists to Grenada to conduct studies related to the construction of military projects the Marshal informed the Grenadian side that the team of specialists would be sent in one
month's time and that they await an indication from Grenada
confirming readiness to accommodate the specialists.

Finally, towards the end of the meeting the Marshal of the
Soviet Union and Chief of Staff of the Soviet Armed Forces
proposed a toast 'from the bottom of our hearts' — in his
words — to Major Louison on the eve of the 10th Anniversary
of the New JEWEL Movement and the fourth Anniversary of
the Grenada Revolution.

In his turn, Major Louison expressed thanks and appreciation
to the Marshal for the kind words about the Grenada Revolution; Major Louison also expressed thanks for the assistance
to the Armed Forces of Grenada and then raised a toast towards the strengthening of relations between the two countries, parties, people's, and their armed forces.

Marshal Ogarkov was thankful for the warm meeting and
reinforced both toasts by raising a final toast for the growth
and further strengthening of the relations between the Soviet
Armed Forces and the People's Revolutionary Armed Forces of
Grenada.

In conclusion, it should be pointed out that the entire meeting was conducted in an atmosphere of warmth, friendliness, simplicity and unpretentiousness.

The meeting ended with warm embraces.

Bernard Bourne

[signature]

Minister-Counselor

VI-4
Meeting with East German Prime Minister
5/25/83

This memorandum, originating with the Grenadian Embassy in Moscow, describes a meeting between the Grenadian ambassador and Willi Stoph, Prime Minister of East Germany. The East German leader emphasized that, in the view of his government, "Cuba, Nicaragua, and Grenada were the countries of greatest hope in the Caribbean region and it was their intention to seek to stabilize and support these revolutionary processes." The Grenadian ambassador replied that his government, for its part, was "working resolutely to improve the chances for progressive change in the other Caribbean islands [and] held regular meetings with the progressive parties in the region."

EMBASSY OF GRENADA IN THE USSR

Dobryninskaya Ulitsa 7   *Telephone*
Apartment 221   *237-25-41*
Moscow   *237-99-05*
USSR

YEAR OF POLITICAL AND ACADEMIC EDUCATION

MEETING WITH PRIME MINISTER (CHAIRMAN OF THE
COUNCIL OF MINISTERS) OF THE GDR, 20/5/83, 1:30p.m.

The Prime Minister welcomed the Ambassador and congratulated him on his recent presentation of Credentials. He said that the formal conditions were now established for the development of close relations between Grenada and the GDR which after all were very new having started in June 1982 with the visit of the Prime Minister.

The Ambassador thanked the Prime Minister for his welcome, extended greetings from Prime Minister Maurice Bishop - who had found memories of his very warm reception in the GDR.

The Prime Minister responded that the GDR also had warm memories of Prime Minister Maurice Bishop's visit and he assured the Ambassador that the GDR will do everything necessary to fulfill all agreements reached between the GDR and Grenada and would, to the extent of its capacity, give further aid. He said that in the view of the GDR Cuba, Nicaragua and Grenada were the countries of greatest hope in the Caribbean region and it was their intention to seek to stabilize and support these revolutionary processes.

The Ambassador informed the Prime Minister that the GDR analysis of these countries was in line with the analysis of our Government and Party on these matters. Even so, we were working resolutely to improve the chances for progressive change in the other Caribbean islands. This required us to held regular meetings with the progressive parties in the region. In the case of Grenada the internal counter-revolutionary activity was under control, but US imperialism was attempting to promote counter-revolution externally. Our people have demonstrated their determination to resist all imperialist intervention and by their hard work have demonstrated their determination to build the revolutionary process.

The Prime Minister said that the Government, people and Party of the GDR are impressed with the progress made by the Grenada revolution. He was informed about our further plans for co-operation in the field of radio and he was of the view that this was a particularly important undertaking. He hoped that it would be implemented quickly. The Prime Minister promised the full support of his office in the successful implementation of the duties of the Ambassador.

The meeting ended.

VI-5
Grenada-Soviet Relations: A Summary
7/11/83

This confidential report by Grenadian ambassador to Moscow W. Richard Jacobs, personally typed by him, was transmitted to Maurice Bishop, Bernard Coard, Unison Whiteman, and NJM politburo member Ewart Layne, dated July 11, 1983.

Jacobs frankly describes the alignment of Grenada with the Soviet Union in international affairs. He states that one of the main reasons for Soviet support was that "Cuba has strongly championed our cause." He notes that in Moscow Soviet Latin American expert Kasimirov had closely questioned him on the nature of the Grenadian meetings with U.S. National Security Advisor William Clark. Kasimirov expressed dissatisfaction that the Grenadians had not coordinated this visit with Moscow. Ambassador Jacobs concludes by recommending that Grenada "continue our international support for the Soviet line."

Along the way, Jacobs here commits other fascinating indiscretions. For example, he states that Soviet personnel considered the New Jewel organization to be a "communist party." Even more significant is his assertion that "for Grenada to assume a position of increasingly greater importance, we have to be seen as influencing at least regional events. We have to . . . be the sponsor of revolutionary activity and progressive developments." Proposing that: "to the extent we can take credit for bringing any other country into the progressive fold, our prestige and influence would be greatly advanced," Jacobs suggests Grenada act to impose a Soviet-Cuban direction on the neighboring states of Suriname and Belize.

The worthy diplomat also let slip the reality of Soviet domination in former colonies like Grenada, which do not cease to suffer a classically-dependent status although they may pass from the Western to the Eastern camp. Thus, he notes problems with East Germany over payments for bananas, a typical "third world" cash crop exported by Grenada.

In addition, Jacobs offers insightful remarks on the special relationship between the ruling parties in Soviet-controlled nations. As he points out, "party-to-party" relations, which tend to evade the eyes of the outside world, assume an importance for such states that is equal or superior to the relations between the governments. Such matters as ideological education (cf. the "Lenin School" documents, VI-6 and VI-7) therefore have a special significance; through party-to-party contacts the Soviets seem able to exercise a far greater degree of control than usually exists in the relations between a great power like the U.S.S.R. and a dependent nation such as Grenada.

The term "national democratic, anti-imperialist stage," referring to political developments in underdeveloped countries, is generally construed to indicate a left-wing regime with a strongly pro-Soviet orientation, but which has not yet completed the process of transition to a full Soviet-type state, either for political or economic reasons. This is further reflected in ambassador Jacobs' complaint that Grenada is not yet included in the "'inner group' of members of the socialist community."

"Popular democracy" and "democratic centralism," in this context, indicate specific Soviet political concepts. "Popular democracy" is normally defined as a system in which political activities are monopolized by "popular" organizations, i.e. mass structures claiming to speak in the name of the "people," such as the Communist parties, or state-controlled trade unions or youth organizations. "Democratic centralism" indicates the system of internal organization of the Communist Party, in which members are ostensibly guaranteed the right to free expression so long as they agree to accept the orders of the upper echelon of party leaders.

EMBASSY OF GRENADA IN THE USSR

Dobryninskaya Ulitsa 7   *Telephone*
Apartment 221   *237-25-41*
Moscow   *237-99-05*
USSR

Typed personally by W. Richard Jacobs.
Distribution as follows: Minister Unison Whiteman
                        PM
                        Deputy PM Coard
                        PB Member Ewart Layne who is in
                        the USSR   ●

                        11th July 1983

CONFIDENTIAL

Grenada's relations with the USSR

   Our relations with the USSR are influenced by a number of
inter-connecting factors. Among the more important are:
1. Perceived ideological direction of the NJM Party and the
   PRG
2. The management of state affairs.
3. The development of state to state relations.
4. Grenada's role in the world (region).
5. Our relationship with other members of the socialist community.
6. Relationship between the NJM and CPSU.
7. Our activity in international organizations.

Perceived Ideological directions - PRG

   Grenada is regarded as being on the path of socialist ori-

entation. There is a general acceptance among Soviet authorities that we are at the national democratic, anti-imperialist
stage of socialist orientation. The USSR assigns a special place
to these types of countries in its foreign policy. This is, of
course, also the case with other socialist countries. In terms
of their priorities, the countries of socialist orientation come
right after the socialist community. Therefore, whatever, the
internal debate, it is important that we continue to maintain
our public assessment of our stage of development as the national democratic, anti-imperialist stage of socialist orientation. After all the PM himself made that assessment when he
was here in Moscow as well as during his visit to Berlin. This
has recently been reinforced by the Foreign Minister during
his visit to Vietnam, Kampuchia and Laos. So it seems to me
absolutely necessary that we maintain this line. This is made
all the more important by the very high priority that is placed
on consistency of analysis here.

— NJM

The Comrades responsible for Grenada in the International
Section, have told me that they operate on the basis that the
NJM is a "communist party". Given the relatively low level of
these comrades (Nicholi etc.) one is not so sure about the au-
thoritativeness of this statement though, I doubt that they
would make a statement like that without the necessary
authority. In any event, my clear impression is that we are
being treated as a fraternal party — i.e. a M-L Party. My impression too, is that the CPSU delegation that visited in March
formed a positive impression of the work of the NJM and have
communicated that impression. The CPSU is in a position to
know almost everything about the NJM — its size, programme, objectives, orientation etc. and they cannot fail to
recognize and accept the authenticity of our credentials. The
problem of protocol - the proper level at which our leaders
should be met etc. remains. This could perhaps be explained
on two levels: 1. They sometimes adopt an over-protective attitude towards us and argue that if we meet at too high a level
the USA would use use this as an issue to further squeeze

Grenada. (This is one of the explanations floated as to why the
PM did not meet with Andropov in April). 2. Although we are
regarded as a fraternal party we are not in the "inner group"
in members of the socialist community - their highest party
officials are reserved for these levels of encounters. Their
answer as to why Nicaragua is treated differently - and at a
higher level - would presumably be that Nicaragua is already
under direct US attack and it is necessary for them to openly
show solidarity. They would like Grenada to avoid that direct
attack. The core of the matter however, is that they regard
Grenada as a small distant country and they are only prepared to make commitments to the extent of their capacity to
fulfill, and if necessary, defend their commitment. (I recall on
one occasion explaining the situation in St. Vincent to the
Party comrades. Their response was that this is all very interesting but St. Vincent is so far away!!)

Recommendations

1. The Soviets have a correct perception of our ideological line
both at the Government and Party levels. We should continue
along these lines.

2. The problem of "protocol" has to be solved but it must be
handled gently. At the diplomatic level, we could keep on insisting that counterparts meet. To the extent that this is not
achieved, the principals could mention it in passing - not a
substantive point, just in passing. We must not fail to mention
the matter to their Ambassador at social activities. Gestures
are also important - cutting conversations short with junior
people etc. Receprosity is also important. PB members should
not be easily available to low-ranking Soviet officials on visits.
As a rule, the PM in particular, and I would also say the Deputy PM should only entertain courtesy calls not exceeding 15
to 30 minutes.

The management of state affairs

The Soviets have been burnt quite often in the past by giving support to Governments which have either squandered

that support, or turned around and become agents of imperialism, or lost power. One is reminded of Egypt, Somolia, Ghana
and Peru. They are therefore very careful, and for us sometimes maddingly slow, in making up their minds about who to
support. They have decided to support us for two main reasons. 1. Cuba has strongly championed our cause. 2. They are
genuinely impressed with our management of the economy
and state affairs in general. They are impressed with our
commitment to planning, the absence of corruption, the ethic
of hard work among the leadership, the ability of the leadership to spread this ethic among the population, the willingness to sacrifice. They are also impressed with the policy on
the communication media, the close links with the masses,
the practice of popular democracy and the implementation of
the policy of democratic centralism as a guiding principle and
not a dogma. Also of importance is the stability of our leadership.

Recommendation

The Soviets are very impressed with our management of
state power. We should continue along this line with a continuing emphasis on the "step by step" approach.

Development of State to State Relations

The principal item here is the implementation of the
Agreements signed in July 1982. In the area of Trade and Collaboration — this is generally being implemented in accordance with the agreements. Some collaboration agreements
however, have been delayed as a result of procrastination on
our part. In particular, the sattelite dish agreement has not
yet been signed by our side. As far as the Soviets are concerned, this is the centerpiece of our July agreements, the
only negotiable items in it are how we house and transport
the technicians, and how we pay them in local currency. The
other items are fixed. The credit for this project cannot be utilized for any other project. We really need to get on with this
matter. The same holds true for the Fifteen Teachers project.
In any event, the reasons for not signing these agreements

promptly, should be routinely communicated to the Embassy. We are not infrequently faced with the question as to what is the state of affairs on this or that project and we are placed in the very embarassing position of not being able to answer. Meanwhile, our Soviet colleagues who ask these questions often know the answer because their Embassy in Grenada has informed them. But even with these shortcomings, I would say that we are OK in this area of trade and collaboration.

State to state relations are also fundamentally influenced by the development of relations in other fields as well. We have a good record of collaboration at the military and trade union levels. These are positive factors in the development of our state to state relations. A lot more could be done at the NYO and Peace levels. It is important always to remember that plans for visits and interchanges should be made at least one year in advance. The NYO level is developing satisfactorily.

One of the most difficult areas is at the University and Technical education levels. As in all the above, the Soviets assess the level of state to state relations by, among other things, the extent to which we are willing to share our experiences with them, and learn from their experiences. When trade unionists, youth, women and pioneers come to study in the USSR, we are in effect signaling to them that we recognize that we can learn from their experiences and thereby sending the correct ideological message as well. The same holds true for our University and technical students. The presence of ten of our top planners has made a very favourable impact on the development of our state to state relations. But the same is not true in the area of the University and Technical education. To date we have been offered 80 (eighty) University or Technical scholarships — 20 in 1981, 20 in 1982 and 40 in 1983. We have accepted eighteen (18) of which two of our students have given up the course. Of the remaining sixteen (16) at least eight (8) do not have the minimum requirements for entry to the level of education they expected to receive upon leaving Grenada. This, it seems to me, is requesting more than we know that we can absorb. It is much better to ask for five scholarships and fill four than to ask for 40 and send only four people. This gives the impression, false as it may be, that our students prefer not to study in the USSR. It introduces a certain question mark and works in a negative way on state to state relations. Of course, it need hardly be mentioned that the behaviour of our students can also have an effect on state to state relations, and we must therefore be careful to select highly motivated students.

The establishment of the Grenada-Soviet Friendship society has a positive effect on our relations. It is now critical that this organization function.

State to state relations are very seriously affected by the use that is made of the aid and assistance rendered to Grenada at the material and technical levels. In the case of technicians, it is important that proper provisions be made for their stay in Grenada and they be fully utilized for the entire time of their stay in Grenada. In general we have received very good feedback on this aspect and the technicians are full of praise for the enthusiasm and commitment of their Grenadian hosts.

In the case of the use of materials, the feedback has also been generally good. But there have evidently been some lapses, and we must always take care to ensure that we order the correct item with full information and specifications for everything associated with its use. The case of the first set of tractors which arrived without the necessary attachments simply because the Soviets did not know what "attachments" we were talking about; the case of waterpumps going unused because of no hose; and the case of military vehicles without spare-parts in part because of poor specifications on our part — all contribute to a negative impression. There seems to have been some slip-up also in relation to the AN-2. The information needed for certification should certainly have been requested before the completion of the assembly of the plane. The Soviets have serious concerns about the operation and maintenance of the AN-26. We have assured them that we have a suitable stand-by agreement with the Cubans on this one, but it is urgent that we select and dispatch as soon as possible ten (10) people — at least — to be trained for the operation and maintenance of this aircraft.

An important aspect of the development of state to state relations is the operation and functioning of the Embassy. All countries use the quality and quantity of personnel assigned as diplomatic staff to particular Embassies as an indication of the nature of a country's priorities in domestic and international affairs. The Soviet Union is no exception in this regard. Their own Embassy in Grenada is not only an indication of their resource base, but equally a reflection of the fact that they have considerable interest in the development of relations with Grenada.

I have on a previous occasion pointed out that for any Embassy to operate efficiently, the following officers are absolutely essential — Ambassador, Deputy (at the level of 1st Secretary or above) Secretary to the Ambassador, Accountant. This is emphasized even more in the case of the Embassy in Moscow by the fact that the Ambassador is accredited to nine other countries — GDR, Bulgaria, Checoslovakia, Hungary, Korea, Rumania, Mongolia, Poland, Yougoslavia and Afghanistan — ten in fact — and at least the first five plus the USSR are countries with which we have some serious relations. This means that the job requires a lot of travel. Both inside and outside the USSR, I would say that about 60% of the Ambassador's work is representational. This responsibility requires two essential elements 1. Information from Grenada 2. Sophisticated analyses of the information available from each country. The first one is lacking but I am confident that a political decision can correct this situation. The second requires a person of high cultural level with some formal training and/or experience in international relations. Equally, we need someone with the appropriate training to undertake the task associated with the maintenance and development of our trading relations with the socialist community. Because of the structure of the diplomatic corps in the USSR both of these people need to be at the level of 1st. Secretary or above. We have a mountain of experience in the proper selection of these people. The fact is that a trained person can absorb and apply the experience to which he exposed in a creative way. An untrained person can be little more than a messenger, and length of service becomes a repetitive experience. It is important too, to recognize that particularly in the socialist community, training is highly valued and contributes to the development of the kind of prestige necessary to achieve our objectives.

All members of our leadership with whom I have raised this matter of staffing agree that we need additional staff at the Embassy in Moscow. This matter should be given the most urgent attention. Inadequate staff prevents this Embassy from developing state to state relations to the level necessary to preserve and advance our interests.

I mentioned earlier about the representational role of the Ambassador and the need for information for this task to be properly performed. I wish to draw on the example of the PM's recent mission to the USA. I was in the GDR at the time of the mission and I happened to hear on VOA a report of the PM's mission just before a meeting with the Foreign Ministry. The PM's mission turned out to be the main item on the agenda. I was able to handle the issue because as part of the information package on the March mobilization, the PS (Foreign Affairs) had sent an up-to-date package on our relations with the USA. When I returned to Moscow, the issue was raised by Kasimirov — Director of the First Latin American Department — who handles Grenada's affairs in the Foreign Ministry. Basically, he wanted to know what was the nature of the meeting with Clark. I told him that thus far the results are confidential. He said to me in the usual light vein of types of conversations that if he were friends with the American Ambassador he could get the information from him!! The basic point that he successfully got over to me is that in the circumstances of our relations with the USSR and their and our relations with the USA, it would have been courteous to inform them of the intention to visit. I agree with that. The contents of the discussion with Clark is another matter since, among other things, I am certain that the USA could break our code if they wanted to. Kasimirov told me that he first read of the visit in the newspapers and that he first heard that the PM had a meeting with Clark when the Canadian

Ambassador, who was on a visit to his office, mentioned it to him. I feel sure that either his Ambassador in Grenada or USA would have informed him of this but the basic point that he is making is that he would have expected the information to come from me.

The other piece of information which is really crucial for our state to state relations deals with the IMF loan that I understand that we are negotiating or have signed. Now, when the PM raised the possibility of a US$6 million with Gromyko in April he made the point that we could get the money nowhere else. I have been monitoring the response here and the latest thing that they told me is that we may get a reply by mid July. I assume that the IMF loan has nothing to do with the airport project and therefore we are still going ahead with the US$6 million request which is strictly for the airport. But this is only an educated guess on my part. I have no hard information, and it would have been appropriate to let the Soviets know through our Embassy here that we were about to apply for this loan. Of course as I understand it, they have no problem with us going to the IMF. But the communication of this kind of information adds to a stable, reliable friendly state to state relations atmosphere. And equally important, it developes an expectation of recoprosity — they will give us information in the future.

Recommendations

1. We should make every effort to implement all collaboration and personnel-exchange agreements. In the case of personnel exchange, when it is not possible for the Grenada party to fulfill the agreement, the Embassy must be promptly informed. No individual should arrive in the USSR without previously informing the Embassy.

2. Both the Embassy and an appropriate Unit in the Ministry of Trade should monitor the implementation of trade agreements on a monthly basis and exchange this information. The Embassy and the Ministry of Planning should do the same thing with other collaboration agreements. (I have in the past

received such a monitoring report from the Macro-Planning Unit. But only on one occasion.)

3. We should as a matter of principle never request materials and opportunities that we are not in a position to utilize within a defined period.

4. A political decision should be immediately communicated to the International Department of the Party or the PS (Foreign Affairs) to keep the Embassy informed on all important issues.

5. Urgent steps be taken to recruit three new members of the diplomatic staff for the USSR Embassy with the appropriate qualifications.

Grenada's role in the world (region)

By itself, Grenada's distance from the USSR, and its small size, would mean that we would figure in a very minute way in the USSR's global relationships. Our revolution has to be viewed as a world-wide process with its original roots in the Great October Revolution. For Grenada to assume a position of increasingly greater importance, we have to be seen as influencing at least regional events. We have to establish ourselves as the authority on events in at least the English-speaking Caribbean, and be the sponsor of revolutionary activity and progressive developments in this region at least. At the same time, we have to develop and maintain normal state to state relations with our neighbours and concretely operationalize our good-neighbourlyness policy. The twice per year meetings with the progressive and revolutionary parties in the region is therefore critical to the development of closer relations with the USSR. In order to keep both the Embassy and the Soviets informed of the outcome of such meetings, perhaps a good model would be for a member of the CC to pay a visit to the USSR after each such meeting. The mission of such a person could without difficulty be mixed with other activities. We must ensure though that we become the principal point of access to the USSR for all these groups even to the point of having our Embassy serve as their representative while in the USSR.

Equally important is our relationship with those neighbours who the Soviets regard as our potential adversaries. We have not been making a big deal of the Regional Defence Force but the Soviets never fail to mention that to their mind this is one of the most serious future dangers that we face. It is perhaps possible to use the CC on some kind of good-will mission to the other islands as a preliminary to the signing of some type of treaty of Friendship and Co-operation with them. It seems to me too, that we need to maintain a high diplomatic profile in these islands.

Of all the regional possibilities, the most likely candidate for special attention is Surinam. If we can be an overwhelming influence on Surinam's international behaviour, then our importance in the Soviet scheme of things will be greatly enhanced. To the extent that we can take credit for bringing any other country into the progressive fold, our prestige and influence would be greatly enhanced. Another candidate is Belize. I think that we need to do some more work in that country.

Recommendations

1. Establish a system of informing the Soviets of the outcome of the meetings between NJM and the progressive parties in the region.

2. Maintain these party to party meetings.

3. Examine the possibility of concluding formal treaties of Friendship and cooperation with our neighbours.

4. Explore ways and means of influencing the international behaviour (voting at UN etc.) of Surinam and Belize.

Our relationship with other members of the socialist community

It is well to remember that there is a constant and very

detailed consultation process that takes place between members of the socialist community. For example, on my recent mission to the GDR (June 1983) they made it very clear to me that they had been briefed on the PM's discussions with Gromyko, and this is to be expected. As a result, our performance in various aspects of our relations with members of the socialist community directly affects our relations with the USSR — not to mention the fact that it directly determines the relationship between Grenada and the country involved.

There have been some positive points that has promoted our image throughout the socialist community. Among the most recent are: 1. The excellent to very good performance of our students who went to the CPSU Party school — this has become generally known. 2. The excellent contribution made by comrade DeRiggs and the generally good impression made by the Grenada delegation at the Berlin Conference on Karl Marx — this is a constant cause of congratulations in verious countries. (Incidentally, as a further indication of the communication problem, it is worth noting that I have not yet received a copy of this presentation which I am sure will serve as a good guide of policy.) 3. The fact that I have been presenting credentials and participating in the important occasions of the states involved. But there have also been negative factors. I think chief among them is the very slow process of implementing the agreements signed between Grenada and Bulgaria and GDR. This is very bad for our relations with the countries involved as well as for the USSR because they not only look at the process of implementation of our bi-lateral agreements with them, but also with the rest of the community. In particular, the GDR has floated the view with me that we appear to want to rewrite a solemn agreement agreed to by their President and our PM. (This refers principally to the method of paying for the bananas.) This, to them, is entirely inconceivable. My own view is that once the agreement is signed at that level, there is no going back and even if it is disadvantageous to us we just have to implement it. It is indecent to be seen as wanting to revise an agreement arrived by the two Heads of Government. I have no evidence that this view regarding our apparent desire to revise a solemn agreement has been communicated to other members of the community, but I would be very surprised if it has not. In any event, I have not formed the impression that there is any such generalized view within the community and it is of course in our interest to ensure that we retain the reputation as honest brokers who keep their word regardless. It is worth noting also that any effort to revise an agreement signed by the two Heads of Government below the level of Heads of Government will be next to impossible and could only serve to undermine the prestige and authority of the office of the Prime Minister.

As far as the relations with the other socialist countries are concerned, it is useful to have our people visit there as frequently as possible as well as to have state officials visit us as frequently as possible. I think that officials who travel to Eastern Europe should as a matter of policy include on their itinerary, at least one other socialist country in a planned and rotational way so that we get to touch as many bases as possible. If we are informed of such visits at least ten days in advance, we can get the host country, I am sure, to stand most of the costs. The benefits to us will be very great. As a rule, our officials have made a very positive impression on their hosts.

Recommendations

1. Continue high profile, well prepared participation in important events of the socialist community, eg Karl Marx Conference and World Peace Council.

2. Implement agreements between Grenada and other members of the socialist community promptly and faithfully.

3 Encourage officials to visit at least two countries in Eastern Europe during official missions to this part of the world.

Party to Party Relations

In the socialist community, it has emerged that there is a very close inter-relationship between party to party and state to state relations. Many of the things that the party was able to arrange in Cuba (eg airline tickets and special considerations of several kinds) are passed on to the state here. Further, as we discovered during the PM's mission and after, there is such an intimate linkage between the party and state at all levels, and notably at the highest levels that the distinctions that we have been inclined to make are not applicable in the socialist community.

One of the direct consequences of this is that the perception of party to party relations is fundamentally influenced by the nature of state to state relations and it is important to constantly keep this in mind.

Of course the implementation of the party to party agreements is paramount. By and large, we have implemented these agreements faithfully. Our first batch of party school students, although they were some two years late, have made a very good impression. Our implementation of the rest and recreation agreements have been good for our relationship. But there are a number of negative points. I think the most telling is the fact that Comrade Strachan undertook during his mission here in December to send a team of party mobilizers to the USSR for a couple of weeks to experience the Soviet experience. As is known, these people were not sent. This did some damage which could have been minimized if we had received some instructions to explain to the CPSU comrades that this undertaking was not possible at the moment. As it is, they cancelled it when the time ran out. Another example, has to do with the Public address system. We said that we needed it urgently for March 13th. 1983. They rushed it down by air to Cuba at the end of January, as promised, and the P.A. system stayed in Cuba for a very long time. I am not even sure if it has arrived as yet. They have brought this matter to our attention on a number of occasions, we have sent messages to Cuba and Grenada to try and co-ordinate our excuses by we have received no response.

We have to insist too that they stick to their agreements, for example, they agreed with Comrade Strachan to send down to Grenada "a high level delegation" — in March 1983 — you know of course, the very low level that was sent. They also agreed to send two people for rest and recreation in 1983, and we must make sure their undertakings to supply books, magazines, newspapers, films and projection equipment for the political education programme. We have to stick them to their word. I can raise it here at the diplomatic level but it will be twice as effective when it is repeated at the party political level.

The problem of what might be called counterpart protocol remains. That is, we have never been able to meet with our strict counterparts at the party level when we have our leaders here. On 27th June, I had a very frank and friendly discussion with Boyko Demitrov — the former Bulgarian Ambassador to Grenada who is now Director of International Relations in the Party. He told me that even Bulgaria sometimes faces this problem and that Grenada has to face the reality that it is a question of size, distance and priorities. I think that he is correct. But we then have to deal with these realities. Inorder to elevate our priority in the socialist scheme of things, the recommendations contained in the section dealing with our role in the world (region) becomes all the more relevant. In addition, we have to raise and discuss with the highest authorities, <u>global</u> and regional issues rather than parochial or national issues. In other words, our legitimate beginning operations have to be cast in the larger world context. We have in fact done this in the past quite successfully, linking our national requests to a global analysis. What we need to do now, it seems to me, is to become the spokesman for a broader constituency — perhaps the countries of socialist orientation. It is in this context that I have prepared the attached paper dealing with a task of last resort sponsored by the socialist community for countries for socialist orientation. This will give us an opportunity to discuss the highest issues of policy both with the countries of socialist orientation and with the socialist community, lift our profile, and tighten our priority. Here we can clearly see the close link between party to party and state to state relations.

All that is said about the CPSU holds true for the other parties as well. We have a very sympathetic hearing in Bulgaria with Boyko Demitrov and we should perhaps draw ever closer to the Bulgarian Party.

In the GDR, we also have made a good impression and there is great sympathy there for the NJM. Four comrades will be coming for rest and recreation in 1983.

I doubt that we will encounter the protocol problems that we have found in the CPSU. But we must at all cost continue to regard relations with the CPSU as the highest priority.

Recommendations

1. Strictly implement all agreements and initiatives on implementation on the other sides as well.
2. Send prompt explanations when it is not possible to implement an agreement.
3. Seek to become spokesman for the countries of socialist orientation.
4. Develop even stronger relations with the Bulgarian and GDR parties by sending delegations etc.

International activity

From the point of view of our relations with the USSR, our international activity is important from the following perspectives:

1. The consistency of our political line.
2. The influence of Grenada in the international community.
3. The degree of support offered to the positions taken by the USSR.

Our performance is assessed at the following levels:

1. The United Nations and its agencies — UNESCO, UNCTAD etc.
2. Organization of American States
3. Non-aligned Movement
4. Missions in various countries (Embassies).

It is very difficult for me to assess their view of our performance in the UN, its agencies and the OAS because, we receive only the minimum of information on our voting and performance etc. But during the period of the threats etc. in
March 1983, they advised us to play a more active role in the
UN especially at the Security Council and spoke approvingly of
Nicaragua's performance at the Security Council. But I suspect
that we need a bigger staff at the UN to do the kind of job that
would impress internationally. The same probably holds true
for the OAS. They have however, praised our role in the Zone
of Peace resolution and activity.

At the non-aligned movement, they have a high valuation of
our role. You will recall that before the New Delhi Conference
they gave me a detailed briefing on their positions and when
Comrade Whiteman visited afterwards they expressed admira-
tion for our performance. I think however, that we must insist that we form the inner circle of the advisers to Mrs. Gan-
dhi in line with our leading role in New Delhi especially in
regard to the New International Economic Order and the
Small States Conference. We have an excellent case — especially since Guyana did not participate when they were invited
to in May 1983 in New Delhi. The Guyana Ambassador here
tells me that the Foreign Minister decided that the Heads of
Mission meeting then taking place in Guyana was more important.

As far as our Embassies are concerned, the most important
thing is that they carry the same line on all matters —
economic and political, internal and external. To do this successfully, we need to have a common fund of information.
Obviously, each mission would have its area of specialty and
would have more information on that area than any other
Embassy. But a regular series of directives, instructions and
information from the Party or the Foreign Ministry would ensure that a common line is maintained throughout.

As far as the role of the mission in the USSR is concerned,
the reality of size came to me very early in the game. It therefore became necessary to establish ones influence in the corps

by making strategic associations and alliances. Latin America — our natural constituency — lacks cohesiveness and leadership. The Dean of the Latin American group — Venezuela is lazy and uninterested in leadership. The Cuban Ambassador is not very out-going. So I have had to maintain individual relationships especially with Cuba, Nicaragua and Mexico. Ecuador is also a good man. The African group is much more cohesive and influential in Moscow. They have also been very welcoming. My informal inclusion in the group has raised Grenada's profile and influence in the corps as a whole.

The socialist countries to which I am accredited are a[illeg.] area of interest. Of these, Bulgaria is the Dean and has little time for socio-political interaction. Checoslovakia, GDR and Rumania have been particularly warm. We have it as a high priority to establish and maintain the closest personal and official relations with these countries. And although the Korean Ambassador for example, is regarded as a recluse, I have had him over to dinner and he has reciprocated, as is the case with many of the others.

On the whole, I have formed the view that the USSR is satisfied with the degree of support that they receive from Grenada. Indeed, I would say that they have every reason to be satisfied especially if our vote on Afganistan for example, is recognized as one of two Latin American votes (the other being Cuba) in their favour. Considering the risks that we have taken on this and other matters, it might be fair to say that their support for us is actually below our support for them. We must therefore work to establish a balance of interests. This might best be done by gentle reminders at critical stages by members of our leadership. We might also seek to develop our links with what has been called the "middle" countries like Yugoslavia and Greece for example and strengthen our links with "off centre" countries like Korea, Rumania and Hungary. But these calculations have to be done very carefully and in a very sophisticated way. We have to think them out very carefully.

Recommendations

1. Continue our international support for the Soviet line.

2. Strengthen our political efforts in the UN and OAS and their agencies.

3. Seek a more critical role in the non-aligned movement.

4. Examine the desirability, ways and means of developing closer relations with the "middle" and "off centre" countries.

5. Provide all missions with a regular common fund of knowledge so that there can be a guarantee that a common line is being pursued on all matters.

VI-6
Report on Grenadian Students at Moscow Political Training Course
5/23/83

This report was submitted by Grenadian ambassador W. Richard Jacobs. It describes training received by Grenadian students at the international political school run by the Soviet Communist Party. This school, well-known to scholars of Communism as the "Lenin School," has traditionally trained the leading cadres of pro-Soviet Communist parties, both in and outside the Soviet bloc.

EMBASSY OF GRENADA IN THE USSR

Dobryninskaya Ulitsa 7	*Telephone*
Apartment 221	*237-25-41*
Moscow	*237-99-05*
USSR	

Course name: WCM — World Communist Movement
SPP - Social Psychology and Propaganda
- Historic Experience of the CPSU

Name of Students

School name	Real name
Femr Achebe	Derrick James
David Gill	Sam Braithwaite
Justin Lorainey	Fabian Outram
Bill Jordan	Anselm DeBourg
Francis Che	Glen Noel
Bernadine Peters	Rita Joseph
David Allen	Ian Lambert
Dave Gordon	Andre Mc. Queen

John Franklyn   Ronnie Spooner
       -                   William St. Louis
       -                   Gordon Raeburn
       -                   Roy Cooper
       -                   Patrick Superville
       -                   Fred Burris

EMBASSY OF GRENADA IN THE USSR

Dobryninskaya Ulitsa 7   *Telephone*
Apartment 221   *237-25-41*
Moscow   *237-99-05*
USSR

Report of meeting with Acting Rector of the CPSU party school
Gaiduz Oleg P. 23rd, May 1983

This meeting between the Acting Rector and the Ambassador was arranged at the request of the Ambassador to receive
a confidential assessment of the performance of our students
during the six-month course just completed.

The Acting Rector informed the Ambassador that normally,
it is necessary to apply to the International Department of the
CPSU in order to receive an official report of the performance
of the students. However, in this case, since this was the first
batch of Grenadian students he would be prepared to make
available to the Party (NJM) the confidential assessments of
their teachers as well as to communicate to the Ambassador
in a confidential manner, the general opinion of the teachers
regarding the overall performance of our students. The
Ambassador thanked the Acting Director for his cooperation
in that matter and pointed out that he will also request an
official report from the CPSU.

The Acting Director reported that since this was the first
group of Grenadians to attend the school, it was the policy of

the administrators and teachers to pay very close and careful attention to the performance and behaviour of the students. After a collective assessment of the students, he could inform the Ambassador that he was expressing the unanimous opinion of the teachers and administrators of the school.

The students fully covered the syllabus of the six month course. It was the view of the school however, that the students would have benefited more from a one year course.

As a whole the students were well disciplined and oriented towards collective work. Minor evidences of indiscipline were never repeated once they had been identified and explained.

The internal relations of the group were generally good. Friction was kept to a minimum, problems were resolved in time, and due to the excellent leadership of Rita Joseph, the collective maintained a very marked cohesion throughout the course. It is worthy of note that Comrade Joseph was greatly helped in the exercise of her responsibility and authority by the following Comrades: Gordon Raeburn, Ronnie Spooner, Ian Lambert and Fabian Outram.

Comradely relations between members of the group steadily improved over the period of six months.

Attendance at classes was excellent, but punctuality was occasionally weak.

All comrades displayed a conscientious attitude towards their work.

With the sole exception of Fred Burris, our students actively participated in classroom discussions. They always adopted a very serious attitude towards the work, asked relevant questions and all except Burris have been assessed as having achieved good to excellent knowledge. Burris was satisfactory.

All the students made consistent efforts to link up the theoretical points with the tasks to which they have been assigned by the NJM. This was particularly true of Ian Lambert, Rita Joseph and Roy Cooper.

There was a marked difference in cultural levels of the students as well as in levels of health. Both Fred Burris and Andre Mc Queen (David Gordon) were ill for long periods. A Report on Mc Queen's illness is enclosed.

The group took several good initiatives, and undertook the responsibilities associated with these initiatives. Three examples: Celebration of the 10th. Anniversary of the NJM, 4th. Anniversary of the Revolution, Round table solidarity Conference of the Amaricas.

As part of their practical work, the group had a permanent link with the CPSU Party committee of the October factory. They went to the factory on several occasions, participated in voluntary work on two occasions and had a lecture on the cost accounting procedures of the factory. The management of the factory was pleased with the students' performance and the students were satisfied with their experience.

The two most outstanding students were: Rita Joseph and Ian Lambert. The weakest student was Fred Burris. The teachers considered that Burris would be well placed in an area of work requiring inter-personal relations with non-intellectual workers. He can carry out instructions and is very tenacious in his determination to implement agreed procedure, but he is neither an intellectual nor initiator.

The Acting Rector said that the performance of our students demonstrate a real thirst for knowledge and he recommended that the NJM think very seriously about the establishment of a Party School as a top priority. He pointed out that there were very positive achievements as a result of the establishment of the Party School in Yemen, Afganistan, Angola, Mozambique and very soon Ethiopia. In this context he suggested that the NJM might think of sending students who could qualify as teachers in the future Party School.

In closing the Acting Director said that he would like to emphasize that the teachers and Administrators had come to develop great respect for the abilities of Rita Joseph as a leader. In the beginning they were a bit apprehensive about her ability to manage thirteen men and she was a bit shakey in the beginning, but as time went on, it emerged that it was a wise decision.

[signature]

W. Richard Jacobs

VI-7
Report of Lenin School Student
10/8/83

In this originally handwritten letter, an NJM member studying at the "Lenin" educational facility in Moscow describes the curriculum and activities pursued by the students (see previous document). Aside from personnel drawn from such "liberated" countries as Nicaragua, Angola, and Mozambique, this report notes the presence at the school of "comrades" from other Soviet-leaning nations, including Ethiopia and Syria, as well as from South Africa, Colombia, England, and Denmark.

"RSDLP" is the Russian Social-Democratic Labor Party, predecessor of the Soviet Communist Party. A "subbotnik" is a workday donated to the state, usually falling on a Saturday (from the Russian **subbota***).*

---

8 October 1983
Moscow

Cde. Strachan,

Attached is the first report from the group for our first month's activity. Other things have happened since then but I will include them in the next report which I hope to send down with whoever comes to represent us at the November 7 activity.

Everything is basically alright — the course is going fine, but plenty work — writing, reading reporting, etc.

Since writing the report, Cde. [illeg.] has left for Moscow Central [illeg.].

We are anxious for a reponse to the report and further directives.

Greetings to everyone!

[illeg.]

[signature]

Hazel-Ann

REPORT TO N.J.M. ORGANISING COMMITTEE
FROM PARTY CELL AT CPSU INTERNATIONAL
1st - 30TH SEPTEMBER, 1983

1. Introduction
2. Course Outline
3. Internal Structure
4. Cell Assessment
5. Non-Academic Activities
6. Moscow Party Branch
7. Needs
8. Issues for Party's Attention & Decisions
9. Conclusions

I. INTRODUCTION

1.1 The Comrades comprising the party cell [illeg.] International Leninist School, as [illeg.] are — [illeg.] Neckles, Albert Alexander [illeg.] Bernadette Smith, [illeg.] Hazel Ann [illeg.]

1.2 We left Grenada 27th August for [illeg.] Havana. Flight problems resulted in our [illeg.] days in Cuba and arriving in Moscow [illeg.]

1.3 This report covers the period 1st [illeg.] They will continue during the acade [illeg.] monthly basis.

2 COURSE OUTLINE

2.1 Our classes started on September 6th with the Russian language which lasted for three (3) weeks amounting to fifty (50) hours. We completed this course by performing an Auction Sale in Russian for the school audience of mainly new students — Friday 30th.

2.2 The school week is from Monday to Saturday, with General Lectures on Monday and specific topics on the other days — up to Saturday.

2.3 Our present course is comprised by the following topics:
   i) Historical Experience of the CPSU
   ii) Internal Relations
   iii) Political Economy
   iv) Philosophy
   v) Theory & Tactics of the World Revolutionary Movement

The following gives an idea as to the subject matter we have completed or are presently doing under each topic:

NO.	TOPIC	SUBJECT MATTER/SUB-TOPIC
1.	Historical Experience - CPSU This topics ends on the 3rd week in March and our "Final Talks" is one week later.	— Formation of RSDLP — The Leninist Stage in the development of Marxism — Historic Destinies of Marx's Teachings — Ideological and Theoretical Foundation of the Leninist Party — Features of the Party of a New Type — Sections of "What Is To Be Done?"
2.	International Relations This is short — Only 48 hours ending 1st week in December. No "Final Talks."	— Structure & General Features of International Relations — What is International Relations? — Peaceful Co-Existence concept — Proletarian internationalism — The three (3) sub-sections that exist in International Relations

		— Problems of War & Peace
		— Disarmament: USA-USSR Negotiations
		— War, Nuclear Weapons
3.	Political Economy This ends 2nd week in April; "Final Talks" one week later.	— Economic Map of USSR
		— Capitalist Mode of Production & Stages of its development
		— Capitalism's Place In The History of Society
		— History of Society
4.	Philosophy — Finishes 4th week in May; "Final Talks" in 1st week of June.	— Emergence of Philosophy
		— Development of Philosophical Thinking in Ancient Greece
		— What is Philosophy?
5.	Theory & Tactics of the World Revolutionary Movement. Finishes 2nd week of May; "Final Talks" 3rd week of May.	— Lenin's definition of Strategy & Tactics
		— Sections of the Communist Manifesto: chapters 1 & 2
		— The First, Second & Third Internationals
		— The World Revolutionary Process In The Contemporary Epoch

2.2 Apart from these five topics, another three will be added upon completion of the initial five. The following explains:

NO.	TOPIC	STARTING DATE	COMPLETION DATE
1.	Party Organisation	4th week of December	3rd week of June
2.	Theory of Management of National Economy	4th week of April	3rd week of June
3.	Social Psychology & Propaganda	2nd week of December	2nd week in June

2.3 We are expected to participate in a theoretical conference from 3rd February - 27th March on the topic — "A Revolutionary Party Is The Vanguard of Our Time." If possible, we will appreciate the Party's assistance in this regard — ideas for approach, content, creative application to our situation, etc.

2.4 Besides the theoretical party the school's plan is for us to participate in practicals. There will be two such activities.

---

3. CELL STRUCTURE

3.1 The following comrades represent our collective at these school committees:

i)	Monitors	: Merril
ii)	Hostel	: Deborah
iii)	Canteen	: Neckles (?!)
iv)	Sports	: Albert
v)	Culture	: Bernadette
vi)	Group Leaders	: Hazel-Ann

3.2 Our cell meetings are held forthnightly to discuss:

  i) Reports
  ii) Criticism & Self-criticism
  iii) Any Other Matters

For the period, we have had two such meetings — 5 and 19 September, each for a duration of about 90 minutes.

3.3 We have developed a system for checking individuals' level of preparation for classes by organising a study chart for comrades to mark their level using a scoring system of 0-5. However, we have to improve on the level of supervision of this to ensure that this works and achieves its objective.

3.4 Additionally, the cell meets four nights weekly for the purpose of collective study which entails revision of the subjects covered for the pervious days and preparation for the next days class. It takes place on Monday, Wednesday and Friday from 9:00 p.m. - 11:00 p.m. and Sundays from 10:a.m. - 12:00 noon. But the Sunday time may vary depending on whether school activities are organised for that day.

4. CELL ASSESSMENT

4.1 The cell is close and very united. We have not had any internal problems as yet.

4.2 Cde. Neckles up to now has not been able to start his classes as yet because of ill health. The doctor's report is that he has high pertension and is sick with his heart. He has been kept in the isolation unit at the school, but is due to leave for the Central Moscow Hospital for medical treatment. No indication as to how long he will remain there has been given as yet.

This is an area of concern for the group and one the Party will have to consider because the doctors have said that he must not study hard, but the work here requires hard study and already he has lost one month. The relevant decision will have to be taken by the Party.

4.3 Deborah Roberts was hospitalised for two weeks because of additional problems. She has now returned and is 'picking up' what she has missed in the period.

5. NON-ACADEMIC ACTIVITIES

5.1 We have had thorough medical examinations by — general physician, eye, bone, skin and ENT specialists, neurologist and dentist. We are [illeg.] to X-ray and heart examinations during the coming month.

5.2 The cell has been brought on two excursions organised by the school:

i) Sunday, 11 September — Lenin's house in Gorky where he lived from 1918-1923.

ii) Sunday, 18 September — Tour of Moscow: Red Square, Kremlin, etc.

5.3 We attended activities hosted by the English and German collectives to celebrate their respective parties' anniversaries.

5.4 Our cell has developed contacts with our colleagues in the Nicaraguan, Angolan, Mozambique, Ethiopian, South African, Syrian, Colombian and Denmark collectives. In particular, we have developed close contacts with the

Jamaican collective, and also have contacts with other groups.

5.5 Our active participation in sports has not started as yet. The same goes for culture.

5.6 On October 18 we will take part in the Soviet Subbotnik — Soviet Voluntary [illeg.] work.

6. MOSCOW PARTY BRANCH

6.1 So far, we have attended one meeting and study session of the branch. All comrades have paid their September Party dues.

7. NEEDS

7.1 We need the following items for activities we will be having:
  — Party, Revolution, National Flags (all sizes)
  — Posters
  — Party Emblem
  — View cards
  — Large pictures or posters of leadership
  — buttons or tokens
  — Party Literature — Jewel, Posters, etc. . . .
  — Important taped speeches of the leadership
  — Updated list of achievements
  — local craft and other items — . . .

7.2 Analysis of the present political situation

7.3 Regular newspapers and other literature

8. ISSUES FOR PARTY'S ATTENTION & DECISIONS

8.1 Resource material and ideas for our participation in the theoretical conference (Earliest)

8.2 Issue of Cde. Neckle's illness [illeg.]

8.3 We are all anxious as to whether arrangements made for salary payments are working properly.

8.4 . . .

8.5 A deputy leader of the group needs to be designated.

8.6 We would appreciate a critical response to this report.

9. CONCLUSION

9.1 The Party cell has been informed of the recent analysis, decisions and thinkings of the Central Committee.

9.2 We first of all, congratulates the C.C. on having reached this conclusion and for what it signifies. We believe that it is one of the most (if not the most) positive developments in the Party's history because it really shows the Marxist-Leninist character or tendency of our Party and is a concrete manifestation of our proclaimed adherence to the Marxist-Leninist principle of constructive criticism and self-criticism from the highest to the lowest bodies within the organisation.

9.3 For us, what we can do towards the solution of the crisis is of paramount importance for us to know. In the meantime, we have discussed the issue and have decided that under the present conditions, we pledge to take a more serious and Leninist approach to our ideological training.

9.4 Our other specific questions, comments and suggestions have been done through the Party Branch.

9.5 We take this opportunity to express our deep concern about the situation as analysed by the cc; our confidence in the Party's leadership and our collective ability to avert the situation through hard, organised, systematic, self-critical, Leninist-type work. The CPSU International Leninist NJM Party Cell repledges our commitment to the Party; to building a strong Party on Marxist-Leninist principles and to the defense and building of the Revolution along the lines that would bring us to achieving Socialism.

    Long Live our Party!

                    Hazel-Ann
                    Moscow

                    [illeg.]

AGREEMENT

ɪn cooperation between the New JEWEL Movement
of Grenada and the Communist Party
of the Soviet Union

ᴇ Central Committee of the New JEWEL Movement of Grenada and the Central Committee
ɔommunist Party of the Soviet Union,

ɟided by the desire to deepen relations between the two parties in ᴇ ꜱpirit of friendship
idarity,

ɔting that common commitment to the ideals of peace, national liberation, democracy and
ɪc socialism creates favourable opportunities for cooperation,

ɾoceeding from common goals in the struggle against imperialism, neocolonialism, racialism
action in all their forms and manifestations,

ᴇasserting their constant striving to render internationalist support to all peoples fighting for
freedom, independence and social progress,

ɑnd considering that inter-party cooperation is a most important basis for the development of
y relations between the peoples of Grenada and the Soviet Union,

have signed the present Agreement under which both parties declare their intention:

1. Steadfastly to extend and deepen their cooperation at all levels.

2. Continuosly to exchange experience in party work and party guidance of the social, eco-
ɪ and cultural development of their countries, including regular exchange of information and
ɪials on the aforesaid topics.

3. Regularly to exchange delegations of party workers, to conduct consultations and ex-
ɡes of opinion on international matters, problems of the world revolutionary process and
ᴢnt-day social development, and other matters of mutual interest.

4. To promote cooperation in the training of party and government cadres and in furthering
political competence.

5. To develop contacts between the party press and other mass communication media, to in-
the public of their countries about the activity of the two parties, and of their home and fore-
policy, and resolutely to combat hostile imperialist and reactionary propaganda.

6. To promote all-round development of inter-state relations and ties between mass or-
ɪisations of their countries.

7. Periodically to coordinate and implement concrete plans of inter-party ties, including ini-
ivesᵗhat are not covered by the present Agreement.

ɪR THE NEW JEWEL　　　　　　　　　　　　　　FOR THE COMMUNIST PARTY
ɔVEMENT OF GRENADA · · · ·　　　　　　　　　　OF THE SOVIET UNION

Moscow 27 July 1982

СОГЛАШЕНИЕ

о сотрудничестве между Коммунистической партией Советского Союза и партией Новое движение ДЖУЭЛ Гренады

Центральный Комитет Коммунистической партии Советского Союза и Центральный Комитет партии Новое движение ДЖУЭЛ Гренады,

руководствуясь стремлением углублять отношения между двумя партиями в духе дружбы и солидарности,

отмечая, что общая приверженность идеалам мира, национального освобождения, демократии и научного социализма создает благоприятные возможности для сотрудничества,

исходя из общности целей в борьбе против империализма, неоколониализма, расизма и реакции во всех формах и проявлениях,

подтверждая свое неизменное стремление оказывать интернационалистскую поддержку всем народам, борющимся за свою свободу, независимость и социальный прогресс,

учитывая, что межпартийное сотрудничество является важнейшей основой развития дружественных отношений между народами Советского Союза и Гренады,

подписали настоящее Соглашение, в соответствии с которым обе партии заявляют о своем намерении:

1. Неуклонно расширять и углублять свое сотрудничество на всех уровнях.

2. Постоянно осуществлять обмен опытом партийной работы, партийного руководства социальным, экономическим и культурным развитием своих стран, включая регулярный обмен информацией и материалами по указанным вопросам.

3. Регулярно обмениваться делегациями партийных работников, проводить консультации и обмен мнениями по международным вопросам, проблемам мирового революционного процесса и современного общественного развития и другим вопросам, представляющим взаимный интерес.

4. Содействовать сотрудничеству в области подготовки партийных и государственных кадров и повышения их политического уровня.

5. Развивать контакты между партийной печатью и другими средствами массовой информации, знакомить общественность своих стран с деятельностью обеих партий, их внутренней и внешней политикой, давать решительный отпор враждебной империалистической и реакционной пропаганде.

6. Способствовать всестороннему развитию межгосударственных отношений и связей между массовыми общественными организациями двух стран.

7. Периодически согласовывать и осуществлять конкретные планы межпартийных связей, включая в них и те инициативы, которые не были отражены в настоящем Соглашении.

За Коммунистическую партию
Советского Союза

(подпись)

27 июля 1982 года

За партию Новое движение
ДЖУЭЛ Гренады

(подпись)

Agreement in English and Russian between Soviet Communist Party and the Grenadian New Jewel Movement

MINISTRY OF INTERIOR

~~PRIME MINISTER'S~~
~~BELMONT~~
~~GRENADA~~

BUTLER HOUSE
ST. GEORGE'S
GRENADA
WEST INDIES

TEL: 3383 3020

17th Feb 19 82

TO: Commander Andropov
        Chairman of the Committee of State Security
        Member of Politburo

FROM: General of the Army Hudson Austin

Dear Comrade,

Warmest revolutionary greetings to you, the Communist
Party of Soviet Union and all Soviet people, from the
Political Bureau of the New Jewel Movement, Government, Armed
Forces and all the Grenadian people.

Let me first of all extend our deepest sympathies to your
Party and people on the passing away of comrade Suslov a true
Bolshevik and hero of revolutionary people worldwide, I WRITE AT THIS TIME, TO
~~Secondly, I write this letter in the form of a~~ request ~~to~~
assistance in the strengthening of our Ministry of Interior.
This request stems from discussions HELD BETWEEN Cde. Vladmir
Klimentov, then attached to the Soviet Embassy in Jamaica,
~~During the course of these discussions held with~~ held Comrade
Maurice Bishop, Chairman of the Central Committee of our Party
the New Jewel Movement, Prime Minister and Minister of Defence
and Interior of the People's Revolutionary Government, ~~and~~
~~and~~ Comrade Liam James, Member of the Central Committee of our
Party and Head of the Ministry of Interior and myself.

Request to Soviet Union for training in counter-
intelligence (document II-1), first page

MINISTRY OF DEFENCE

FORT RUPERT

GRENADA

ST. GEORGE'S

WEST INDIES

TELEPHONE: 2265 2178

17th February 19 82.

TO: MARSHAL DIMITROV USTINOV,

MINISTER OF DEFENCE,

USSR.

FROM: MINISTER OF DEFENCE, MAURICE BISHOP.

Dear Comrade,

Revolutionary greetings to you, the Communist Party of the Soviet Union and all Soviet people, from the Political Bureau of the New Jewel Movement, Government, Armed Forces and all the Grenadian people.

I am writing this letter to you in reference to training for personnel of the Grenadian Armed Forces in your country.

Based on Article Three of the Signed Protocol between the Government of Grenada and the Government of the USSR of 27th October, 1980 in Havana, Cuba, I hereby make the following request –

1. Military preparation for twenty(20) Junior Officers in the following areas in courses lasting a period of one year;

.../ -2-

Request to Soviet Union for military training (document II-11), first page

The hopeful beginning: Maurice Bishop's rebel forces
during the 1979 anti-Gairy coup (Wide World photo)

Sir Eric Gairy (Wide World photo)

Maurice Bishop with Fidel Castro (Bettman
Archive photo)

Bernard Coard (Bettman Archive photo)

Unison Whiteman addresses the Organization of
American States (Wide World photo)

Jacqueline Creft, companion of Maurice Bishop, executed with him

Hudson Austin (Wide World photo)

Russian construction machinery on site of airport project (Wide World photo)

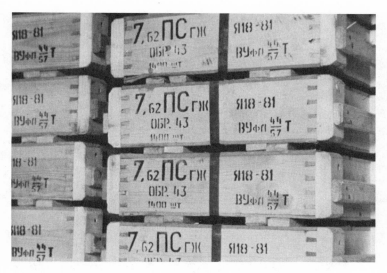

Russian ammunition captured on Grenada
(Wide World photo)

The final act: Russian armored cars, following
the orders of Coard's faction, attack Fort Rupert,
minutes before the killing of Maurice Bishop
(Wide World photo)

A closer view of Russian armored cars approaching Fort Rupert as civilians flee (Wide World photo)

Bishop's killers (see "Interviewing George Louison," by Bernard Diederich, *Caribbean Review* [Miami], Fall 1983)—This poster was issued by the intervention forces (On Victor Husband, see document III-6)

Marshal of the Soviet Union Nikolai V. Ogarkov (see document VI-3) discusses defense policy (Wide World photo)

VII
GRENADA AND THE SOCIALIST INTERNATIONAL

One of the most complex problems of Grenadian politics, revealed by the following documents, consists of the role played by the Grenadian government party in a coordinated attempt to disrupt the activity of the Socialist International, the worldwide organization of Socialist and Social Democratic parties.

Founded in the late nineteenth century, the International was the leading force in the left and labor movements until the end of the first world war. As in the past, the International today is dominated by the large Socialist parties of Western Europe, which use the International both as a kind of clearinghouse for political activities and as a forum for international policy debate. In the latter role, the International has become increasingly important in the Central American and Caribbean region, and in the Western European controversy on East-West relations.

Since the 1960s, the International has been marked by a split between its "left," led by the West German Social Democratic Party, along with the Dutch and Scandinavians, and its "center-right," consisting mainly of the Portuguese, the Spanish, and the Italians. The French Socialist Party has tended to hold to a middle course between the left-wing Germans and the right-wing Portuguese. The British Labour Party, meanwhile, although an affiliate of the International, has traditionally stayed out of most S.I. activities.

Increasingly, the main point of conflict in the International has been the question of socialist attitudes toward the Eastern Bloc. Historically, the Socialist International has been committed to the defense of Western democracy. In recent years, however, the West Germans and other leftists argued that the Western democracies should be more accepting of the realities of undemocratic rule in the Soviet sphere, and should steer away from alignment with the United States and from support for U.S. defense goals. The Portuguese, on the other hand, having wit-

nessed a serious Communist attempt to overthrow their nascent
democracy in 1975, were active Atlanticists.

With regard to Central America, the left wing of the International has criticized U.S. efforts to contain the activities of the
Sandinista regime in Nicaragua, while the center-right has
warned of the growth of totalitarianism in the region. However,
a change seems to be taking place: at the time of the publication
of this volume, the German Social Democrats appear to have
moved significantly away from their previous stance in en-
thusiastic support of the Sandinistas. Faced with the probability
of a hardening of totalitarian trends, in July 1984, the German
Social Democratic Party chose to give official support to the
democratic opposition group, the Coordinadora Democratica
Nicaraguense, in its boycott of the Nicaraguan elections. Simultaneously, Carlos Andres Perez, the social-democratic ex-
president of Venezuela who is consistently mentioned in the
Grenada papers as a Cuban nemesis, came out in full support of
Nicaraguan anti-communist revolutionary Eden Pastora Gomez.
(La Nacion, San Jose, Costa Rica, 19–25 July 1984).

With the Socialist International thus becoming ever more important as a forum for peace efforts in Central America, it is
probably not surprising that, through whatever means, pro-
Soviet forces would attempt to intervene directly in the S.I. to
influence the course of the debate. Documents appearing here
show that the Grenadian New Jewel Movement, which became a
member of the S.I. in 1980, served as a specific weapon of the
Cubans, the Nicaraguans, and their Soviet mentors. The New
Jewel Movement joined a secret pro-Soviet faction in the
International that included the Nicaraguan Sandinista party,
another S.I. member. The secret faction operated under the discipline of the Cuban Communist Party, which naturally is not
and could not become a public participant in the Socialist
International. The secret faction also brought together the People's National Party of Jamaica, led by Michael Manley, which
ruled that Caribbean island until 1980, and the Movimiento Nacional Revolucionario of El Salvador, a major component of the
Salvadoran guerrilla movement, led by Guillermo Manuel Ungo.

The documents on the S.I. discovered in Grenada include a
report on the S.I.'s discussions on Central America (document

VII-1) written by NJM member Unison Whiteman. This memorandum proves the existence of an overall strategy pursued by leftist forces in the Caribbean and Central American region to resolve the conflict in El Salvador in an unequivocally Marxist direction.

The same themes are visible in the rest of the Grenada-S.I. materials, including the minutes of the secret regional caucus, and the Fennis Augustine report on the S.I. presidium meeting in Bonn in 1982.

VII-1
Memo
Panama S.I. Meeting
3/3/81

The report on the Socialist International deliberations on Central America was prepared for the use of the NJM leadership.

Bernt Carlsson is a representative of the Swedish Social Democratic party. Carlos Andres Perez is the former president of Venezuela and head of that country's Accion Democratic party.

As noted in the introduction to this section, the Salvadoran Movimiento Nacional Revolucionario (M.N.R.), and the People's National Party of Jamaica (P.N.P.), appear here. At this meeting, the Salvadoran M.N.R. was represented by Hector Oqueli. The P.N.P. is headed by Michael Manley, prime minister of Jamaica until 1980.

TO: N.J.M. Leadership
FROM: Comrade Whiteman
SUBJECT: Emergency S.I. Meeting in Panama
DATE: March 3, 1981

The emergency S.I. meeting of Latin America and the Caribbean took place in Panama on Saturday, 28th February and Sunday, 1st March. Basically, it was a one item agenda; the situation in El Salvador.

There were representatives of the following countries:

Argentina, Barbados, Bolivia, Chile, Costa Rica, El Salvador, Ecuador, Guatemala, Grenada, Honduras, Panama itself, Peru, Puerto Rico, Dominican Republic, Venezuela, Uraguay and Nicaragua. P.N.P. was absent. From Europe came Spain, West Germany, France, Portugal and Sweden arrived. Brent Carlsson, Secretary General attended. Media coverage was wide.

The Conference was designed to counter these two carefully worked out tactics by the United States:

(1) To project the struggle of the people of El Salvador as a direct East West ("Communist - Capitalist") confrontation as a means of completely wiping out from the consciousness of the world the domestic causes, the oligarchy, the semi-feudel system, the incredible poverty of the masses.

(2) To show that the freedom fighters ("Marxist hardliners") do not want a negotiated settlement, that they prefer the bloodshed.

Because of airline difficulties, I missed the first day of the Conference. Although S.I. has a clear concensus on El Salvador, somehow Carlos Andre Perez insisted on adding the names of Cuba and the Soviet Union to the resolution demanding an end to the supply of arm to El Salvador! (He claims that he is not anti-Cuba or anti-Communist but that S.I. must appear to be objective and even handed. He also claims that he whole heartedly supports the El Salvador liberation struggle. This is strange because there was a quiet meeting where the military commanders in the field explained their need for support in this critical situation and Carlos agreed with them).

For hours he persisted. Sweden and Grenada spoke out forcefully on the issue. Grenada pointed out that the U.S. supply of arms to the junta is a notorious fact, that the U.S. officially and publicly stated this; that S.I. should not speculate on where the freedom fighters are getting arms from; that, in any event, we should not equate arms for the oppressors with weapons to defend the people in their just struggle.

Finally, the El Salvador Comrades said they were prepared to accept a compromise formula that names no country but makes it clear that it is the U.S. that is being condemned. The house accepted this approach.

It should be noted that Vernon Walters, the ex-deputy C.I.A. Director insisted on presenting to the meeting (he is on a tour of the region to drum up support for a U.S. invasion of El Sal-

vador and he happened to be in Panama by "coincidence")
proof of Cuban and Soviet arms supplies. This offer was not
accepted.

As a means of defeating the second U.S. tactics ("hardliners,
not wanting to negotiate"), the Conference offered the services
of S.I. Chairman, Willy Brandt as mediator in the conflict.

This initiative ensures that the U.S. cannot propose someone
favourable to their own interest. Brandt is sympathetic for the
freedom fighters but the U.S. will have difficulty rejecting him
for he is a Nobel Peace Prize Winner with stature world wide.

This counter tactic would therefore give the comrades time to
carry on the military and the political struggle together.

Another resolution expressed support for the Nicaraguan and
Grenada revolutionary processes and solidarity with the Government and people of Panama who were undergoing pressures from the U.S. There was also support for Michael Manley and for the independence of Puerto Rico.

A Working Group for Latin America and the Caribbean was
chosen. The members are Jose Pena Gomez, Carlos Andres
Perez, Hector Oqueli, Bernt Carlsson, N.J.M. and P.N.P. This
group will propose to S.I. structures and a work programme
for the region.

For a number of reasons, I proposed a regional conference in
Grenada in May. The conference enthusiastically accepted. Delegates from all over expressed interest in coming to Grenada
to the meeting and this will be extremely useful to us also. If
the N.J.M. Bureau ratifies this, plans for the conference will
have to begin soon after the Festival.

The General Secretary, Bernt Carlsson, will be visiting us for a
few days on April 18, and Pierre Schori sometime in May.
These are also two important visits for us since they are stal-
wart supporters of the revolution in S.I. and internationally.

.   .   .   .

Many of the leading comrades will be at the Aruba meeting. They look forward to seeing Comrade Maurice.

The next two major S.I. (International) events are the Party Leaders' Conference - Amsterdam - April 29, and the Bureau meeting - Tel Aviv on June 11, and 12. I strongly recomend that Comrade Maurice attend one of these.

P.S. On my way back from the Conference I noted the following from press reports:

(1) That the mission of Vernon Walters to the region has been considered a failure. Of course, he claims that his objective was not to gain support for a U.S. invasion of El Salvador but merely to explain and give evidence of Cuban and Soviet military involvement.

(2) That the big four Latin American powers: Argentina, Brazil, Venezuela and Mexico have issued a statement in Buenos Aires rejecting any U.S. intervention in El Salvador.

(3) That Duarte has agreed to participate in the mediation talks as proposed by Socialist International.

(4) That Bernt Carlsson is on his way to Washington to discuss the mediation offer with the State Department.

(5) That the U.S. has just announced a massive step up of military aid to El Salvador. (Many U.S. Senators, even Senator John Glenn who once supported such a policy are now opposed to this).

(6) It seems that both sides are applying the tactic of talk more, appear the one more willing to talk, but fight harder.

VII-2
Report
Bonn S.I. Presidium Meeting
4/1/82

This memorandum was delivered to Grenadian Foreign Minister Unison Whiteman by Fennis Augustine, reporting on a later meeting of the S.I. to discuss further Central American issues. At the meeting it is clear that the Grenadian representatives again served as agents for the Cubans and Soviets in seeking support for the Sandinista government in Nicaragua and for the guerrilla movement in El Salvador. The Grenadians also express distaste for the S.I.'s "unilateral and self-seeking mention of the subject of elections in Grenada."

The Chilean Radical Party, mentioned here, unlike the Grenadian NJM or the Jamaican P.N.P., has never been considered a Marxist or even a very left-wing party; it represents liberal intellectuals and business people. On the P.N.P., see the introduction to this section and the note to document VII-1. Felipe Gonzalez is the head of the Socialist government of Spain. Ed Broadbent is the head of the New Democratic Party in Canada.

To: Cde. Unison Whiteman, Foreign Minister
From: Cde. Fennis Augustine, High Commissioner

Report on Meeting of the Praesidium of Socialist International
held in Bonn, West Germany on 1-2 April 1982

I arrived at the Tulpenfeld Hotel, Bonn where most of the delegates were staying at about 4.00 p.m. Unfortunately, I was unable to obtain accommodation at that hotel. Arrangements were subsequently made for me at Astoria Hotel, a reasonable distance away from Tulpenfeld.

After settling in, I returned to Tulpenfeld. There was a meeting with the Cuban delegation, the Nicaraguan delegation, the British delegation which was headed by Michael Foot, leader of the Labour Party, the Guatamalan delegation, the Venezuelan delegation headed by Carlos Cuidros [Andres] Perez, a member of the Swedish delegation and Guillermo Lingo [Ungo] of the El Salvador delegation.

Before these meetings I spoke to representatives and later on Bernt Carlsson Secretary General of the Socialist International seeking observer status for Grenada at the meeting. The decision was firm that only members of the Praesidium and specially invited guest could attend. (The composition of the Praesidium is; President, General Secretary, six Honorary Presidents, and twenty-one Vice Presidents).

ISSUES:

The special meeting of the Praesidium was called because of the confusion existing in S.I. over a number of issues, one delegate said to me that if nothing is done about the present situation S.I. would lose credibility.

(a) The most immediate was the cancellation of the Bureau meeting which was to take place in Venezuela, when the party Democratic Action bowed to American pressure and refused to invite Nicaragua. It was cancelled on the personal intervention of Bernt Carlsson and Willy Brandt.

(b) The declaration by Nicaragua of a state of emergency, seen in the context of the debate taking place within S.I. as to the principles involved in Social Democracy i.e. elections, two party system, human rights question, freedom of religion, freedom of speech (free press).

(c) Disarmament - The recent visit of the S.I. disarmament committee to the Soviet Union within the context of world disarmament.

(d) The East - West conflict as it is seen being aggravated by Poland, Afghanistan and the debate about the relationship with Cuba.

The meeting started at 09.45 on the 1st April, although a number of delegations had not yet arrived. Some of the late arrivals were, French delegation, Israeli delegation, Austrian delegation, Jamaican delegation (only Michael Manley attended Cde. Paul Miller did not attend), Danish delegation and the Netherland delegation and the Chilean delegation Radical Party (Cde. Anselmo Sule was the only delegate attending)

Central America and the Caribbean was down for discussion in the afternoon session (see agenda attached) it generated the most interest.

My information is that the discussion on Central America and the Caribbean went very well, this is substantiated by the fact that:-

(a) There appear to be some dissatisfaction with Felipe Gonzales's report on Nicaragua - one delegate referred to the report as somewhat vague.

(b) A committee was appointed to draft resolution on the area (resolution attached) the composition of the committee was Ed Broadbent, Canada; Carlos Perez, Venezuelan; Michael Manley, Jamaica; and later on Gunselmo Sule was coopted.

(c) A decision was taken that Willy Brandt should appoint a committee to visit the area and report back (I asked Brent Carlsson that Grenada be included in the itinerary of the committee).

(d) It was decided that the S.I. Secretariat will continue to invite Nicaragua to attend its meeting, implication being disapproval with Democratic Action of Venezuela over its decision to exclude Nicaragua from the Bureau meeting in November.

I had a short discussion with Michael Manley — his stay was extremely short — he advised that based on the letter he received from Maurice, Grenada's case was put firmly by him. My understanding is that this was so, although there appear to be some confusion on the invitation. In a follow up discussion, Brent Carlsson informed me that N.J.M. will have to send our individual invitations to Sister Parties.

On the East/West question — it appears that the meeting supported West Germany's position on Ostpolitick and to press for constructive dialogue on disarmament.

Comments

Most sister parties seemed well disposed towards Grenada, although some have reservations on what they see as the Marxist thrust of the N.J.M. I believe that close relationship with Cuba will continue. Nicaragua's position is a little more difficult, although there was a great degree of understanding and sympathy for them by the time the meeting was finished.

.   .   .   .

VII-3
Report
Secret Regional Caucus
1/7/83

*This exceptionally important document was submitted to the New
Jewel leadership by Chris de Riggs, NJM participant in a meeting
held in Managua, Nicaragua, of the secret regional caucus set up by
Cubans to intervene in the Socialist International.*

*The Frente Sandinista de Liberacion Nacional (FSLN) is, of
course, the currently ruling party in Nicaragua. On the M.N.R.,
Chilean Radical Party, and P.N.P., see the introduction to this
section and notes to documents VII-1 and VII-2. W.P.A. is the
Working People's Alliance. ALDHU is a Latin American human
rights group. The U.D.P. (sic) is the New Democratic Party, Canada's third major political force.*

REPORT ON MEETING OF SECRET REGIONAL CAUCUS OF
[word missing] HELD IN MANAGUA FROM
6TH—7TH JANUARY, 1983

The following Organizations were represented:-

F.S.L.N.	- Nicaragua	- Antonio Marguin [Jarquin]
M.N.R.	- El Salvador	- Hector Oqueli
R.P.	- Chile	- Freda
P.N.P.	- Jamaica	- Paul Miller
P.C.C.	- Cuba	- Silva
N.J.M.	- Grenada	- Chris DeRiggs

. . . .

I. ANALYSIS

i) Regional Situation — the progressive forces are in control.

a) There are fourteen members of the S.I. Committee
for Latin America and the Caribbean.

Of these fourteen, there are seven parties that are generally progressive and some within a Marxist-Lennist trend.

There are three (3) new parties that have recently gained consultative observer status in S.I. They are:

(i). Puerto Rico.

(ii). W.P.A. - Guyana

(iii). P.L.P. - St. Lucia

The presence of these parties will help to strengthen the influence of the progressive forces within the Regional Committee. These parties can, in effect, function like full members of the organization. We must always consult with them and keep them informed.

2. EUROPE IN RELATION TO LATIN AMERICA

a) There are sharp divisions among the European parties in their outlook on Latin America.

b) Our friends in this area are prepared to accept the Latin American Revolutionary process as being palatable if restricted to the Latin American context.

c) There is a great amount of misunderstanding about Latin America both among our friends and our enemies — some amount of fear and uncertainty.

d) Many of the European S.I. parties expect us to understand the concept of "the Soviet Menace".

e) Some European parties are concerned that, by the Latin American presence in S.I., they have let in a [illeg.]

f) Many European Parties are willing to hold discussions with us at levels which indicate the contradictions among themselves -

   - the difference between Kryski of Austria and Braudl of Germany on the P.L.O. question.

g) Our strongest allies in Europe are the Nordic S.I. parties and that of Holland. There is also good potential with the U.D.P. of Canada.

h) Our principal enemies are to be found among the parties of Soares and Horgo in Portugal and Italy respectively — the Social Democrats of the U.S.A. are also our sworn enemies.

i) The reason why the European parties did not allow W.P.A. and P.L.P. to get beyond the consultative membership status is because of their fear of the growth of membership with parties that they do not control.

j) A Mission to Europe comprising of our most trusted forces in Latin America and the Caribbean can be strategically valuable before the Sydney Congress. It can help to assure our friends and confuse our enemies.

DECISIONS

1) The next meeting of the Broad Latin America Region S.I. Committee will be in any one of the following places:-

Las Paz - Bolivia
Mexico
Caracas
Canada

Michael Manley of P.N.P. and Anselmo Sule of P.R. will coordinate with B. Carlson of the S.I. Secretariat on this matter. Member parties will be informed accordingly.

2. A broad resolution on the Latin American and Caribbean situation will be passed at the meeting of the Regional Committee.

Agenda for this meeting will include:

a) Analysis of current political situation.

b) Attitudes to S.I. in Latin America

c) Issues for Sydney:

    i) New situation

    ii) Expansion of S.I.

d) S.I. Latin America Comtee:

    i) Structure

    ii) Staff

    iii) Officers

e) Christian Democracy in Latin America.

f) Actions to strengthen ALDHU.

g) Sydney Resolutions.

3. Hector Oquel of M.N.R. of El Salvador will draft a Resoultion on Latin America and the Caribbean by 31st January, 1983. This Resolution will be specifically for the Sydney Congress and will address only the most major issues.

The following guidelines will be the basis for the Resolution:-

(a) The Basle Resolution - including such themes like Peace and Non-Intervention, Anti-Militarisation in the Region, Anti-dictatorship, the settlement of disputes, etc.

(b) Solidarity with Nicaragua, Grenada and the F.D.R., F.M.L.N. and M.N.R. of El Salvador.

(c) A limited number of other key issues in the Region.

(d) The creation of a platform and frame of reference in S.I., the approach on the Latin America and Caribbean Region until the next Congress in Belgium (in the subsequent 2 years).

4. Subject to the approval of N.J.M., the next meeting of the Secret Regional Caucus of progressive S.I. parties will be in Grenada around the 13th and 14th March. This meeting will have strategic value in that it will provide the opportunity to:

i) Assess the results of the tour of Europe by the selected parties, and

ii) Conduct a final assessment on issues related to the Sydney Congress — questions of tactics and levels of co-ordination can also be discussed

. . . .

Submitted by,
CDE. CHRIS DE RIGGS.

VIII
CRISIS IN THE PARTY:
MINUTES OF THE NJM CENTRAL COMMITTEE

Once in power, the NJM organized itself as a communist party around a Politburo and Central Committee (C.C.). Nearly all government positions were held by NJM members, the most important ministries by "veterans" such as Bishop (Prime Minister), Selwyn Strachan (C.C. member and head of the militia), Hudson Austin (C.C. member, general of the army, and Minister of Communications), and Unison Whiteman (C.C. member and Minister of External Relations). Bishop, however, remained the unchallenged leader of the movement—largely, it seems, because of his charisma. Gairy had been a popular figure, especially among peasants, and Bishop was able to supplant him in the role of Grenadian hero on the strength of his magnetic oratory and personality.

In time, high-ranking party members came to view Bishop's leadership, and thus his "personality cult" among the "masses," as an obstacle to the revolution. As early as April 1982, criticisms of party administration on the part of Deputy Prime Minister Bernard Coard and his wife Phyllis (C.C. member and head of Radio Free Grenada) strained relations within the C.C. so badly that Coard resolved to resign. In October he made his intention public, sparking a period of self-criticism within the party. Already, Bishop's resignation was discussed in the context of a choice between a petit-bourgeois and communist route (document VIII-1). By summer of 1983 disaffection was growing. C.C. members complained of "deep petty bourgeois manifestations" and the failure of the party to "transform itself ideologically and organizationally" (document VIII-2). It seems, in short, that the NJM was not "making the transition" to the next, fully socialist stage of the revolution fast enough for some leaders. In the emergency meeting of late August (document VIII-3), Hudson Austin complained that even dedicated party workers were resigning their posts in disillusionment. The minutes reveal that blame for demoralization began to be laid at the door of the C.C. itself, and that tension was growing between NJM factions and their foreign Communist patrons.

The opposition to Bishop, led by the Coards and Minister of Interior Liam James (chief of security), raised its banner at the extraordinary meeting in September. The economic program was faltering; the propaganda apparatus was a flop (for instance, the masses had gone "backward ideologically" on the issues of "the Korean airliner and Afghanistan"; and the party itself was "crumbling." The root cause of these disasters was judged to be the C.C. itself, which (under Bishop's leadership) had taken "the path of right opportunism." This would "lead to the total disintegration of the party" unless the crisis was addressed on strict Leninist lines and the NJM "tightened" its relations with Cuba, East Germany, and the U.S.S.R. Phyllis Coard blamed Bishop by name for being irresponsible, disorganized, and providing no guidance. The C.C. then voted to invite Bernard Coard to rejoin the C.C. on a level of equality with Bishop and substitute joint for personal leadership within the committee. Bishop, finding himself in the minority, voted in favor of joint leadership (document VIII-4).

How should we interpret these events? Had the Coards been plotting against Bishop for years, or only since the period of "self-criticism" began in 1982? Was this a rebellion of disgruntled *apparatchiki* against an ineffective leader, or were other forces at work? The Coard faction perceived the crisis as a split between "petty bourgeois" and "real Leninist" factions over the nature of the revolution, accused Bishop's supporters of deviationism and called for firmer discipline if the NJM were to become a true Marxist-Leninist Party. On the other hand, Bishop considered himself a Leninist at least since 1979 (see Part III), and it was he who planted Grenada firmly in the Soviet camp. Did Bishop arouse suspicion because of his personal failings alone, or because he was not sufficiently Marxist-Leninist, or because of his meeting with U.S. officials earlier that year, or because he had lost the confidence of his foreign allies? The documents do not permit us to do more than speculate. In any case, the September decisions threatened to reduce Bishop's role to that of figurehead. That they did not go further might have been due to Bishop's abiding popularity.

On September 25 Bishop appeared to "surrender" to his critics. He admitted his errors, promised to purge his petit-bourgeois tendencies, and looked forward to working with Coard in the effort "to build a Marxist-Leninist party that can lead the people to socialism and communism" (document VIII-6). From September 27 to October 8 Bishop was abroad on state visits to Czechoslovakia and Hungary, and an unscheduled stop in Havana, where he conferred with Fidel and Raul Castro. Upon his return to Grenada, Bishop tried to recoup. He refused to implement "joint leadership," while his supporters rallied the militia and public with rumors that Coard intended to assassinate their leader. The opposition countered at the C.C. meeting on October 12. Coard's supporters called for Bishop's ouster and a purification of the party: "In the coming days we would not be talking about whether you are a party member or not, we will be talking about whether you are a communist or not" (document VIII-7). The C.C. then apparently voted to place Bishop under house arrest, and on October 14 Hudson Austin and Selwyn Strachan informed him of his expulsion from the Party.

VIII-1
Central Committee Meeting
10/15/82

*During the meeting described in these minutes, Bernard Coard's
theatrical "resignation" from the NJM central committee was de-
bated. The vagueness of the political points addressed reflects the
way such internal "theoretical" verbiage is often employed in Soviet
systems to mask struggles between personalities in which genuine
political or intellectual differences may play little role.*

*Following his "resignation," Coard apparently secured the re-
moval of two Bishop allies, Vincent Noel and Kenrick Radix, from
the Central Committee.*

*The demand for "stringent Leninist measures" implies an in-
crease in discretionary decision-making powers assigned to the
highest levels of party leadership.*

*On "democratic centralism," see note to document VI-5,
"Grenada-Soviet Relations, A Summary."*

MINUTES OF THE EXTRA-ORDINARY MEETING OF THE
CENTRAL COMMITTEE OF THE NJM NEW JEWEL MOVE-
MENT — FRIDAY 15th OCTOBER, 1982

Present:

Maurice Bishop	Ewart Layne
George Louison	Phyllis Coard
Selwyn Strachan	Leon Cornwall
Unison Whiteman	Kamau McBarnette
Kenrick Radix	Caldwell Taylor
Hudson Austin	Fitzroy Bain
Liam James	Ian St. Bernard
Chalkie Ventour	Ian Bartholomew
	Chris DeRiggs

On Tuesday 12th October, 1982, the Central Committee of
NJM was convened by CC Chairman Cde. Maurice Bishop in an

extra-ordinary plenary to discuss a letter of resignation from Cde. Bernard Coard, Deputy Party Leader and to examine the issues raised in the letter related to the state of the Party and the crisis in the work of the higher organs.

Within the period of the meeting, the CC held four sessions totalling 32 hours. The crisis in the work of the higher organs was analysed, the performance of each member of the CC was assessed and a number of decisions on the way forward were taken.

Subsequent to two hours of initial deliberations, the CC settled on an approach to the meeting. Cde. Strachan was asked to summarize his discussions with Cde. Coard in relation to the matter of his resignation. Cde. Strachan made the following points: —

   i) Cde. Coard had indicated that his decision to resign from PB and CC was taken 6 months previously;

   ii) His decision to resign from CC was primarily on account of strain but this was hastened by certain developments — linked to this was the undermining of his authority as Chairman of the OC.

   iii) He had made reference to the slackness of the CC and its unwillingness to speak up on issues, the lack of preparation for meetings by CC comrades, and the unwillingness of the CC to study.

   iv) In order to take corrective action it would result in personality clashes with the Chairman of the CC.

   v) His presence was a fetter to the development of the CC if viewed dialectically.

   vi) His resignation is not negotiable.

   vii) In the final analysis stringent Leninist measures are required.

The meeting also listned to what was explained to be the main theoretical options presented by Cde. Coard to the Central Committee: —

   i) His own resignation

   ii) He remains and tolerates slackness of CC and PB

   iii) Put all members of CC into work committees

   iv) Expand the Political Bureau

The meeting moved to address itself to the issues raised by Cde. Coard in his conversation with several CC members. Cde. Layne was asked to comment on resolutions and decisions taken by the Central Committee since April, 1981 relating to the introduction of Leninist measures in the Party. Cde. Layne pointed to the following: —

April, 1981: The resolution of the CC addressed itself to: —
   a. Tight chairmanship
   b. [word missing] application of high standards of discipline and self-critical approach by all committees
   c. The setting up of a Secretariat and appointment of Recording Secretaries.

September, 1981: Analysis was done on: —
   a. state of comrade's health
   b. lack of personal work plans

Decisions: —
   a. CC would meet once per month
   b. OC would draft schedule of rest for comrades
   c. CC members would do personal work plans

December, 1981:
   a. There was a lack of follow up work and a failure to implement major decisions.
   b. Information on decisions taken was not sent down to all levels of the Party.

April, 1982: The CC considered problems related to: —
   a. discipline   e. arrogance throughout the party
   b. study   f. work performance of members of
   c. standards   the higher organs
   d. planning   g. [word missing] of information

June, 1982: The OC analysis of the Party has indicated that:
   i) There was a collapse of nearly all areas of Party work, name: —
   a. workers   c. women
   b. youth   d. state

In this period the mood of the masses had been described as lower than May Day. The work of the OC had been described as bureaucratic and giving no guidance to work committees.

July, 1982: In discussing the present state of the Party, the following weaknesses were pointed out: —

a. control mechanisms were not working
b. there was looseness in Party organization
c. activities were controlling the work of the CC
d. a Party School was required for Party members to master the science of Marxism-Leninism

The CC agreed that there were certain recurring, glaring weaknesses: —

i) the improper functioning of Central Committee and Political bureau
ii) the lack of control at the level of Central Committee

Comrades also cited additional evidence of the crisis: —

i) lack of collectivity in building the Party — few PB and CC comrades were giving serious thought to the work and this resulted in low levels of participation in the work;
ii) PB and CC had been "ducking" the real issues;
iii) there was dead weight at CC and PB level and this urgently had to be addressed;
iv) the CC was not studying while seeking to tackle the most explosive issues of the Church and the land.

The CC also addressed itself to the Basis for the crisis:

1. Material Basis: The material basis for the crisis could be found in the backward and underdeveloped nature of our society and the consequent existence of a large petty bourgeois influence in our society. This predominant petty bourgeois composition of the society as a whole reflected in the practical work of the CC.
2. The Political and Ideological Basis: As seen in the failure of the CC to study for close to one year which has weakened the extent to which the ideology of Marxism-Leninism acts as a guide to the actions of the members

of the higher organs. This failure to study is definitely linked to the non-Leninist manner of functioning, slackness, timidity and "ducking" from making principled criticisms.

3. The Organisational Basis: Seen in the poor functioning of many Party structures, the non-Leninist practices of comrades of higher organs, the inadequate functioning of other Party members in work committees, the lack of reporting, and the objectively based — inability of the O.C. to deal with all matters of discipline further feeds and allows petty bourgeois tendencies to dominate the life of the higher organs of the Party.

CROSSROADS

The CC concluded that the Party stood at the crossroads: —

i The first route would be the petty bourgeois route which would seek to make B's resignation the issue. This would only lead to temporary relief, but would surely lead to the deterioration of the Party into a social-democratic Party and hence the degeneration of the Revolution. This road would be an easy one to follow given the objectively based backwardness and petty bourgeois nature of the society.

ii The second route is the Communist route — the road of Leninist standards and functioning, the road of democratic centralism, of selectivity, of criticism and self-criticism and of collective leadership. The Central Committee reaffirmed the position taken by the General Meeting of September 12th and 13th, 1982 — the Party must be placed on a firm Leninist footing.

VIII-2
Central Committee Plenary
7/19/83

Nine months after Bernard Coard's "resignation," the "July plenary" session of the NJM central committee, from which this report was developed, seems to have represented a turning point for the party leadership. As will be seen from the discussions in the documents that follow, Coard's supporters later expressed consistent dissatisfaction with the conclusions produced by this meeting.

However, in the report itself, it is difficult to detect the sources of these complaints. On its face, the "July plenary" produced little or nothing of a controversial nature. The most convincing argument would seem to be that Coard's followers were to become irritated over the failure to carry out with sufficient speed the decisions specified here. But this criticism may have served as a mere cover for Coard's drive toward more power. Thus, references to "petty bourgeois manifestations and influence" in the NJM may represent no more than the use of political insults to mask personal competitiveness and factional maneuvering.

We should note here the proposal for introduction of political education "for all primary school students" (cf. document IV-3, "Analysis of the Church"). Perhaps more importantly, the NJM leadership suggested that the Grenadian private sector be encouraged to pursue investment opportunities under the U.S.-sponsored Caribbean Basin Initiative, but added that "this area must be closely monitored to ensure that the capitalists are not provided with an effective new base for covert activity by the USA."

<u>CENTRAL COMMITTEE REPORT ON FIRST PLENARY SESSION</u>
<u>13—19 JULY, 1983</u>

Historically the Central Committee has met on many occasions to analyse all areas of the Party, State and Mass Work. This, however, is the first full scale, wholistic plenary of the C.C.

Between Wednesday 13th July, 1983 and Tuesday 19th July, 1983, the C.C. of N.J.M. spent six and a half (6 1/2) days in plenary — a total of 54 hours assessing all areas of Party, Mass and State work. The strengths and weaknesses of the Party's performance were highlighted and a number of conclusions were made.

SECTION I

A(i) <u>Main Feature</u>

> In its analysis of the present political and economic situation, the main feature was identified as follows:-

>> The continued failure of the Party to transform itself ideologically and organisationally and to exercise firm leadership along a Leninist path in the face of the acute complexities and difficulties facing the Revolution on all fronts — economic, political, social, military and international.

> <u>THE PARTY</u>

> Over the period under review our Party has demonstrated many weaknesses — ideologically, politically and organisationally. At the same time, the emergence of deep petty bourgeois manifestations and influence in the Party has led to two ideological trends, . . . In the face of all of this, there was a slowing down of the important task of Party Building.

(ii) OTHER FEATURES OF THE PERIOD

The complexity of the period is further demonstrated by the following:-

. . . .

REGIONAL

(a) The continued victories of FMLN in El Salvador.

(b) The growth of left and progressive organisations in the Caribbean, together with the growing positive sentiments towards Grenada in the OECS countries and the growth of our mass base in the Caricom territories as a whole.

(c) The improving relations with World Socialism and some Caricom countries.

(d) The growing contradictions among and within Caricom countries.

(e) Our improving relations with some key Latin American countries eg. Columbia and Argentina.

(f) Growth in formal and informal relations between Grenada and other Caricom countries making it objectively more difficult for U.S. imperialism to achieve their strategic objective of isolating Grenada.

(g) Our developing relations with Trinidad.

. . . .

REVIEW OF THE LINE OF MARCH

During the plenary, the CC reviewed the Line of March of the Party which was laid down in September '82. It was agreed that the Line of March is correct and will continue to be pursued in this upcoming period.

. . . .

Re (2) IDEOLOGICAL WORK

(a) Workers Education Classes will commence in the private sector.

(b) The appropriate steps re the implementation of this decision will be worked out by the Workers Committee and the Ministry of National Mobilisation.

(c) A special programme for these classes will be developed by the Socialism Tutors Committee.

(d) The ideological work among the farmers to be stepped up.

(e) The NYO to make more creative use of their radio programme on RFG.

(f) Political education for all primary school students.

(g) Political education for all teachers.

. . . .

REVIEW OF PARTY COMMITTEES & PILLARS OF THE RE-
VOLUTION

The Central Committee further analysed all other areas of Party work:

(1) ECONOMY

The Central Committee analysed the economic sectors of the country and noted the following:-

(i)   Problems/Difficulties: Continued serious negative effects of cash flow on capital programmes with:-

a. Threat to halt investment on key investment projects eg. Airport, GFC, Machinery Pool, Agro-industries, etc.

b. Have shaken the confidence of broad sections of the masses and provided the basis for some vicious rumours.

(ii)   Continued weak performance of the productive
        sectors — eg. Agro-Industries, Fisheries,
        Tourism.

(iii)   The failure of one of our most strategic sector
        to get moving — marketing (export).

(iv)   1983/1984 will be difficult years and requiring
        maximum efforts of the Party on the economic
        front hence the ideological work has to be
        stepped up to combat consequent difficulties
        that these two years will pose for us.

(v)   Extreme difficulties in mobilising external fi-
        nance and receiving already promised
        amounts.

On the positive side:-

(i)   Continued progress in the structural adjust-
        ments of the economy:-

        a. increased domestic savings.

        b. continued positive reduction in the food im-
            port bill, from 27.5% in one year to 25.5%.
            At March 13, 1979, it was 40%.

        c. sizable sections of our overall imports con-
            tinue to be capital goods for investment and
            not for consumption.

        d. decrease in the rate of inflation and holding
            down.

        e. drop in unemployment — increase in jobs.

(ii)   The rise in the production and export of tradi-
        tional crops.

(iii)   Continued good performance in export of non-
        traditional crops.

(iv)   Further growth in the state ownership of the
        banking sector.

(v)   Bringing under state control of approximately
        5000 new acres of land.

(vi)   Improved performance of GFC.

(vii)   Continued good performance of MNB on the
         commercial side.

(viii)   Continued growth in the capital programme
         despite all the difficulties.

(ix)   The commencement of long term trade with
         the socialist community.

(x)   Continued progress in state planning.

(xi)   Acquisition of Holiday Inn — Grenada Beach
         Hotel.

(xii)   Grenada's improved credit rating.

(xiii)   We have been able to mobilise massive external
         assistance over the first four and a half years
         of the Revolution.

After much deliberations, the Central Committee concluded:-

(i)   The creation of a Ministry of State Enterprises,
         with Cde. George Louison as the Minister and
         two Boards of Directors: the productive sphere
         headed by George and the non-productive by
         Lyden Ramdhany.

(ii)   The major projects for collaboration in the up-
         coming two years will be:-

         a. a new 20 m watt power station to be sought
             from the USSR;

         b. Tourist development:

             seven (7) 150 room hotels through joint
             ventures, dummy companies and the
             bourgeoisie.

         c. Water expansion, with Soviet assistance.

         d. Road network (40 miles of main roads, farm
             and feeder roads with assistance from Cuba
             and the CDB.

         e. The industrialisation of the geographic reg-
             ions — agro-industries, etc. from Bulgaria,
             DPRK and Czechoslovakia.

(iii)   The continuation of our land policy and the study of the possibility of the state securing more land for agriculture.

(iv)   A Ministerial delegation led by Lyden Ramdhany to visit Lybia re a grant. A three man Party delegation led by Cde. Nelson Louison to visit Lybia.

(v)   The private sector must be encouraged to explore opportunities in the area of investments by the CBI. However, this area must be closely monitored by the Party to ensure that the capitalists are not provided with an effective new base for covert activity by the USA.

(vi)   Ensure that our Caricom partners continue to give us limited solidarity on the trade and investment position of the CBI.

(2) INTERNATIONAL WORK
Foreign Affairs

The C.C. analysed the international relations work of the Party and State and concluded that there was a significant improvement in the quality of this work.

The C.C. noted that the main feature of the international situation was the increased aggression of U.S. imperialism under the leadership of the Reagan Administration which is planning to deploy nuclear weapons in Western Europe leading to a heightening of East West tension and a grave danger to peace and World civilisation.

The C.C. noted that regionally, there is the beginnings of a shift in the balance of forces in Caricom towards Grenada, as a result of:-

a. the continued economic problems of Caricom countries

b. Some Caricom countries are contesting seats in regional and international organisations.

c. the increasing respect on the economic front for
    Grenada's achievements.

However, it is too early to determine how long this
will last.
The C.C. concluded that in seeking to greatly improve
this work there is need to:-

1. Step up the work in the USA, Western Europe and
    the Caribbean, especially Trinidad.

2. Reorganize the Ministry of Foreign Affairs to en-
    sure national and strategic deployment of the staff.

3. Ensure greater co-ordination between Ministry of
    Foreign Affairs and the International Relations De-
    partment of the Party.

4. Develop a team in monitoring of Foreign Affairs to
    study International Relations.

5. Follow up on all new relations established during
    the Comrade Leader's U.S. visit — responsibility: In-
    ternational Relations Department.

6. Ministry of Foreign Affairs personnel to study the
    economies of other countries in the future.

7. Organise scholarships in international relations
    for Grenadian students.

8. The international relations department to intensify
    its work with the parties and friendship societies
    worldwide bearing in mind the need for material
    assistance and to develop political tourism.

9. Ensure that the MDC's particularly Jamaica and
    Barbados which are co-ordinating closely with US
    imperialism do not succeed in isolating Grenada
    now in developing a strategic imperialist control in
    the region. Hence we:-

i.   must move rapidly to firm up relations with
        Caricom countries through more attempts at
        co-operation;

ii.   need to be discreet and cautious with left op-
        position parties in OECS states;

    iii.   must work towards special relations with Guyana;

    iv.   must maintain Party relations on a careful level;

    v.   must ensure that our Ministers seek to know the Caricom countries personally;

    vi.   must establish a consulate in Trinidad.

10. Ensure that we move rapidly to firm up relations with the Socialist World.

. . . .

VIII-3
Emergency Meeting of Central Committee
8/26/83

We note, in this discussion of growing problems in the NJM, both the growing tendency toward C.C. self-criticism and toward friction with Communist allies. The East Germans seem to have become irritated at coming to Grenada under less than standard "fraternal" conditions. Their complaints, perhaps echoed by the Cubans, may have contributed to the Coard group's ambitions.

Characteristically, the NJM is again exhorted to further follow the Soviet model in internal party life, by studying the history of the Soviet party and rereading "Standards of Party Life," a Soviet work.

"Pinero" is Manuel Pineyro, head of the Cuban Communist Party's hemispheric affairs section, the "America" department.

MINUTES OF EMERGENCY MEETING OF N.J.M. CEN-
TRAL COMMITTEE DATED 26TH AUGUST, 1983

COMRADES PRESENT

Maurice Bishop   Selwyn Strachan
Hudson Austin   Unison Whiteman
Liam James   Tan Bartholomew
Ian St. Bernard   Kamau McBarnette
Fitzroy Bain   Leon Cornwall
Chris Deriggs

COMRADE ABSENT

Phyllis Coard — Excuse — ill

AGENDA

1. Concern of Party Membership

Central Committee Chairman and Party Leader Comrade Maurice Bishop called the meeting to order at 8.00 a.m. He asked Comrade Cornwall to summarise the concern expressed by a member of senior party member.

Comrade Leon Cornwall reported that he had held discussions with some senior party Comrades in order to get their views on a number of issues. This, he said was based on his own feelings that we do not have an effective way of assessing the feelings of party membership on key matters.

Comrade Cornwall summarised the feedback as follows:

(i) Some conclusions of the C.C are not correct.

(ii) Some C.C Comrades are not functioning properly, are in a state of rut or performing in a weak manner.

(iii) He had been told by a Comrade from the G.D.R. that the state of work is bad.

(iv) Similar allegations were made by Cuban Comrades Carlos Diaz and Pinero.

(v) Comrades in the Armed Forces complained that they were not happy with the level of party guidance even after C.C deliberations and the recent general meeting.

(vi) There was a feeling among some party Comrades that the C.C did not criticise itself in a serious way before the G.M.

(vii) Cde. Cornwall concluded by recommending that C.C look into these concerns.

Other Comrades reported on the feedback that they had received.

. . . .

Comrade Tan Bartholomew:

"Fraternal Comrades had raised certain concerns with him: conversation between Carlos Diaz Kamau and himself special concern over Army/ Militia, Youth. . . ."

"Concern over the presence of G.D.R Technical delegation down here for a month and having nothing to do, while having to live in unsatisfactory housing at the risk of their personal security

— noting that this can tarnish our image in the
eyes of fraternals."

.   .   .   .

"Lack of supervision of the work among police,
control by RightWing elements, lack of respect for
party among police, demoralisation among newly
recruited police making it difficult for transformation of this section of the Armed Forces to take
place."

.   .   .   .

Comrade Hudson Austin:

"Comrades are in a serious state of demoralisation.

Good Comrades are asking to leave

Comrades are saying that at the end of five (5)
years they are not materially better off."

.   .   .   .

Cde Fitzroy Bain:

"We need clarification as regards the depth of the
criticism of the C.C.

There is division between party and masses —
Concern over the image of the party before the
masses."

.   .   .   .

SUMMARY REMARKS BY CDE. MAURICE BISHOP:

(i) The meeting inspite of its short duration has been useful.

(ii) In agreement with Owusu that we are faced with the
threat of disintegration.

(iii) Agrees also with analysis that Comrades of the party are afraid to raise criticisms.

(iv) Agrees with the postponement because of the need for C.C members to adequately prepare themselves.

(v) By way of preparation C.C members should do the following:

   (a) rap with party members, particularly senior party members on all the critical issues.

   (b) rap with key section of the masses with the following in mind: —

   — the increasing disrespect for the party among certain sections of the masses.

   (c) rap with leading mass orgs. activists, leading militia types, consistent participants in zonal councils, leaders of party support groups.

(vi) July C.C resolution should be discussed in work committees and study groups.

(vii) C.C members should research on the history of the party during the last five or six years. Minutes and conclusions will be useful to look at.

(viii) There is reasonable basis to share the concern that many key decisions of the party, if not the majority have been made informally outside of higher organs.

(ix) We should study the history of the C.P.S.U.

(x) We should re-read Standards of Party Life by Pronin.

(xi) We should reflect on the individual strengths and weaknesses of all C.C members. We should also think about the specific responsibilities of C.C Comrades both at the party and state levels — This should be in writing.

The meeting ended around 10.00 a.m.

Minutes taken by
Cde. Chris DeRiggs.

VIII-4
Extraordinary Meeting of Central Committee
9/16/83

In this meeting, the Coard group finally won its main battle within the NJM elite. Still, little credible evidence exists of significant political differences between Bishop and Coard. In all the documents, the conflict is subsumed in declarations and accusations that, although appearing serious and elaborate, are in fact, vague and insubstantial. Coard's "activism" seems less a matter of doctrine or policy than of simple ambition.

Apparently, Bernard Coard no more sought a truly collective leadership than Maurice Bishop. To increase the "firm Leninism" of the New Jewel movement, as Coard's followers demanded, could only mean more political dictation from the top. If Bishop indeed represented a more moderate variety of one-party socialism, this in no way lessens Bishop's loyalty to overall Soviet and Cuban political and military leadership. Both Bishop and Coard sought to fulfill Soviet policy goals in the Caribbean and Central America; both defended the totalitarianism goals of the 1982 "Line of March" speech. Coard was simply more ruthless—and impatient.

"Right opportunism" is a standard Soviet political insult usually referring to acceptance of situations as they already exist. Its opposite is "left sectarianism" or revolutionary adventurism.

In this document we find expressions of concern for a growing disillusion on the part of the "masses." The term "economism," for example, which appears here, refers in Leninist parlance to the tendency of workers to consider their immediate wage and other economic needs ahead of the demands of Marxist ideology. But while the participants in this session warned emphatically of the dangers represented by the low level of enthusiasm of the Grenadian people for the NJM regime's programs, there is little independent evidence of dangerous dissatisfaction among the Grenadian "masses" during this period. Coard's group seems to have fostered an exaggerated atmosphere of crisis, to support his claims of a need for increased personal power. Significantly, the party elite voted not to inform the "masses" of the decision to adopt "joint leadership."

"Brutans" may be Karen N. Brutents, a Soviet ideologist.

EXTRAORDINARY MEETING OF THE CENTRAL
COMMITTEE NJM
14-16 SEPTEMBER, 1983

MEETING STARTED 1.00 P.M.

COMRADES PRESENT

Maurice Bishop   Phyllis Coard
Selwyn Strachan   Leon Cornwall
George Louison   Kamau McBarnette
Unison Whiteman   Tan Bartholomew
Liam James   Fitzroy Bain
Chalkie Ventour   Chris Deriggs
Ewart Layne

COMRADES ABSENT

Hudson Austin   —   (out of country)
Ian St. Bernard   —   (sick)

(1) ANALYSIS OF THE PRESENT STATE OF THE PARTY AND
REVOLUTION

Cde. Ewart Layne lead off in the discussion. He said that had
received minutes of the last C.C plenary, all documents and
report from the P.B and C.C. Therefore his assessment is based
on these reports and feed back from the ground he had picked
up during his short time home.

The situation is that the revolution now faces the greatest
danger since 1979. There is great dispiritiveness and disatis-
faction among the people. Though not in an open way it can
be recognised. The state of the party at present is the lowest it
had ever been. The international prestige of the party and revolution is compromised e.g the C.C delegation visit to the S.U.

We are faced with the tasks of Managing the state sector in
great economic difficulties, to build the economy in the face of
tremendous pressure from imperialism. Politically, to raise
the consciousness of the working class and working people in
the face of resistance from imperialism and to build the party
into a Marxist Leninist vanguard in a country that is domin-
antly pettit bourgeoise and to carry the proposed constitution
to the people in two years time.

Militarily, to organise the defence of the revolution in the face of a qualitatively stepped up aggression from imperialism who for years has attempted to carry out its policy of becoming more and more into a "gun Boat" policy. The small Caribbean islands are being drawn into an alliance against Grenada and all the left organisations in the region.

We have to develop an army with more complicated means. Tighten our relations with the World Socialist Movement especially Cuba, S.U, G.D.R, of which relations are becoming more and more complex. To steer off isolation but not at the extent of departing from the correct path, and to carry out all tasks of social development.

In the face of all these tasks the party is crumbling, all mass organisations are to the ground, organs of people's democracy is about to collapse. The internal state of the party is very dread. There is wide protest against the higher organs, prestige has fallen in the eyes of the party members and the masses. The C.C has proven its inability to give leadership to the process e.g this time the C.C cannot determine the stage the revolution is at. The style of the C.C is becoming more and more formalistic. The growth and carrying of working class elements into the party is low. The style of leadership is carried out by directives (members says that democracy is dead in the party). Decision making is characterised by spontainety.

The C.C is on a path of right opportunism and is very dishonest to its members e.g in the conclusions of the July plenary was reported that C.C has advanced, every single committee mass orgs were criticise except the C.C and P.B. The failing to match up with incentives to the participants in C.P.E was not criticised. When Cdes have failed to accomplish tasks and accuses others for this it very serious. For soon ideological justifications will be found for these mistakes.

The C.C criticised the NYO for their short comings, at the same time Cde. Tan Bartholomew has been given additional responsibility of C.P.E and St. Patrick's P.C.B. He said that the tasks given to the NYO in this period are giant tasks which is impossible to accomplish in the end it will only lead to the fustration of the Cdes in this area.

In his view the main problem is the C.C. The C.C has diverted from the correct path. This will lead to the total disintegration of the party and the collapse of the revolution; at the same time when the work on the economic, military and international fronts becomes much more difficult.

The C.C needs to take a serious view, frankly criticise itself inorder to move out of this serious dangers in the interest of the masses and the revolution.

Cde. Ventour supported the points made by Cde. Layne. He said that the party is facing disintegration. Cdes are complaining of the amount of tasks, some are showing signs of resignation, Cdes are afraid to speak up, they show timidity and fear to express their positions. He said that this can make the C.C lose a lot of prestige. Cdes do not agree with the C.C lose a lot of prestige. Cdes do not agree with the C.C conclusions of July. They are also raised that the months have passed and there is no implimentation of the conclusions. There is a serious drift away from the party by the key supporters of the revolution, the vocal Cdes are now passive, they are not prepared to fight the reactionary lines on the ground. Community work is not going as was expected, he graded it as poor to fair. The militia is non existent. In some respects the masses have gone backwards ideologically using the present positions on the Korean plane incident and comparing it with the position of the masses on the Afganistan in the early days of the revolution. He said that people are getting their lines from VOA.

Cde. Leon Cornwall also agreed with the analysis made by Cde. Layne. He said that the honey moon period of the revolution is over. In the past 4½ years progress was seen in many areas and the masses were on a high, now the work is becoming much more difficult and complex. The C.C has failed to develop a perspective on how the revolution must develop. The C.C has given too much unrealistic tasks and in pushing Cdes to accomplish it they become fustrated. A striking feature in this period is the absence of the masses in the activities of the revolution because of tne deep frustrations which exists. He said that there is confusion among the party masses, we do not know how we are going to come out of this situation because the party has not develop a prospective. We tend to push things down Cdes throat and fustrate them.

All areas of mass organisation work has fallen, which is related to our lack of prospective on how to implement solutions. The serious economic difficulties we face is also affecting the people.

He said that Cuba had similar problems in their development but they were able to develop a militant mass bases because of the strength of the party in developing a perspective and its work.

.   .   .   .

He also agreed that the C.C is on a right opportunist path referring to the conclusions of the July plenary. He continued to say that if the C.C is to gain any respect we must move away from this path. He said that this problem is as a result of the low ideological level of the C.C and the party in general. Cdes see the conclusions of July as a set of administrative measures. There is no system to ensure that Cdes understand the lines of the party. No perspective on the development of the G.M's. He thinks that the solution is an ideologically clear and steeled C.C and party which can explain the lines of the party and can impliment it in all areas.

Cde. Fitzroy Bain agreed with the position of the Cdes. He said that the strongest supporters of the revolution are demoralised, the party has set too much high standards for the people, we had expected social benefits to do the work for us. Cdes who leave the army are spreading unfavourable lines which is difficult to fight back, it is affecting the credibility of the army in the eyes of the people. There is presently a very low surface mood among the masses which will soon affect their basic mood.

Party Cdes bramble the masses, a small amount of our firmest supporters are leaving the country. The mood of the party is also lower than the masses at this time, there exist a level of mistrust, resentment and fustration among party Cdes. They are not convinced on the lines given by the C.C on Cde. Coard and Cde. Radix. Cdes set double standards in the party e.g when Cdes of the C.C do not do any house to house Cdes do not have any respect for the D.C, they also show a willingness to resign. Cdes of the Workers Committee are saying that their [illeg.] is at stake, they attend too many meetings, they have no time to visit workplaces and given very little time to address the trade union work. Cdes refer to the case of Sydney Francis and Valentine Sawney who were disciplined recently in saying that Cde. Austin committed a similar offence and he was not disciplined Party Cdes are just going through motions, they lack the spirit to fight on the ground. They criticise the supervision of the C.C, they say that communication from the C.C is weak. They refer to the July Conclusion saying that meetings were held with M's [Members] and C.M's [Candidate Members] no meetings were held with A's [Applicants] but at the same time A's are expected to carry out the decisions and tasks from the July Plenary.

Cde. Bartholomew agreed with all the points made so far saying that the C.C has not been giving leadership to the process. The party has been dishonest with its members on a number of issues which has shaken the confidence of the party masses. The C.C does not report frankly, the flow of information is a major problem, internal party democracy has been destroyed and decisions are handed down without involving the full members.

Timidity is a major problem in the party, Cdes are afraid to speak out frankly because when they do they are termed in different ways. Members and C.M do not understand basic norms of party life. Cdes were not consulted when the three Cdes of the C.C was brought onto the P.B. Cdes do not know the members of the Central Committee. The D.C has not played the role it had been assigned to do, it has developed a very arrogant attitude towards Cdes, it has not developed ways of assisting Cdes that come before the D.C. The masses have lost confidence in the party, irregularities takes too much time before it is solved, e.g water and electricity problems police and soldiers who left the army are going to Trinidad. They complain about the condition in the army. The economic problems are not explained to the people and the Church has grabed a number of people in this situation. He also reported an incident of Militia Cdes guarding a Church in this period. He said that the party has not yet developed a policy for dealing with the Church. The revolution has lost its ability to manners counters who are very active. He referred to the 300 turn out in the [illeg.] indoor rally in Sauteurs as a very weak turnout in the context of the amount of mobilisation done. Mobilisers were actually chased in some areas.

Cdes complain of the lack of stability in the leadership of the NYO. He accused the party of bleeding the youth movement. The best Cadres are pulled out at a time when the youth movement is in problems. Leading Party Cdes have contributed to the discrediting of the youth Cdes terrorize the youth calling NYO "Not yet organise". We are not yet clear on the relation of the party are tied up for NYO activities they do not turn up and failed to give any excuse. He continued to say that the international prestige of the NYO is very poor there is the possibility of loosing seat on the Bureau of W.F.D.Y. He raised the problems experienced by the G.D.R. Cdes now in Grenada. His view is that Cde. Goddard is given too much work as a result he cannot focus on the youth work in St. George's.

He said that the main problem is in the C.C. The C.C need to make frank decisions and communicate to its members frankly.

Cde. Chris De Riggs registering his agreement with the points made referred to the 19 characteristics of pettit bourgeois party that party identified in the weekend of the fedons group seminar highlighting the points on (i) inconsistency (2) insufficient planning (3) vascillation (4) agreement in principle windbagism in practice (5) inadequate vision of the future (6) crisis management (7) poor attitude towards criticism (8) lack of a perspective of the future. He said that all these points charaterise the New Jewel Movement at this time. He

pointed up the fact that the C.C has failed to accept the failure
for the work which in his view is very dishonest. This attitude
has discourage Cdes from criticising the higher organs, the
reason being that Cdes were not encouraged to think critically
of the higher organs. He also refered to the line of march
document pointing out that no criticism were made of the
higher organs. He said that there has always been a tendency
for the party to pay very little attention to the economy which
has relevance to the question of social benefits and the overall
development of the revolution. The C.C needs to prepare lines
of educating the people on the present situation with I.M.F
and the present salary negotiations of the armed forces, the
social problem still remains. There is a serious lack of C.P.E
and ideological work in the Armed Force.

Cde. McBarnette said that . . . [t]he revolution is suffering
from a serious fall of its active supporters. The party must
seek to consolidate. The church has capitalise on our weaknesses using the tactics and strategies of the party. Cdes at
this time shows deep fear to criticise the party. The basis
must be laid for frank and open criticism in the party.

Sister Phyllis Coard said that we hope to recognise that the
situation is very serious. The mood of the party members can
be graded as one (1) or lower. The mood of the masses can be
graded as 1.5. The work of the P.C.B can be described as unsuccessful though there have been slight improvements in St.
George's, St. David's and West Coast, it is still very very bad in
St. Andrew's and Carriacou. All programmes of the Revolution
are in a very weak condition, while propoganda work is still
very bad. The mass organisations are showing less participation in the political work. During the months May to August
strenuous efforts were made to revive the work but only a
modest 5% improvement was recorded. She analyse the situation as the failure of the leadership of the Committees and
failure of the C.C to exercise leadership.

The militia is non existent, the army is demoralise the Cdes have genuining complains, growth in militarisation and deep economic problems.

No long and short term goals are set for the propoganda Committee and the masses are moving backward politically.

The Poor quality and low moral of the party is communicated to the masses because party Cdes live and work among the masses, they also display a harsh attitude to the masses. The masses are demoralise because of the party's failure to manners the situation. Party members cannot beat back the reactionary lines on the ground. There are also varing trends among party members, at the level of committees there is dog fight going on. The pettit bourgeois elements are using the situation to excuse themselves from criticism. However, some members have become more proletarian in their approach. Members are demoralise by having to carry out unrealistic tasks and decisions. The C.C has failed to analyse the problems correctly and come up with a long term plan development. Cdes sees the July conclusions as being very dishonest.

The question of the ideological development of the C.C is an issue that we need to make a decision on. If this is allowed to continue the party will disintegrate in a matter of 5-6 months with Cdes resigning, applcants cannot make, workers do not want to join the party as a result the few remaining members will become every burdened, & fustrated the party will collapse and the revolution cannot continue without the party. The revolution can be turned back within one year. The international support of the working class is lessening. The party need to put the interest of the working people first and foremost.

Cde. Bishop said that in some ways Cdes contributions have began to address tomorrows agenda.

He said that he is struck by the levels of thought and preparation of Cdes as evident in their various contributions. Though some conclusions are a bit pre mature, they are however, correct he agreed that the main problems lies in the C.C, in his view it have to do with two main factors.

(1) Low ideological levels, insufficient knowledge and awareness

(3) The lack of perspective as evident in a number of C.C
meetings e.g 16th July. However, points are coming out
more sharpely today.

The lack of proper application of strategy and tactics has led
to our party paying no significant attention to the views of the
party and the masses; there is clearly no channels for communications which has lead to a breakdown of collective leadership. He said that it was premature to move from monthly
meetings to wholistic pleanry. The C.C has not been able to
receive oral and written reports from the party. Decision were
taken outside of the C.C, we have not set up systems for implimentation and verification. The C.C is very adhoc in its approach to the work. The consistant over ruling of decision
leads to a lack of clarity regarding the role of the higher organs, and inability for the C.C to provide guidance monitoring
and supervision of the work. This is as a result of the increasing complexity of the work.

The C.C has not been able to rise to the challenge of the increasing complexity this has led it to take a number of unrealistic decisions.

The C.C has made a number of mistakes over the past 18
months because of the weak links with the masses we became
bureaucratic and too formalistic in our approach. Visits to
work places have disappeared, increasing non attendance at
zonal councils and parish meetings, visit to communities to
meet people at an informal level, decrease in the number of
discussion and meetings with people in all areas of work, failure to participate in public activities, village meetings have
disappeared. We have not paid sufficient regards to the material base on the country. Changes in the economy, change in
social wages and the predominant P.B [petty-bourgeois]
Character of the masses and society as a whole our propaganda positions have consistently fed economism. We have
failed to point out to the masses that this period requires a
number of sacrafices and if we are not prepared to build the

economy through hard work we will not make it. We have to take the blame for the over economic expectations of the people. We need to develop proper lines on these questions for the people.

He said the mood among the farmers is very low they criticise and attack workers for not producing.

The mood of the agricultural workers is also very low pointing to his last visit to one of the state farms.

His understanding of the criticism and complain from the party has to do with the lack of channels of communications for the membership to raise their complains and grievances which we need to address. He agreed that a lot of criticisms have developed to leading Cdes in the party. He shares the overall concerns that Cdes have arrived at.

.   .   .   .

Cde. Louison said that he was shocked on his arrival in the country to see the state of the roads which is in the worst state it has ever been since the revolution. This he said is because of the continued decline of the work of the party. He also pointed out to a split in the P.F.U Executive as evidence of the present situation. He said that having listen to a number of Cdes he agree that there is a lot of problems in the leadership. He also pointed to the low ideological level of the C.C and the continued slow rate of development of a number of Comrades on the C.C. There is also a clear lack of contact with the masses among some of the C.C. Comrades. he feels however, that sufficient weight has not been given to the objective situations and the problems in the economy which we have failed to explain to the masses. He also pointed to the fact that while we are loosing links with the masses the middle class types have been coming to the revolution for jobs. He said that this is due to the lack of propaganda work to reach the masses. He said that he is still to be convince that the ideological levels of the masses have gone backwards. Some Cdes gives a panicky impression in the way they make their points.

.   .   .   .

Cde. Whiteman said that he is shocked at the mood in the country. He pointed to the failure of the two indoor rallies in St. George's as an indication of the present situation. He said that there is not enough two way communications in the party, too much directives is given regardless of Cdes work plans and schedules and unrealistic targets are set especially in C.P.E. The propaganda work has been too idealistic especially on the economy. He has never seen the road in such a bad condition before. We have not been able to detect how the enemy operates he feels that there must be some counter revolutionary network in the country. Too much time is spent on small issues instead of fundamental issues e.g the church. He said that we do not fully grasp how the church is working at this time and what tactics and strategy must be employed to counter them. We do not fully know how the masses think and the house to house is not effective in achieving this. His view is that that the leadership must spend more time in house to house in order to know what the people are thinking, we also need to think of how to build and substain the mass organisations in the face of economic difficulties.

He described the directive to remove all party Cdes children to public schools as a wrong approach, he said that the decision battle has not come yet, we have to focus on the major contradictions instead of these minor points. He suggested a second leadership structure that can read and summarise reports, he feels that the Leadership spends too much time reading reports.

. . . .

Cde. Liam James leading off said that this is the last chance for the C.C to pull the party out of this crisis and on a firm M.L path. This crisis is not only among the masses but in the party membership as well. Over the past few months one could have seen that the party and the C.C was not moving forward. The way forward is to take an honest, cold blooded, objective and scientific approach to the situation.

Within the C.C there are many problems all Cdes must be criticise for the levels of disorganisation, low ideological level and failure to put the party on a firm M.L. footing. These weaknesses are so evident that party Cdes are saying that certain Cdes must be chopped from the C.C. It is clear that party Cdes have lost their level of respect for the C.C The removal of the Cdes from the C.C will no way solved the problem in his view all the Cdes of the C.C are by far the best Cdes in the party, what is needed is firm Leninism. He pointed out that the most fundamental problem is the quality of leadership of the Central Committee and the party provided by Cde. Maurice Bishop. In his view the Cdes has great strength, his ability to inspire and develop Cdes, his ability to raise the regional and international respect for the party and revolution; he has the chrisma to build the confidence of the people both in and out of the country, and to put forward clearly the positions of the party. Today these strengths alone cannot put the party any further in this period. The qualities he lacks is what is needed to push the revolution forward at this time:

(1) A Leninist level of organisation and discipline.

(2) Great depth in ideological clarity.

(3) Brilliance in strategy and tactics.
    These qualities which are essential for M.L leadership has prove to be lacking in the Cde. at this time.

Cde. Layne said that based on all analysis, discussions and on conclusions it is quite clear that the C.C has not been able to give ideological leadership to the process. If we are to be honest and frank throughout the crisis we go through more and more Cdes coming to realise that we face a real possibility of the revolution being turned weak.

It is clear that Cde. Bishop lacks theses qualities put forward by Cde. James. Despite his strengths, the strengths that he lacks is vitally needed to steer the revolution off the dangers and to come out of the crisis. The salvation of the revolution calls for us to take a mature proletarian decision to save and carry the revolution forward. . . .

THE ROLE OF THE C.C

Cde. Bishop said that on many occasion we have tried to look at the role of the C.C. He referred to the documents of June '81 and subsequent minutes of the C.C that dealt with its role.

He proposed that the C.C move to meetings once per month and to have three wholistic plenary, each year.

He said that the montly meetings must be seen as a medium of analysis, exchanging information of various sections, and pre-schedules should cover special areas of party and state work. He sees that at the end of October the main topic being C.P.E, in November the study commission we will also have to determine the role of the C.C secretariat is key in operationalizing the sub committee in terms of reports from various bodies etc. Also getting to the party guidelines on major issues ensuring conclusion and resolutions are drawn up after our delebration and be circulated to the membership.

To develop and maintain links with the masses the leadership must personally get on the ground among the people, step up participation in zonal and parish councils, visits schools, monitor and push production. The role of the C.C must be worked out in this regard. Develop mechanism for accounta-bility, and to review constant feedback from the membership and to ensure channels of communications with them.

The C.C must do a constant evaluation of the progress made by members, receive reports from C.C on the re rationalisation of the work, prioritise the work of Cdes on the C.C and set targets to be achieved on a weekly monthly and yearly basis.

.   .   .   .

Cde. Layne made reference to the Ethophian Party and the method they took to develop their party, he said that even though their method cannot be applied immediately so that it can be develop in the future, we need to have a policy for the development of Cdes in the party, Cdes will make mistakes but they will be helped and pulled forward.

He said that the struggle for socialism is won, lost or divided in the array. The party must now be organise in the work places. Cdes with state post must be prepared to carry out the lines of the party in the work places. We have experience in mobilising the masses but we do not know how to build the party. We have to lay the basis for taking a strategic approach for the building of a M.L party learning from the experience of other parties.

Cde. James agreed with the postions of . . . Cde. Layne, he made the following proposals: —

1. The C.C must become fully accountable to the members, so that Cdes can evaluate the work of the C.C on a whole and the C.C members.

2. All C.C Cdes must be based in the country at this time until the situation is resolved.

3. The C.C and party must study Brutans.

4. Recall the conclusions of the July Plenary.

5. Proposed a modle of joint leadership, marrying the strengths of Cdes Bishop and Coard. He went to define the responsibilities of the two Cdes.

The following postions were voted on:

1. On Cde. James proposals

   For   —   9

   Abstain —   2

   Against —   2

2. Formalisation of Joint Leadership:

   For   —   9

   Opposed —   1

   Abstain —   3

Cde. Austin abstained because he was not present for the full discussion for the greater part of the meeting.

3. How to inform the Membership:

   (A) Tell members only through minutes

   For   —   10

   Against —   1

   Abstain —   2

   (B) Tell all three categories in one meeting:

   Against —   11

   Abstain —   2

(C) Tell all categories in two meetings M's and C.M's the A.'s

   For   —   9

   Against —   2

   Abstain —   2

   (D) Informing the masses:

   Against —   9

   Abstain —   3

   Cde. George Louison — non participate.

VIII-5
Central Committee Plenary
9/20/83

In this set of originally handwritten minutes, the NJM leadership, reflecting the increased influence of the Coard faction, discusses areas in which Coard's followers had made suggestions for "improvement." While none of the proposed changes was substantive enough to reflect serious political differences with the Bishop group, it is of great importance to note in Coard's remarks a concern to increase the party's economic control over the Grenadian workers.

Coard's use of the term "idealism" carries a pejorative meaning, denoting in Marxist polemics, an outlook in conflict with "materialism." In the original Marxian discourse, this was construed to describe a contrast between those who view the movement of world history as a product of the development of ideas (idealists), and those who analyze intellectual concepts as the effects of history (materialists). In the Leninspeak utilized by the NJM, however, these distinctions have degenerated into vacuous labels.

SIXTH SITTING OF CENTRAL COMMITTEE PLENARY

Date: Tuesday September 20th 1983   Duration: 8:10 a.m.
                                                      to 10 a.m.

Present   Absent

Cdes Bernard Coard   Cdes Maurice Bishop
      Selwyn Strachan   George Louison
      Hudson Austin   Chris DeRiggs
      Liam James   Ian St. Bernard (sp?)
      John Ventour
      Ewert Layne
      Phyllis Coard
      Kamau McBarnette
      [two names illegible]
      Leon Cornwall
      Unison Whiteman

. . . .

Cde. Austin . . . stated that

—the membership is concerned over the lack of clearly defined party rules with stated sanctions. This leads to many
inexpediencies especially in a case where the Armed Forces
has a Code of conduct thus party members who are in the
Armed Forces see this contradiction.

—The Party school is urgently needed because study circles
are not enough. We should not delay. We can start using one of
the buildings the party has under control and ask fraternal
socialist countries for assistance in tutors.

—The party secretariat is too small. Also we need departments in the secretariat with specialists on different regions
of the world who can brief comrades when they travel. He
stated he was surprise to see how deep the personality cult is
in Korea where the leader is worshipped almost as a god.

Sister Phyllis stated her agreement with Cde. Austin on the
need for party cdes. to [illeg.] of the political direction of parties and government e.g. many social democratic groups come
to Grenada and speak progressively and comrades mislead
comrades in telling them things they shouldn't.

Cde. Strachan stated his support for Cde. Bernard's proposal
and those of other cdes. He further stated that this is the best
CC meeting and for the first time in 10½ years the highest
body in the party is seriously sitting down and discuss how to
build the party since party building is a science.

. . . .

Cde. Tan stated that the party must have a system for supervision and control. He drew on the example of the UJC of Cuba
where in their secretariat there is a room with maps, charts
and telephones so that constant supervision over all the work
can take place.

. . . .

The meeting was adjourned at 10:00 a.m.

SEVEN [remainder illeg.]

Date: [illeg.]

Present   Absent [illeg.]

Cdes. Bernard   —sick
       Selwyn
       Hudson
       Liam James
       Ewart
       John Ventour
       Unison Whiteman
       Phyllis Coard
       Kamau McBarnette
       Fitzroy Bain
       Tan
       Leon Cornwall

.   .   .   .

Cde. Bernard pointed out that for the record he had personally raised a number of times with the Cuban Comrades the
need for advisors in party building, [illeg.] and ideological
work ... However, there has not been a positive response so
far. Cde. Bernard went on to make further points. He stated
that over the years we have been guilty of unbelievable
ideelism, since we have been adding new tasks every without
    a. expanding the party
    b. training existing party comrades to raise their quality
    c. reorganising our method of work to be [illeg.] efficient
    d. involving more non party people in party tasks

Cde. Bernard then called for the CC to move to the other aspect
of the agenda — he stated that for our entire history our party
has operated on the [illeg.] principle then after the revolution
the sectional principle this was correct because we had a very
high unemployment problem and needed to reach people
where they live.
Cde. Layne stated that we need to look [illeg.] question of the
party being opened at the workplace there is a reason for this
since we need to push production.
He further stated that we have a problem and an incorrect

view of seeing political work as thing done only in the afternoon out in the villages. However, by failing to conceptualise
political work at the workplace we find that we overlook problems at the workplaces that can be solved and instead we have
to go on the village to explain to the masses why such problems exist.

Cde. Bernard then pointed out several reasons why party
work at the workplace is important.

a.   we would have control over the employment policy
b.   We can solve problems
c.   We can struggle against economism
d.   We can struggle for the use of modern science and
     technology
e.   We can struggle for the improvement of management
     and organisational standards at workplaces
f.   We can struggle to improve labour intensity
g.   We can struggle for the best use [illeg.] of raw materials
h.   it has implications for emulation and [illeg.] solving
i.   it can strengthen the trade union and revolutionary
     class consciousness
j.   We can mobilise the workers for military GPE etc.
k.   We would ensure that the working class conspection of
     the party is strengthened

He went on to state that the largest concentration of workers
on Grenada is in the villages not the workplaces therefore we
must determine what mode we use whether exclusively workplace based, village based or a combination of the two. . . .

VIII-6
Extraordinary General Meeting
9/25/83

These minutes describe a "crisis meeting" of the New Jewel Movement's leadership cadres at which the "joint leadership" of Grenada by Maurice Bishop and Bernard Coard was politically and psychologically confirmed.

This document strongly suggests that Bishop was undermined less by political differences with the Coard faction than by the dynamic of ideological competitiveness within the party elite. Each speaker attempts to outdo the others in Marxist rhetorical flourishes, none of which appears particularly meaningful. Coard seems to have harnessed deep feelings of intellectual inferiority and resentment that dwelt in the personalities of most of the NJM stalwarts, and to have turned to his advantage the possible failure of Bishop's group to contend adequately with the cadre's posturing yearnings for self-esteem.

It is worth noting that Hudson Austin here explicitly poses himself as the "Grenadian Jaruzelski," arguing that "the lesson of Poland showed that . . . only the Armed Forces was able to rescue the situation."

This document was first published in its totality in Caribbean Review *(Miami), Fall, 1983. Copyright © 1983 Caribbean Review Inc., Florida International University, Miami, FL 33199.*

Sunday, September 25th, 1983

The meeting began at 9:00 am chaired by Cde. Liam James, member of Political Bureau [PB] of New Jewel Movement [NJM] Central Committee [CC].

Agenda
1. Distribution of documents
2. Chairman's remarks
3. Central Committee report to GM
4. Discussion
5. Workshops for individual study and discussion
6. Plenary discussion

The documents distributed to the members were: a. Minutes of Extraordinary Meeting of the Central Committee of NJM— Tues. 12th—Fri. 15th October 1982; b. Extraordinary Meeting of the Central Committee NJM 14-16th Sept. 1983; c. Central Committee report to membership.

Cde. Liam James as chairman made brief remarks pointing out that this General Meeting [GM] is a very serious one and every member must approach the deliberations of the meeting in a spirit of frankness, since it has been called resulting from the comments picked up from the party's membership regarding the problems faced by the party and revolution and their disagreement with the conclusions of the regular plenary session of the Central Committee held from July 18-23rd, 1983.

He further emphasized and stressed that all comrades must show a high level of security consciousness with the documents and their contents, emphasizing that this is an internal party matter and must not be discussed outside of party bounds.

Central Committee Report

The Central Committee report to the membership was presented by Cde. Ewart Layne, member of the Political Bureau of NJM Central Committee. The report was characterized with a spirit of frankness, straightforwardness, criticism and self-criticism. It pointed out that the present crisis faced by the Party and revolution is the worst ever in four-and-one-half years since we are faced with the reality of the degeneration of the party. Its possible disintegration in six months, and the resulting overthrow of the revolution that can come in one year's time if we don't take effective measures to remedy the situation. The report gave concrete evidence which testified to the fact that this process is already in train.

.   .   .   .

The report analysed that the Central Committee's main problem is that of the weak quality of leadership provided by Cde. Maurice Bishop, Chairman of the Central Committee and

leader of the party. It frankly pointed out that Cde. Maurice
Bishop has tremendous strengths that are necessary for the
process, but these by themselves cannot carry the party out of
its present crisis.

· ·

The report also pointed out that the weak functioning of the
Central Committee, its vacillatory positions, the unwillingness
of its members to study, think, take hard decisions and struggle for their implementation have led Cde. Bernard Coard to
resign from the Central Committee September 1982. . . .

It is based on the above that the Central Committee reported to the GM its decision to establish a model of joint
leadership of the party by marrying together the strengths of
Cdes. Maurice Bishop and Bernard Coard with the areas of
work spelt out for each Cde. . . .

The Central Committee also made six other conclusions and
decisions, and demanded of every party member that they display, uphold and struggle at all times for nine principles
which, together with the model of joint leadership, are decisive for overcoming this grave crisis and putting the party on
a Marxist-Leninist path. These nine principles enunciated are:
1. Iron discipline; 2. Firmly uphold and apply the principle of
democratic centralism, emphasising criticism and self-
criticism and collective leadership; 3. Leninist level of organisation; 4. Open warmth and selflessness in dealing with the
masses; 5. Sink but don't drown amongst the masses; 6. Kill
all arrogance; 7. Greater scientific thought and reflection on
the problems and difficulties of the party and revolution; 8. An
end to all vacillation; 9. Bold, firm and a creative style of
thought and action. . . .

After the Central Committee's report, Cdee. Liam James called
on the members to be frank, open, cold blooded and objective
in their deliberations and overcome the tendency to be timid.
He then pointed out to the members the reason for Cde.
Maurice Bishop's absence, stating that since the CC meeting

on Friday 17th Sept., Cde. Bishop said he needed time to think and reflect on the Central Committee's conclusions and would be able to meet on Friday 24th Sept., in the CC plenary to put forward his position. However, Cde. Bishop did not turn up on the appointed date and gave the same reasons for his absence at the General Meeting.

Cde. James then read a note from Bernard Coard which stated that he understood that Cde. Bishop would be absent from the GM and as such he felt it was not fitting for him to be present since this may inhibit free and frank discussion. However Cde. Coard pointed out if the GM requests his presence he would be willing to comply.

.   .   .   .

Cde. Ewart Layne said that Cde. Bishop's attitude to the criticism by the CC and its decision was petit bourgeois in character. He pointed out that the CC warned Cde. Bishop that if he responds in this way to criticism, this could only discourage Cdes. from openly criticising him and would only guarantee that we don't come out of the crisis and thus the disintegration of the party and the eventual loss of state power.

Cde. Layne informed the GM that Cde. Bishop asked for time to reflect, which was given to him up until Friday 23rd.

He also said he need[ed] to know Cde. Coard's views. This he knew by Monday 19th based on the records of the meeting held by the CC with Cde. Coard. In addition Cde. Coard held a direct personal talk with Cde. Bishop and reiterated his position on the matter, namely, that emotionally his preference is to remain outside of the CC, but given the dangers of the revolution at this time he is willing to return to the CC and PB at whatever level determined by the CC.

Cde. Layne went on to state that, however, the CC has no communication from Cde. Bishop on his position although he continues to do his state work normally, operating from his residence while failing to attend the CC meeting on Friday

23rd. This, Cde. Layne pointed out, could only be seen as contempt for the CC, contempt for democratic centralism on the
part of Cde. Bishop.

. . . Cde. Unison Whiteman, on a point of order, informed the
GM that Cde. Bishop turned up on Saturday 24th for a CC
meeting at 1:30 pm, but the meeting did not take place. Cde.
Liam James explained to the GM that the meeting was specifically to discuss and agree on the Central Committee report to
the GM but the document was not yet rolled off. Thus it was
not possible for the meeting to be held.

Cde. T. Stroude asked whether Cde. Bishop sent an excuse
for his nonattendance to the Friday 23rd CC meeting.

Cde. Selwyn Strachan said that Cde. Bishop informed him
that he had not finished reflecting and he had nothing new to
say. Thus he wanted more time to reflect. He also said that he
went to bed late on Thursday night.

.   .   .   .

Cde. Basil Gahagan called on the GM to take a decision to call
for Cde. Bishop. A vote was taken: 46 Cdes. for, one against and
one abstained. A delegation headed by Cde. Ian St. Bernard,
member of NJM Central Committee, and consisting of Cdes.
Basil Gahagen, Marie Francois, Keith Ventour, Chester Humphrey and Wayne Sandiford left to convey to Cde. Bishop the
will of the GM.

At 11:10 am Cde. B. Coard arrived; at 12:42 Cde. Ian St. Bernard reported to the GM on behalf of the delegation. Cde. St.
Bernard pointed out that the delegation met Cde. Bishop and
explained the position of the GM after they had heard the CC
report. Cde. Bishop said he preferred for the delegation to
carry to the GM his position. He said he read the CC report
and had not yet formulated his position on it. He outlined his
position on joint leadership saying he has always accepted
this and referred to the Joint Coordinating Secretaries established in March 1973 when NJM was formed. He stated that
as leader of the party and revolution he accepts the blame for

the weakness of the CC. When asked to come to the GM to explain his position he was not favourable to this; however after some insisting by the delegation he said he would reach at 12:30. Cde. St. Bernard said that in his opinion Cde. Bishop would come.

. . . .

At 12:52 Cde. Bishop arrives.

Cde. Fitzroy Bain said that one member of the delegation said Cde. Bishop said that there were things in the CC report he was not in agreement with, what were they?

Cde. Marie Francois asked Cde. U. Whiteman for an explanation about his abstention in the voting. Cde. Whiteman said that Cde. Bishop had some concerns some of which have not been addressed, thus demanding that he comes here is not correct. Cde. Spooner asked — "What were those concerns?" Cde. Whiteman responded that one concern is that he needs to adjust psychologically, and secondly there were certain important points not reflected in the minutes. Cde. P. David said that the GM concerned about Cde. Bishop's absence and thus he should explain.

Cde. Bishop in response said that he assumed that the CC would explain his position to the GM. He added that the discussions in the CC plenary has raised concerns to him. When stripped bare and until he has completed his reflections then he can face the GM with a clean conscience. He is now relatively confused and emotional. There are several things that concern him and thus require a lot of mature reflection. He said that he shared the basic CC conclusion on the crisis in the country and party and that the source of the crisis lies in the CC. He added that he firmly believes that the more authority and power one had then the greater the responsibility and duty to accept criticism and that the overall responsibility for failures belongs to that person. He pointed out that the concept of joint leadership does not bother him because of his history of struggle especially from the 1973 merger which gave rise to NJM. He said that many comrades had criticised

him in relation to his acceptance of joint leadership in the
past in the form of Joint Coordinating Secretaries. However
the masses have their own conception and perception that
may not be necessarily like ours who study the science. Our
history shows that the masses build up a personality cult
around a single individual. He admitted that his style of leadership has led to vacillation, indecisiveness in many cases. He
confessed that maybe his conception of leadership is idealistic
because of the historical abuse of power and one-man leadership. He and his contemporaries have distaste for one-man
leadership and he has a strong position on this. He further
pointed out that his style of leadership is in error since it calls
for consensus, unity at all cost and this cause[s] vacillation.
And he is not sure that he has overcome this.

Secondly he said that he feels strongly that the party must
have a clear position on areas of demarcation of responsibility
and systems of accountability. He is of the view that some
Cdes. held strong reservations and they should have raised
them in an open and principled way. He said that if they held
them for long and then sudden[ly] spring them then there
must be need for reflection.

He informed the GM that in the July CC plenary there was
assessment held and that many points that are now being
made about him were not made then. He stated that he is always open to criticism but he should have been approached
first before the meeting so he would be able to work out a
clear and cogent response. He went on to say that there is a
fine line separating a petit bourgeois and a scientific response.
He felt that if he had those conclusions on a member he would
have checked them before although this may not be a scientific position.

He also said that he is concern[ed] about the minutes being
given to the GM. If minutes are given which show what each
member of the CC has said it can develop ideas of groupings
and fractions and vacillations in the CC. He is afraid that it
would eventually reach the masses and reaction and would
thus undermine the revolution and give rise to suspicions

that there is a power struggle in the CC. He said that if we are
to rebuild links with the masses, then by solving the problem
by being frank it would undermine the confidence of the leadership. He sees this clearly and thus not understand why
other CC members cannot see this. He pointed out that in the
past the CC has decided on not communicating sensitive matters, e.g. on defence. He said that at the emergency CC meeting
a large part of that meeting was spent discussing whether
Cde. Valdon Boldeau, the CC recording secretary, should be
present at the Extraordinary CC Plenary. At the emergency CC
meeting some Cdes. had apprehension but now, two weeks later, they have no apprehension in giving the minutes to the
GM.

He then said that he is concerned about what is the real
meaning of the CC's position. He is having horrors. If it is
what he is thinking of then he does not see himself as being
on the CC or on the CC as a leader. He said that the CC pointed
out that his strengths were the ability to agitate the masses,
to articulate the position of the party and government to the
masses, and to hold high the banner of the revolution in the
region and internationally, and his weaknesses were lack of
Leninist level of organisation and discipline, brillance in
strategy and tactics, and all that have been said. But the CC
said that precisely those qualities he lacks are those required
to carry the revolution forward because those he has can't
take it further. Thus the strengths of two Comrades are to be
married together. He is suspicious that comrades have concluded that the party must be transformed into a Marxist-
Leninist party and thus he is the wrong person for the leader.
He can't accept this compromise; it is unprincipled. He
explained that for him to put out his strengths it must be as a
result of a deep conviction, love for the poor and working
people, and out of a feeling of confidence from the CC. He is not
satisfied because the totality of points made is pointing him in
a direction he is trying to run from. It is not joint leadership
but a compromise in the interim. "What is the genuine substantial preference of the comrades," he asked?

Cde. Bishop went on to say that only he can solve the problem he is now facing because any assistance and talk about
this not being a case of no confidence will be seen by him as
tactical. He further said that he is considering the option of
withdrawing from the PB and CC but has not yet resolved this.
Therefore the CC as the Vanguard of the Vanguard has a duty
to meet in his absence and come up with clear conclusions on
how to come out of the crisis. He stated that the CC should not
wait for him because supposing after his reflection he de-
cides to withdraw, then many vital weeks would have been
lost. His only concern, he stated, is about certain areas in the
report that concerns him about his role in the future, but the
CC should go ahead and meet and whatever line is taken can
be communicated to him.

Cde. James stated that in his view Cde. Bishop must remain
in the GM and hear from the members. He went on to say that
we must distinguish between emotional and psychological
reactions from decisions of the CC. The CC is the highest body
and its decisions are binding on all — this is a fundamental
Leninist principle.

. . . .

Cde. L. James answered that joint leadership is an internal
party matter and is not to be brought to the masses. Cde.
Bishop would remain as Prime Minister and Commander in
Chief of the Armed Forces. He said that the key to defeating
rumour mongering is the proletarian acceptance, attitude and
disposition of the two comrades. In the past imperialism and
reaction spread rumours about power struggle[s] in the party
but this made no headway because of the closeness of the two
comrades.

. . . .

Cde Layne . . . stated that Cde. Bishop is of the opinion that
there is a plot and conspiracy to remove him but at this time
for tactical reasons we are going half way. This Cde. Layne
considers to be gross contempt for the intelligence of the CC.

For him to feel that under every chair, in every window there is a conspiracy going on is nothing but contempt.

.   .   .   .

Cde. Wayne Sandiford said that he criticises Cde. B. Coard for resigning from the CC and that he is worried how Cde. Bishop is seeing the criticisms of the CC and GM as some kind of conspiracy. He said that he does not want to be part of any conspiracy. He then pointed out that many comrades have been moved from their original areas of work and placed in others. He gave himself as an example of this saying that one morning he was told that he is moved from the Ministry of Trade and is now a full-time Worker Education tutor. This change, although abrupt, he tried to take in a proletarian way and has been making his best efforts. He further stated that in Cde. Bishop's speech he cited four concerns, namely a wrong approach, the minutes going to the membership, he needs time to reflect and that this may be a conspiracy. Cde. Sandiford said that these four concerns are not concerns of principle, they instead reflect Cde. Bishop's petit bourgeois side.

Cde. L. James then suggested that the workshops should begin. Cde. Mikey Prime then said that the GM must decide whether Cde. Bishop leaves the GM or not.

A vote was taken on the matter: 51 Cdes. were for Cde. Bishop staying and one abstained (C. Louison).

.   .   .   .

After the workshops reports Cde. L. James said that the workshops in their reports cited three areas which need clarification. They are Cde. George Louison's attitude at the CC plenary; what is Cde. Hudson Austin's role in the Armed Forces, and what problems Cde. Leon Cornwall experienced as Ambassador to Cuba.

Cde. L. James informed the GM that Cde. G. Louison's behaviour and positions at the CC plenary was right opportunism. He was vulgar and referred to the position taken by one comrade as "a load of shit." He also tried to disrupt the meeting when the majority of the Central Committee was not supportive of his position by taking up his bag and threatening to walk out of the meeting. Cde. James, however said that Cde. G. Louison should further explain his behaviour to the GM when he returns from abroad. He then called Cde. L. Cornwall to explain the problems he experienced.

Cde. Cornwall said that when the issue of all CC members being based in Grenada came up at the CC plenary there were some Cdes. who did not favour this especially on the question of Cde. Layne and himself remaining. Thus he informed the CC that there were some problems he experienced in Cuba mainly caused by the way in which the party was operating that made it unnecessary for a CC member to be based in Cuba as ambassador since a lot of information was being channelled from Grenada to Cuba by our party and government without his knowledge.

He said that this was drawn to the CC's attention several times both in terms of personal talks he had with CC members, reports to Grenada and a long letter he wrote to the CC on these matters. And failure to take corrective action was in fact amounting to a waste of his time as a CC member and a lowering of the image of the party's Central Committee since basic information that any ambassador should know was not being provided to him. He cited the continuous failure for the newspapers to be sent to the embassy and the fact that other embassies were providing him with their newspapers and always asking him for copies of Grenada's. This became a source of personal embarrassment. Also he was not informed except one hour before the plane landed in Cuba when Cde. Bishop was coming to Cuba in March on his way to New Delhi and this information was given him not by Grenada but by the Cuban comrades. This he said is unheard of. Also on several occasions when other leaders of the revolution travel[ed] to Cuba the same occurred. He said that on other matters instead of he as Ambassador to Cuba and a CC member informing the Cuban Comrades they instead were informing him. This, he said, can only be interpreted as if he was not a confidential

person of the Grenada revolution and NJM, and could only
serve to lower the prestige of the CC as well as waste his time
since things were going ahead in spite of his presence in Cuba.
He also cited an example of when he was asked by Grenada to
pass on some information to Cuba and was experiencing difficulties to get that meeting, but instead a Cuban Comrade —
not a member of the CC of the Cuban Communist Party — was
able to fly into Grenada and immediately get a meeting with
four members of our political bureau, including Cde. Bishop,
and deal with the same matter that he was supposed to deal
with. Thus he reasoned because of how we were operating, it
was not useful for a CC member to be wasting his time.

Cde. Hudson Austin pointed out that for more than a year
he had been concentrating all of his efforts as Minister of
Construction on the many construction projects that have
been taking place; as such very little of his time has been
given to the Armed Forces. He explained that in the Ministry
of Construction he works closely with Cde. Mikey Prime, the
permanent secretary, who is the only permanent secretary
that is a party member. He said that there is a clear division
of labour between himself and Cde. M. Prime and that his
Ministry has good relations with the Union which unionises
the workers. However, he said all this has been to the expense
of the Armed Forces and he is very concerned about this. He
said that he proposed in the July plenary of the CC 17 points
for building and strengthening the Armed Forces, and later he
wrote a letter to Cde. Bishop outlining how the Armed Forces
can be strengthened. He said that his concern is great because
the lesson of Poland showed that when the revolution was in
danger and there was chaos in the party and society, it was
only the Armed Forces that was able to rescue the situation.

Cde. Unison Whiteman explained to the GM that he had a
number of reservations on the question of joint leadership for
theoretical and practical reasons. He said he never read about
such a situation. He has heard of a leader and a deputy leader
with the latter having specific responsibilities. He said that
wherever a leader is missing qualities, collective leadership
and not joint leadership solves the problem. On the question

of the minutes going to the membership, he felt that instead of
this a comprehensive report highlighting all the arguments
should have been given.

.   .   .   .

Cde. Fitzroy Bain said that there is a split in views in the CC
on the proposals and that whatever the results it must be for
the party's survival. He said that he had strong feelings and
he had problems with the report read by Cde. Layne. He said
that we have to be careful that we don't move from right opportunism to left opportunism. He asked how can the resignation of the Comrades help the CC? He said that this is to in-
timidate the meeting and that he strongly criticises this. He
went on to say that Cde. George Louison is absent from this
meeting and that Cde. G. Louison has strong feelings on the
matters being discussed; however we have gone ahead and
held the GM in Cde. G. Louison's absence instead of waiting
until he is back. He said that this is not just a case of majority
and minority, since in the past the minority has held views
and the CC has not gone ahead with the position that was held
by majority. He said he is unhappy about labeling comrades
and that more ideologically developed comrades put forward
positions and others like himself, who are of a lower ideological level, feel timid in the face of these. He said that Cde.
Coard's resignation last year exposed the weaknesses of the
party, and when Cde. Coard resigned he had openly called such
a resignation as counterrevolutionary. He said that there has
been caucusing in the CC, that comrades are always talking to
each other and that he has no problems with joint leadership,
but this can mash up the party since there was caucusing. He
went on to say that he does not know if this is a plot, he is not
sure on the caucusing and what comrades said to each other
but if there is a plot we have to crush it. He admitted that the
criticisms of Cde. Bishop are correct and just and that Cde.
Bishop's style of handling the situation and criticisms was
petit bourgeois. He said that he knows that his ideological
level is low and the other comrades have a higher ideological
level but he does not like these things. He ended by saying he

knows that the comrades had well thought-out positions and were frank but he must say what is on his mind.

Cde. Peter David replying to Cde. F. Bain said that the latter is coming up in a subtle way with some conspiracy theory.

. . . .

Cde. U. Whiteman said that his position is clear that Cde. B. Coard should be on the CC and PB but he has never heard or read about joint leadership. He said that maybe he is not being creative but this is his position. He said that someone told him that the General Hospital is having problems because there is no clearly defined head of the hospital.

Cde. Keith Roberts said he is surprise[d] to hear of the positions of certain CC members especially those of Cde. Bishop and Bain who hint that this is a conspiracy. He said that Cde. Bishop must truly accept the criticism in a principled way.

. . . .

Cde. K. Ventour . . . stated that Cde. Bishop now seems more relaxed than this morning (applause). He said that this morning Cde. Bishop seemed to be confused, contemptuous and mistrustful of the party membership. Now he has a more relaxed look and he hopes that it is a good sign that shows his willingness to genuinely accept the CC and GM criticisms and the decision of the CC (applause).

. . . .

The members then called on Cde. Coard and Bishop to speak.

Cde. B. Coard said that today is indeed a historic day in the life of the party (applause). He said that the CC meetings he attended from Monday 19th September surprised him because unlike the past, every CC member was putting forward well though[t]-out, clear and reasoned positions on the way forward for building the party and transforming it into a genuine Marxist-Leninist party. He said that in the past most CC members would be silent in CC meetings and seem not to have ideas on how the party and revolution is to be built. However now he witness[es] a qualitative difference. He also said that the GM showed quality and thought. He said in his many conversations with Cde. Jorge Risket, member of the Political bureau of the PCC Central Committee, Cde. Risket always said that some people come to socialism by their head, others by their heart, and still others by their stomach. He said that in his opinion the members have spoken from both their heads and hearts. Their words have been sincere and it shows a genuine commitment by the members to struggle for socialism and lay[s] the basis for the eventual building of communism. He repeated that a qualitative lift has always taken place in the CC as well as among the membership, thus he is deeply confident in the future of building socialism and communism (applause). He pledged to the party that he would put every ounce of effort in building the process and that he knows that Cde. Bishop would do the same. He said he had known and work[ed] together with Cde. Bishop and that they both owe it to the party, revolution and the Grenadian working people to do all that is possible to build the revolution (applause).

Cde. Bishop stands and embraces Cde. Coard. Cde. Bishop said that it was correct for him to come to the GM and stay and hear the views of the party membership. He said that reflecting in isolation would not have been correct for him since he would have seen things in a lopsided manner. He said that the entire GM had accepted the CC analysis and decision and this has satisfied his concern. He admitted to the GM that his response to the CC criticism and decision was petit bourgeois. He said that the GM has rammed home that the criticism was correct and so too was the decision. He said, "I sincerely accept the criticism and will fulfill the decision in practice."

Cde. Bishop went on to say that his whole life is for the party and revolution and the difficulty he had was because so many things were going through his mind. He said that he agreed with Cde. Moses Jeffrey that he had not shown confidence in the party. But all these things are now behind his back. He said that today is indeed a historic day and a break with the past. He said that party comrades are maturing and are capable of taking strong positions. He said that his desire now is to use the criticism positively and march along with the entire party to build a Marxist-Leninist party that can lead the people to socialism and communism. He pledged to the party that he would do everything to erode his petit bourgeois traits. He said that he never had difficulties in working with Cde. Coard and that joint leadership would help push the party and revolution forward (applause).

At the end of Cde. Bishop's speech the entire GM breaks into singing the Internationale and members filed past to embrace Cdes. Bishop and Coard.

VIII-7
Political Bureau Meeting
10/12/83

In this political bureau meeting of October 12, we sense the beginning of the end. Bishop has returned from his trip abroad and has dragged his feet on implementation of joint leadership. Rather, he and his supporters are accused of spreading rumors in the streets in an effort to arouse public anger against the Coard faction. Coard supporters naturally conclude that Bishop was persuaded to change his mind by those who accompanied him on his trip. After this incident, reconciliation became impossible.

This document suggests once again an important irony in Coard's rise to power. His followers denounced Bishop's "cult of personality," yet Coard had himself proclaimed the epitome of "brilliance." Earlier, we saw the Coard partisans criticizing a similar transgression, "bureaucratism," yet it was Coard who sought to concentrate all power in the highest levels of the party. Finally, when Fitzroy Bain, a leader of the unions, threatened to organize the "masses" of "workers" against the Coard clique, he seems to have become, even more than Bishop, a target for the abuse of the new rulers. Coard's followers, while proclaiming their fidelity to the proletariat, identify the threat to call on the workers for help as a "Gairy attitude," thus equating it with the personalism of the earlier demagogue! This habit of projecting one's own sins upon one's opponents has been a recurring theme in the history of Soviet-style regimes.

Report on the meeting of PB [Political Bureau] and CC [Central Committee] held on Oct. 12th given by Cde. Strachan.

— agenda given

— The PB of CC was very concerned about the situation in the Party. He referred to the CC decision on JL [Joint Leadership] and the basis for this. However, following this Cde. MB [Maurice Bishop] felt that he could not give a decision on the CC decision and wanted time to reflect. We were concerned whether DC [Democratic Centralism] would continue to exist. The CC brought the issue to the MS [Members] which lasted 15 hrs. The meeting was the healthiest meeting in history of party (applause). The cdes. stood up for Principles — the unanimity on the resolution. After when MB reached Hungary there was a change. A meeting was held in Hungary [illeg.]. . . . GL [George Louison] gave a Pb opp. [petit-bourgeois opportunist] report and. . . . played a key role in poisoning the mind of MB and manipulating him not to implement the decision. The conduct of GL was totally unbecoming, it was a vulgar behavior, he was caught lying to the PB and CC. The CC immediately expelled GL (applause and chants). We are in a difficult period. We struggled against one [illeg.] for 28 years [Eric Gairy] and would not allow this in our party (applause). . . . How can a leader allow himself to be manipulated by another Cde. GL said he would appeal to M [masses], obviously the M. would have to decide.

Ian Lambert

A bloodshed could have taken place last night it was the rumours that caused this. They said that the country can have only one PM [Prime Minister] because B [Bernard Coard] is a communist. They said they all come from OREL and [illeg.] by B. to take over power. If there is bloodshed it is MB responsibility. Fr. Martin organized a service. MB has always pointed out where we must stand in class struggle. MB has always said action that is key.

Time and practice would reveal all shades VI [Vladimir Ilyich Lenin] said. Were you ever willing to implement the

principle? GL right wing opp. F. Bain has shown
emotionalism. The struggle for ideas must be in the party.
Who was responsible for the putting the rumour on the
street? Come out and talk the truth.

[illeg. name] —

The CC analysed that the party was in tension as a result of
the minority. The reason for the rumour. The sit. requires de-
cisiveness. The party is not split. He is disappointed in the
content and intent of some cdes. F. Bain has shown little belly,
no principles and has behaved as an unruly peasant. Ideo.
backwardness of the peasantry. He never addressed the principal issue. He threatened to mobilize agric. workers. He can't
speak of resigning. He is like Gairy and this is obj. counter.
What he is asking for is a jail. His behavior is against the WC
[working class]. The agric. workers must know. . On MB — he
would have to be expelled from the party. It won't be easy to
explain to the masses. We have allowed cultism cult of personality. [illeg. sentence.]

.   .   .   .

Peter David

.   .   .   .

He spoke about F. Bain on marching workers against the
party. He called it Gairy attitude (applause). Many cdes. said
that yes that we are moving. Imperialism is watching.

Chris Stroude

We have dealt with this issue too many times and we must
take decisions. All who on the CC that are wavering should be
removed. F. Bain should be removed from CC. He spoke about
honesty and love for masses and GL does not have this. He
shocked about MB. He spoke of his pledge, his vacillation. He
spoke about the PRAF branch meeting. The PRAF [People's
Revolutionary Armed Forces] would not use guns against
the party and revo. The period has steeled us in the PRAF, it
has been practical experience. It is not only officers and NCO
but everyone. The PRAF wants to see socialism (applause).

Headache

In MB speech he said 3 times he fully accept the blame that JL has not been implemented. He never accepted the decision or changed his mind overseas and he has to come with a cover in order to sell his lines to the party. MB should not be surprised when no one checked him. He spoke of the lack of phone communications. GL phone call to Nelson.

A small clique yet very influential and powerful refusing the CC decision. He called Selwyn brave and courageous.

He spoke of the class character of the whole issue. These elements chose to spread the Afghan line because it is a well known anti-C[ommunist] and anti-Soviet position.

He spoke of key opinion makers. MB is personally responsible for spreading the rumour as a pre-condition for murdering CC and chasing the party of the street. He spoke about Donald told HA. This shows that bourg. know where MB is coming from. They see him as the chosen one to defend the [line missing]. GL is jumping off at the first step on the road to Soc. [Socialism]. He is very disappointed in MB.

Andre McSween [McQueen?]

He said that MB said he never had problems with JL because of he and Uni[son Whiteman]. But now he has to reflect. MB said that the members should not get the minutes but now he brought in to masses. MB knows about the level of the masses and this tried to mobilise the masses. He proposed that the strong supporters should be checked. Proposed that F. Bain should be expelled tonight. Now he has no confidence in GL. Because of B. resignation the CC has made a qalitative leap forward. When our party gets out of this crisis it would be a CP [Communist Party] (applause).

GL

Its a historic discussion. On JL he took an open position. He always take an open position. His position has always been WC, in interest of build ML [Marxist/Leninist] party. He explained what happened at CC meeting.

.   .   .   .

He said he didn't engage in anything to turn cdes. against
the CC. The Cdes. in CC said that it is what he didn't say. There
seem to be a report that he and MB was sitting together and
discussing strategy and tactics. This is false.

. . . .

Errol George

... In Hungary MB was in a low mood. GL, Uni, and MB
was in a low mood. GL, Uni, and MB were meeting often when
he left for Gda. MB mood was higher. He felt GL was guiding
MB ...

He told MB about rumours of bloodshed. Debourg told him
there was an Afghanistan line. ...

Yvette Joseph

The CC list for confinement is incomplete. GL should be detained. Jackie [Creft] is moving all over the place.

Timoty

Today he met Fitzy who said that CC is lying on MB.

. . . .

Gordon Rachan [Raeburn?]

... Can we allow one man to hold up the party? (No) Can we
allow a minority to hold the party in ransom? (No) This has led
to tension in the party but also tension in the country. He said
that the issue must not be taken to the masses but the rt. opp. did
so and GL was the main person for doing this.

While there has been a temporary commitment but because of
the deep commitment of party cdes. This struggle is turning out
to be more and more commitment (applause and ovation). In
the coming days we would not be talking about whether you are
a party member or not, we will be talking about whether you are
a communist or not (applause). The rumour has made the work
more difficult but we have to tell the workers the truth
(applause) who want to go to the masses can go they maybe

there for awhile but when the Leninists go the masses they would be there for ever (applause). . . . We have been hiding for years under Gairy now we have to do so under the Pb rt. opp. But we are hiding no longer we will fight out there (applause). Because of the crisis the CC has decided to inform 2 fraternal party—CPSU CC (applause) and PCC CC [Cuban Communist Party](applause). He called on cdes to be sober in their deliberations and to come up with ideas.

Long Live NJM, Leninism, etc.!

IX
THE REVOLUTION DEVOURS ITS CHILDREN

Following Bishop's detention, Bernard Coard became Prime Minister of Grenada and head of the NJM. Five cabinet ministers loyal to Bishop resigned their posts. On October 19 a crowd of Grenadians, possibly led by Unison Whiteman, forced Bishop's release from house arrest and then seized nearby Fort Rupert, where Bishop and his lieutenants set up a headquarters. The Coard government ordered the regular army (loyal to Coard—see document IX-1) to storm the fort, resulting in numerous casualties (wire services reported fifty) among the civilians. Maurice Bishop, Whiteman, and four other loyalists were reportedly captured, marched into the fort's central courtyard, and shot.

The government ordered a 24-hour "shoot on sight" curfew, turned away journalists at the airport, then closed the airport to incoming traffic. The People's Revolutionary Army heralded its fallen soldiers as heroes of the revolution, blamed Bishop and his henchmen for inciting the crowd, and declared the violence that led to his death as proof that Bishop had betrayed the people, become a "criminal" counter-revolutionary, and "did not want Socialism built in this country" (document IX-4). Nevertheless, when the curfew was lifted to permit shopping, riots and looting reportedly resumed.

Fidel Castro reacted to his friend's death in a venomous speech that referred to Coard as the "Pol Pot" of the Grenadian revolution. But Bishop in turn was alleged in Grenada to have courted Castro's sympathy for his campaign against collective leadership during Bishop's recent stopover in Havana. Castro vehemently denied such allegations in his letter to the Central Committee, dated October 15 (document IX-2).

Behind the Coard faction's apparent resentment of Cuban support for Bishop, however, loom Bishop's suspicions of Soviet intrigue on behalf of Coard. In his final "plea of mercy," the imprisoned Bishop supporter, Vincent Noel, recounted a conversation with Bishop on October 11: "After a long pause, the comrade responded by saying that what was at stake was much more than whether he had petit-bourgeois qualities or weaknesses. He said that he had picked up a line which spoke of an 'Afghanistan Solution'" (document IX-3). Indeed, in the Central Committee minutes of October 12, another member recounted that Bishop, while in Hungary, had heard rumours of bloodshed, that there was "an Afghan line." In Afghanistan, one communist regime had taken power under Taraki only to lose the confidence of Moscow, whereupon Taraki was murdered and another, more solidly pro-Soviet communist regime headed by Hafizullah Amin took its place. Hafizullah Amin, in turn, was murdered and replaced by Barbrak Karmal, the current ruler. Whatever the reality in Grenada, Maurice Bishop feared just such a denouement.

The latest document in our collection is the Main Political Department's bulletin of October 20, 1983. Five days later U.S./ Caribbean forces landed on Grenada.

IX-1
Resolution of People's Army
10/12/83

RESOLUTION OF THE PEOPLE'S REVOLUTIONARY ARMED
FORCES BRANCH OF THE NEW JEWEL MOVEMENT

We, the members of the People's Revolutionary Armed
Forces Branch of the New Movement gathered this day 12th
October 1983 unswervingly support the analysis and deci-
sions of the New JEWEL Movement Central Committee at its
Extraordinary Plenary meeting of September 14th - 17th
1983.

We share with deep concern the analysis of the Central
Committee on the deep seated crisis and danger which exist in
our country and party and therefore wholeheartedly stand by
the Central Committee decision to officially establish Joint
Leadership in our Party as the correct scientific mode of leadership of our Party, as a decisive step in pulling our Party and
Revolution out of its present danger. This decision of the Central Committee was unanimously accepted by all members and
candidates of our Party. However, a few opportunist elements
in our party are now unashamedly spreading vicious lying
rumours to obstruct the implementation of the Central Committee decision.

We recognise and uphold that based on the fundamental
Leninist principle of democratic centralism that decision of
our Party's Central Committee have the force of law and form
the basis of the activity and conduct of all party bodies and of
every single party member, candidate member and applicant
regardless of their services and posts. We further unswervingly hold high the principles of criticism and self-criticism
and collective leadership in our Party as the firm guarantee
that our Party will always stay in the correct course and exercise correct leadership and guidance of our Revolution as we

326 THE GRENADA PAPERS

struggle to build socialism. Never would we allow cultism, egoism, the unreasonable and unprincipled desires of one man or a minority to be imposed on our Party thus stiffling inner party democracy and endangering the party and revolution and holding our country to ransom. We demand an immediate end to this and the restoration of Leninist norms of party life and their strict observance by all as the key for the normal functioning of the party.

We, the members of the People's Revolutionary Armed Forces Branch of the NJM. Uphold as the only reasonable basis for party unity the truth spoken by Comrade Lenin when he said, "Discussing the problem, expressing and hearing different opinions, ascertaining the views of the majority of the organised Marxists, expressing these views in the form of decisions adopted by delegates and carring them out conscientiously, this is what reasonable people all over the world call untiy."

We clearly understand that party discipline is nothing less than the active struggle for the implementation of collectively adopted decisions, such as the decision of the Central Committee on Joint Leadership which was ratified by our entire membership. Therefore, we call on the Central Committee and the entire party to expel from the Party's ranks all elements who do not submit to, uphold and implement in practice the decision of the Central Committee and party membership but are bent on holding up the party's work and spreading anti-party propaganda.

The People's Revolutionary Armed Forces Branch of NJM. awaits the decision and orders of the Central Committee!

LONG LIVE THE NJM CENTRAL COMMITTEE — the highest body and authority of our Party and Revolution!
LONG LIVE THE PARTY — NJM!
LONG LIVE LENINISM!
LONG LIVE OUR PEOPLE'S REVOLUTION!
FORWARD EVER   BACKWARD NEVER!

IX-2
Letter from Castro to Central Committee
10/15/83

EMBASSY OF THE REPUBLIC OF CUBA
GRENADA

The Central Committee
New Jewel Movement
St. George's

Esteemed Comrades:

I send you this message motivated by certain references
which, in their conversations with our Ambassador, have
been made by several Grenadian leaders in relation to Cuba.

The supposed notion that on passing through our country
Bishop had informed me of the problems inside the Party is a
miserable piece of slander. Bishop did not mention a single
word to me, nor did he make the slightest allusion to the matter. Completely the opposite. He expressed to me in general
terms and with great modesty that there were deficiencies in
his work which he thought he would overcome in the next
few months.

In reality, I am grateful to Bishop for that discretion, and for
the respect he showed to his Party and to Cuba by not touch-
ing on such matters.

We are indignant at the very thought that some of you would
have considered us capable of meddling in any way in the internal questions of your Party. We are people of principle, not
vulgar schemers or adventurers.

Everything which happened was for us a surprise, and dis-
agreeable. In our country, the Grenadian Revolution and Comrade Bishop as its central figure were the object of great sympathies and respect. Even explaining the event to our people
will not be easy.

In my opinion, the divisions and problems which have
emerged will result in considerable damage to the image of the
Grenadian Revolution, as much within as outside the country.

Cuba, faithful to its moral values and its international policy,
will pay strictest attention to the principle of not interfering
in the slightest in the internal affairs of Grenada, fulfilling the
promises made in the field of cooperation. Our promises are
not to men. They are to the peoples and to principle.

History and developments yet to come will judge what has
happened in these last few days.

I wish for you the greatest wisdom, serenity, loyalty to principles, and generosity in this difficult moment through which
the Grenadian Revolution is passing.

Cordially,

Commander-in-Chief
Fidel Castro Ruz.   15 October, 1983

IX-3
Letter from
Noel to Central Committee
10/17/83

TOP STAFF

17. 10. 83.

Members of the Central Comittee and Party,

There seem to be some confusion as to what transpired on the occasion when I met Maurice last week. I was told by Gemma on Saturday that on enquiring from Owusu she was told that I was being kept at home because no one knew what had been discussed between Maurice and myself on the occasions that we met.

I met and spoke to Maurice three times since he returned from Hungary. Prior to that the only conversations I had with Maurice for months were at the meetings of the workers Committee and sub-committee.

The first time I spoke to Maurice was last Tuesday night at his house from about ten o'clock until sometime after twelve. He telephoned and asked me to come up in response to two unsuccessful calls I had made to him on Monday and Tuesday afternoons.

We spoke first of all about his trip to Eastern Europe and then my trip to Jamaica. We also spoke about the local and regional trade union situation and especially the upcoming C.C.L. Congress. Finally I introduced the discussion of the Party stating that I had picked up from various comrades that he had not accepted the decision of the Party on Joint Leadership.

Maurice denied that he had any problems with Joint Leadership and went into a long history of his acceptance of that principle dating back to the formation of the Movement. He stated that he himself had voted for Joint Leadership at the meeting of full members of the Party, but at that time and at the meeting of the Central Committee he had expressed certain reservations. These reservations were reinforced during his trip and by certain developments since his return.

His first concern was the question of the precise operationalising of Joint Leadership; the second was historical precedent. My response was that 'operationalising' was a detail to be worked out and that ours was a dynamic process which could not be dogmatically patterned after historical precedence. He retorted that it was a tiny detail like a fuse that could cause a car or aeroplane to stall or take off.

The third concern of Maurice was the attitude of comrades of the C.C. to him since his return. He complained that quite unnaturally only one comrade of the entire C.C., Selwyn, was present to meet him at the airport and that Selwyn's greeting had been cold. Further, that no other comrade of the C.C., save H.A., had checked him. Contrary to long established practice neither Owusu nor Headache as chiefs of the Interior and Army respectively had come to give him any report.

I responded to Maurice by suggesting that there may have been a very simple explanation for the number of comrades who met him at the airport. Some comrades may not have been informed or were simply pressed with work. I pointed out that while I was a member of the P.B. I rarely went to the airport either to see him leave or arrive. On the question of comrades of the C.C. checking him I asked Maurice whether HE had tried to establish contact with them. He replied no. I told him that as chairman of the C.C. the ultimate responsibility for establishing contact with members of the C.C. must lay with him. He agreed and said that he was planning to raise that and all his other concerns at a meeting of the P.B. scheduled for the next day, Wednesday 12th.

I queried Maurice as to whether he would raise the fact that only Selwyn met him at the airport as one of his concerns. He said yes. I responded by saying that in my opinion the question of how many people met him at the airport was objectively a petty bourgeois concern and I could not see members of the P.B. treating it in any other way. The comrade replied that that would be correct if it was a single incident standing by itself but it had to be seen within the wider context of all the other things which were happening.

I answered the comrade by saying that if anything was happening other than what I had read in the minutes and been told by party members who were at the general meeting then I did not know. What I did know, I explained, was that several party comrades were accusing him of holding up the work of the party through his non acceptance of Joint Leadership. Some comrades had gone so far as to say that he could not go beyond social democracy. Maurice appeared visibly hurt by that last statement.

After a long pause the comrade responded saying that what was of stake was much more than whether he had petit bourgeois qualities or weaknesses. He said that he had picked up a line which spoke of an "Afghanistan Solution". I was stunned by this. While Maurice was out of the country De Bourg had said to me one day that Chalkie had told him that there would be a solution like Afghanistan if the Chief fucked around on the question of Joint Leadership. At the time that De Bourg told me this I had dismissed Chalkie's remarks as a lot of irresponsible nonsense but Maurice's statement shook me.

I told Maurice that I had heard the Afghan talk before and where I had heard it. He said that in his case he had picked it up as coming from Ram Folkes through one of his personnel security comrade. He did not name the comrade. I said to Maurice that if things had descended to the level of P.S. [Personnel Security] men taking sides and talking of Afghanistan then we were a fraction away from bloodshed and disaster. I assured the comrade that the position that I had adopted on Joint Leadership was based purely on principle and my understanding of the issues involved, not personality. I then questioned him about his personal relationship to other comrades within the C.C. as I was of the opinion that he had good relations with all and in particular Selwyn, H.A., Owusu and Bernard.

He claimed that until recently he had excellent relations with all comrades except Bernard with whom he had had strained relations for about one year. He gave an example of the good relations with Owusu, for instance, and spoke of a report that Owusu had written about the U.S. Trip which report embarassed him (Maurice) because of the hero worship it contained.

As regards Bernard he said that relations had been strained for about one year since his resignation from the C.C. He recounted his years of association with Bernard from school days up to October last year. Her said that when Bernard resigned last year he did his best to get Bernard to withdraw it recognising the many talents of the comrade and his value at the leadership level. But Bernard refused to withdraw the resignation and decided to go to Carriacou instead. During that period he became apprehensive that Bernard was contemplating suicide and for that reason called in Keith Roberts and asked him to follow Bernard to Carriacou and ensure his safety.

Maurice said that as far as he was concerned he could work along with Bernard even if Bernard was chosen outright as leader of the party. But he said that in recent times he had been become increasingly convinced, from all the bits and pieces of evidence available to him, that there were behind the scenes, unprincipled manoeuvres to remove him by a section of the C.C. I again told the comrade that the position I had taken was based on the minutes I had read, the account of the general meeting and my desire, like all other party comrades, to push the party forward. I urged Maurice to formally appeal the decision on Joint Leadership if he had a problem with it and to also raise all the other issues frankly and openly at the meeting of the P.B. the next morning as the situation was grave and could only get worse.

Maurice repeated that he had no problems with Joint Leadership subject to clarification on operationalisation. But,

Maurice went on, the main concern at this time was the behind the scenes manoeuvres against him. I again urged
Maurice to raise that openly at the P.B. the next day. He told
me not to worry that he would deal with everything. The conversation more or less ended there and I left.

That night (Tuesday) I did not sleep. The more I thought
about what Maurice had said the more worried I became. Next
morning instead of going to the International Airport as
usual I went to H.A.'s house and told him of my grave concern
about the situation in the party and in particular the fear of
bloodshed. H.A. said that the situation was worse than I
thought and that I could not be more concerned than he was.

He said that, for instance, there was a meeting of some
comrades in the army that very morning to discuss the situation in the party and he had no idea who precisely had called
the meeting as he had not been officially informed. Further, he
said that the tension among C.C. members was so high that
they had stopped sleeping in their houses. I told H.A. that that
was madness and demanded that the P.B. sit down that morning and fully and completely thrash out all the problems and
suspicions. He agreed. The conversation between H.A. and I
was a very short one. It lasted only for the time it took me to
drive from his house to Fort Frederick in my car.

When I left H.A. I went down to Selwyn to again raise my
concern. Selwyn agreed with my analysis of the serious state
of tension existing within the party but said Maurice was the
one to blame because he had refused to accept in practice,
Joint Leadership as agreed upon by the entire party. He said
that he was hearing about the 'Afghan solution' for the first
time, and, that contrary to that, it was Maurice who had been
planning to kill members of the C.C. He said that within the
past few days a lot of evidence had come to light. For instance,
last year St. Paul had approached another security man to kill
Bernard after he resigned from the C.C. I retold to Selwyn
what Maurice had told me about taking measures to prevent
Bernard from committing suicide after his resignation from
the C.C. and I commented that it seemed to me that the C.C.
was suffering from an overdose of paranoia.

resigned. That the night before (Wednesday 12/10/83) Maurice using George Louison had organised Bourgeois elements in St. Paul's (Bulleu, Donald etc.) to take arms from the st. Paul's Militia Camp to go Mt. Walldale to defend Maurice. That George had been removed from the P.B. and C.C.

I told Chalkie that he was mad that I could not believe what I was hearing about Maurice. Chalkie replied that it was Maurice who was power crazy. After that conversation with Chalkie I must have looked visibly shaken as both Frog (union officer) and my secretary asked me if something was wrong. I asked my secretary to cancel all appointments for the day. I then tried to get both Chess and Naz neither of whom was in office.

As I left the union office I saw Carl Johnson and others in front of the Party Secretariat. I went thereand asked C.J. for Chess. He said that Chess was still at the Power Station. There were all sorts of excited bilateral taking place among party comrades at the secretariat. I left there and went directly back to Maurice's house. He was alone and I was told by the security to go into his bedroom.

I told Maurice about the rumour and related to him what Chalkie had said. He confirmed the unpleasant development but denied having anything to do with the origin of the rumour and organisation of armed vigilante. Maurice gave me a blood chilling account of what had happened at the C.C. meeting the day before. He said that members of the C.C., particularly Chalkie, kept pulling out their weapons threateningly during the whole meeting and that Fitzy had freaked out partly as a result of that. I told Maurice that what was going on was madness, that the membership had a right to know and that he should lay everything bare before the membership in the general meeting planned for that afternoon. He asked me what general meeting I was talking about. I explained that Chalkie [illeg.] told me that there was a meeting of all ranks of the party, from applicants up, to explain the present situation within the party.

Maurice explained that he had been at a meeting of the Central Committee until late the night before and that no such general meeting had been proposed or agreed. He offered it as another example of the plotting against him and said he would not go. I pleaded with Maurice to attend the meeting as any other action may be interpreted by the membership as an admission of guilt. Maurice complained of not feeling well and said he really did not know whether he could stand the emotional strain of a meeting such as the last general meeting.

Eventually I got Maurice to agree for me to get a doctor, namely Bernard Gittens, to attend to him. At the same time, while I went for the doctor he was supposed to start putting his notes together for the meeting that afternoon so that even if he was given sedation by the doctor he would still be prepared at the meeting. As I left to go for the doctor I was worried not only about the state of the party and Maurice's physical health but the possibility of his committing suicide also crossed my mind.

As I was about to enter my car and leave I was approached by one of the Personnel Security men and told that I was under arrest. I was taken to under the mango tree in Bernard's yard and interviewed by Chalkie and Ian St. Bernard. I was told by the two comrades that the Central Committee had decided that I should be arrested for conspiring with Maurice. They could not answer conspiring about what and refused to say if Maurice was still a member of the C.C. In brief I explained to the comrades that I had not been involved in anything resembling conspiracy and was only going to get a doctor for Maurice. I asked him (St. B.) to send to get Dr. Gittens for Maurice while he clarified matters. He told me not to worry that a strong "delegation" would go to visit Maurice in a short while. I was then taken to my house and ordered to stay there or be formally detained. All arms and ammunition which I have always carried were taken away.

About 3.45 p.m. that afternoon I received a note through Chess from Ian St. Bernard authorising me to attend the general meeting of the party. Given the extremely serious nature of what we were there to discuss, one would have thought that the discussions and decisions would have taken place in a calm and sober way. Instead led by members of the Political

Bureau, the meeting was a horrendous display of militarism, hatred and emotional vilification. Never before have I witnessed this trend within our party and on no grounds can this conduct be justified.

This trend has continued in public and on the public media. A horrible lie is being spread that 'Brat' Bullen and the other persons who went to the St. Paul's militia camp to collect arms did so to go and kill Bernard and Phyl. This is a lie known to the whole party. What was said by Chalkie to me on the morning of Thursday 13th and repeated at the general meeting by both H.A. and Owusu was that they had gone to get arms to go and protect 'their Chief' because he was in danger. Let me make it very clear, however, that I disagree fundamentally with the action taken by that group and support the measures taken by the security forces.

In my over 10 years of association with our party never one day have I had reason to despair, not even when I was removed from the Political Bureau in 1981. For 20 years I have dreamt of building a socialist and communist society. We began our march forward with our Glorious Revolution but, today, by our own collective irresponsibility we have begun to cannabilise ourselves.

The crime that we are committing is not only against our Party, People and Revolution. Our crime is against the entire world revolutionary process and the Caribbean masses in particular.

You know no less than I that our Revolution is not irreversible. And while we brutally destroy ourselves, the corbeau [crow] of imperialism and reaction anxiously make preparation to pounce.

For the past four or five days I have stayed at home following the threats of Chalkie and Ian St. Bernard. Several conrades have checked me to find out what happened and my position on various things. I have made it clear that from the time I read the minutes and obtained some specific clarity on a few issues I accepted the decision on Joint Leadership. But even if I did not that is my right as a party member so long as I did not seek to subvert in anyway the Democratic Centralist decision of the party. Or have we now new norms?

For the past four or five days I have allowed myself to be confined as a counter-revolutionary criminal. Perhaps a conscious attempt is being made to push me into adventurous objectively counter-revolutionary activity so that I can be discredited afterwards. But that will never happen!

If I am to be sacrificed to suit the expediency of any person or persons then is is my duty as a communist to prevent it if I can. When I chose the road to revolution above all else including family I knew that I could be martyred at any time. But frankly, comrades, at no time did I vaguely dream that that threat would come from within our own party. My only crime is that I spoke to Maurice Bishop, chairman of our Central Committee and Prime Minister, in a principled way about the same things that all other comrades in the party were discussing in a million bilaterals.

I request that my letter be discussed by the C.C. and be circulated to all members of the party in the same way that the Resolution from the Armed Forces was circulated last Thursday 13th October.

Long live inner party democracy!

Long live our Party!

Long live Socialism and Communism!

Fraternally

[signature]

Vince

IX-4
Bulletin from Main Political Department
10/20/83

BULLETIN FROM THE MAIN POLITICAL DEPARTMENT
20/10/83
THEIR HEROISM IS AN EXAMPLE FOR US

Comrade soldiers, yesterday 19th October, the masses of
people led by Unison Whiteman broke into the home of
Maurice Bishop in defiance to warning shots fired in the air
by the soldiers of People's Revolutionary Armed Forces. They
then took Maurice Bishop into the streets of St. George's. They
wanted to hear Murice Bishop speak. Maurice Bishop, Unison
Whiteman, Vincent Noel, Fitzroy Bain, Jacquelin Creft and
other people of the bourgeois and upper petty bourgeois
strata, known counter-revolutionaries and Gairyites led the
crowd onto Port Rupert, the Headquarters of the People's Revolutionary Armed Forces where they forced through the main
entrance, besting the Comrade Sister who was trying to prevent them from entering and over-running the Army Headquarters and disarming the Officers and Soldiers. Enstein
Louison, former chief of the General Staff who had been sus-
pended was called by Maurice and proclaimed Commander-
in-Chief and Chief of Staff to the People's Revolutionary Armed
Forces. Enstein Louison then proceeded to issue arms and
ammunition to the people. It must be noted that when Einstein Louison started distributing the weapons, Vincent Noel
asked who were the trained militia in the crowd for them to
step forward because there were some men that had 'to be
passed out'. Soldiers on Port Rupert took off their clothes and
said that they could not take part in such an Army. Important
to note that some of the comrade sister Soldiers were beaten
and stripped by Maurice Bishop, Vincent Noel, Fitzroy Bain
and their petty bourgeois and bourgeois supporters. One

heroic sister, Pte. Racheal Abraham then went up to Maurice Bishop and in his face told him that he was responsible for all that had happened.

It is very important to note that when the masses of people called on Maurice Bishop to speak they were told by Vincent Noel that Maurice Bishop could not speak to them because he was in a very important meeting. Comrades, the masses had no intention to cause bloodshed but in their confusion they were led by Maurice Bishop and his petty bourgeois and bourgeois friends as cannon fodder to cause bloodshed. Comrades, it is very important to recognise the heroism of our People's Revolutionary Armed Forces. When WO2 Rapheal Mason and Sargeant Byron Cameron were shot one sister Pte. Patricia Frank tore up her jersey to bandage the chest and leg of those wounded comrades. She then went clad in pants and bra to mobilise a fire truck to put out the flames at Port Rupert. She was prevented from doing this and she later went to get nurses to evacuate a sister who in her fright had jumped over the wall at Port Rupert and was seriously injured. She also went to the hospital to explain to the people there that counter-revolutionaries had opened fire on our soldiers. This is an example of true love and heroism, the qualities that we must develop further.

Pte. Lynessa Frederick stood firmly with weapon in hand preventing the crowd of people from going up to the Armoury to get arms until she was overpowered by them and her weapon taken.

Corporal Nerril Richards greatly assisted in boosting the morale of the comrades there and inspiring them with his staunchness to stand firm.

Comrade Lance Corporal Godfrey Thomas advancing with WO2 Rapheal Mason to give covering fire to OC Mayers in the counter attack was told by comrade Mason that he comrade Mason had been shot. On reaching comrade Mason, Lance Corporal Thomas was pushed by WO2 Mason who told him to continue the advance. Comrade Thomas refused to go on without assisting comrade Mason. While holding comrade Mason, comrade Thomas said he saw a man suddenly rise up from behind a wall with a weapon and he heard a bullet strike the BTR and penetrate comrade Thomas's pants. Comrade Mason then said that he had again been shot and told comrade Thomas that he could not make it and that he should be taken to the hospital. On the way to the hospital, comrade Mason collapsed and told comrade Thomas to take care of his son because he was going to die. Comrade Mason was taken by some civilians to the hospital where he later died. Comrade Thomas then pushed back to meet the BTR and on his way up saw Lance Corporal Martin Simon with his chest streaming blood. Even in that condition comrade Simon warned comrade Thomas that the masses were shooting at them and that he should be careful. While at the same time assisted OC Mayers, who was also shot. Comrade Thomas left comrade Simon in the care of some civilians who took him to hospital. OC Conrad Mayers led the first squad into the attack shouting "For the Defence of the Homeland". He was clearing his way to move further on up the Port when he was shot by a man shooting directly.

REVOLUTIONARY SOLDIERS AND MEN OF THE PEOPLE'S REVOLUTIONARY ARMED FORCES

Today our People's Revolutionary Army has gained victory over the right opportunist and reactionary forces which attacked the Headquarters of our Ministry of Defence. These anti-worker elements using the working people as a shield entered Port Rupert.

Our patriotic men, loving the masses and rather than killing them since we understood that they were being used, we held our fire. However, the leadership of the counter-revolutionary elements, led by Maurice Bishop, Unison Whiteman and Vincent Noel, knowing that we did not want to harm the people disarmed the Officers and Chiefs and soldiers and began arming people who represented their own minority class interest.

Comrades, these men who preached for us that they had the interest of the Grenadian people at heart did not have one member of the working class controlling their criminal operations. These elements although they used the working class and working people to gain their objective did not have any confidence in them and therefore had only businessmen, nuns, nurses and lumpen elements in the operations centre.

The presence of the people shows as clearly where they are coming from. Besides, Maurice Bishop certain that they had won, pointed out to the Officers that he did not want to have socialism built in this country.

These counter-revolutionaries who had given the assurance in the Party before to resolve the crisis peacefully — were on the one hand trying to give assurance to the unarmed soldiers that nothing would happen while on the other hand they were preparing to murder all Party comrades, Officers and Chiefs that they held. Again this truth was borne out when Maurice Bishop openly stated that he was going to build a new Party and a new Army — to defend the interest of the bourgeois.

However, because of the prompt action of the reserve force, guided by the Central Committee of the N.J.M. — these betrayers of the masses were crushed. The timely move of our Motorized Units dealt a devastating blow to these criminals, those opportunist elements who did not want to see socialism built in our country and who were not interested in seeing the masses benefit more and more.

Comrades, today Wednesday 19th October, history was made again. All patriots and revolutionaries will never forget this day when counter-revolution, the friends of imperialism were crushed. This victory today will ensure that our glorious Party the N.J.M. will live on and grow from strength to strength leading and guiding the Armed Forces and the Revolution.

This victory is ongoing progress and for socialism. But in giving this victory, one of our soldiers, Sgt. Byron Cameron was wounded, while O. Cdt Conrad Mayers, WO2 Raphael Mason, Sgt. Darrel Peters and L. Cpl. Martin Simon died a heroes death.

Let our comrades death be an inspiration to us, let it be a sign of the staunchness of our revolutionary Armed Forces and let us use it to strengthen our resolve to defend the Revolution and to build socialism.

Let this moment be proof to counter-revolution of our firmness, discipline and staunchness to the Party, the N.J.M., the working class, working people and to socialism. Let this be testimony of our unity behind our Party and Revolution.

We have won a victory comrades, but let us stand and be united to ensure that we achieve other victories.

LONG LIVE OUR PARTY, THE N.J.M.!!
LONG LIVE THE PEOPLE'S REVOLUTIONARY ARMED FORCES!!
LONG LIVE THE GRENADA REVOLUTION!!
FORWARD EVER!! BACKWARD NEVER!!!

SOCIALISM OR DEATH!!!

GLOSSARY OF ABBREVIATIONS

A	Applicants (to NJM Party membership)
AGWU	Agricultural and General Workers' Union
ANC	African National Congress
AUCCTU	All-Union Central Council of Trade Unions (Soviet)
CBI	Caribbean Basin Initiative
CC	Central Committee
CCC	Conference of Caribbean Churches
CCG	Conference of Churches of Grenada
CCL	Caribbean Congress of Labor
CDB	Caribbean Development Bank
Cde	Comrade
CM	Candidate Members
CPE	Centre for Political Education
CPSU	Communist Party of the Soviet Union
CPUSA	Communist Party, United States of America
DC	Democratic Centralism; also, Disciplinary Commission
DFP	Dominica Federal Party
DPRK	Democratic People's Republic of Korea
FDR	Frente Democratico Revolucionario (El Salvador)
FMLN	Frente Farabundo Martí para la Liberación Nacional (El Salvador)
FSLN	Frente Sandinista de la Liberacion Nacional (Nicaragua)
FWI	*Free West Indian* (newspaper)
GDR	German Democratic Republic (East Germany)
GFC	Grenada Farms Corporation
GM	General Meeting
IMF	International Monetary Fund
M	Members; also, masses
MAP	Movement for Assemblies of the People
M-L	Marxist-Leninist
MNIB	Marketing and National Importing Board

MNR	Movimiento Nacional Revolucionario (El Salvador)
NBIPP	National Black Independent Political Party (U.S.)
NCBL	National Conference of Black Lawyers (U.S.)
NFM	National Farmers' Movement
NJM	New Jewel Movement
NWO	National Women's Organization
NYO	National Youth Organization
OAS	Organization of American States
OC	Organization Committee
OECS	Organization of Eastern Caribbean States
OREL	Organization for Revolutionary Education and Liberation
PB	Political Bureau
PCC	Partido Comunista de Cuba
PFU	Productive Farmers' Union
PM	Prime Minister
PNP	People's National Party (Jamaica)
PRA	People's Revolutionary Army
PRAF	People's Revolutionary Armed Forces
PRG	People's Revolutionary Government
PS	Personnel Security
RFG	Radio Free Grenada
RMC	Revolutionary Military Council
RP	Radical Party (Chile)
SI	Socialist International
SWP	Socialist Workers Party (U.S.)
UJC	Unioń de Juventudes Comunistas (Communist Youth Union—Cuba)
VOA	Voice of America
WC	Workers' Councils
WFDY	World Federation of Democratic Youth
WPA	Working People's Alliance (Guyana)
YCL	Young Communist League (Komsomol—Soviet)
YEP	Youth Education Program

THE GRENADA PAPERS

The U.S.-led invasion of Grenada in October 1983 was an event of major historical importance. Not only did the action mark the sole occasion on which an established Communist regime was deposed by democratic forces, but it yielded a treasure trove of captured documents revealing the inner workings of the New Jewel Regime (otherwise known as the People's Revolutionary Government of Grenada). Never before have the archives of a Communist state been made available to persons not under Party control.

Edited and with major commentary by Paul Seabury and Walter A. McDougall, and with a foreword by the eminent American political philosopher Sidney Hook, THE GRENADA PAPERS is a fascinating selection of the party, state, and police documents which dramatically chronicle the internal affairs of the People's Revolutionary Government (PRG) from its creation in 1979 to its last days in 1983.

"What makes these papers from Grenada doubly valuable," writes Professor Seabury in the Introduction, "is that they permit us intimately to witness both the dynamics of a Marxist-Leninist regime in the early stages of its consolidation and its emerging relation to broader configurations of political power in the Communist world."

Using methods copied from existing Communist states, the New Jewel leaders worked to consolidate